WOMAN
IN MODERN LIFE

THE PASTORAL PSYCHOLOGY SERIES,
NUMBER 5

WOMAN
IN MODERN LIFE

Edited by
WILLIAM C. BIER, S.J.

FORDHAM UNIVERSITY PRESS · NEW YORK

PRINTED IN THE UNITED STATES OF AMERICA
BY THE COLONIAL PRESS, INC.
CLINTON, MASSACHUSETTS

Table of Contents

Preface

The series of Pastoral Psychology Institutes sponsored by the Psychology Department of Fordham University was begun in 1955, and with a single exception, has been presented on an alternate-year basis since that time. The current volume contains a selection of papers presented at the 1965 Institute.

The general aim of these Institutes has been to bring to clergymen of all faiths the insights developed and the findings provided by the behavioral sciences to the extent to which these viewpoints, often provocative, sometimes startling, and invariably illuminating to the clergyman would be of assistance to him in his pastoral work. Topics were selected for the Institutes in which it was judged that the behavioral sciences would be in a position to make a contribution to pastoral work. Thus, the Institutes of 1955 and 1957 treated somewhat briefly a series of topics such as anxiety, guilt, scrupulosity, and personal and sexual development. These topics were later combined to provide the material for the first volume in the series published by Fordham University Press: *Personality and Sexual Problems in Pastoral Psychology*. Subsequent Institutes were limited to single topics which were treated in more detail. The 1959 Institute was devoted to addiction as a pastoral problem, and appeared as volume two in the series: *Problems in Addiction: Alcoholism and Drug Addiction*. The 1961 Institute focused on the teenager and provided volume three in the series: *The Adolescent: His Search for Understanding*. Marriage was the topic of the 1963 Institute and gave rise to the fourth volume in the series: *Marriage: A Psychological and Moral Approach*.

All of the Institutes have conformed to a similar pattern: they have been a week in length, from a Monday through a Friday, during the latter half of June. They were planned to fit, for the convenience both of the faculty and the Institute members, between the academic year and the start of summer school or other summer commitments. In the limited time of one week it is obviously impossible to develop pastoral or counseling skills, and the Institutes have never tried to accomplish this but have always focused on the imparting of information and the cultivation of attitudes, a goal which is attainable within a one-week span. The Institutes have, however, provided a concentrated week-long experience, and the interchange in both formal discussion and informal conversation between the Institute members and the faculty has been an obviously valuable feature for those who attended. Not all of the faculty members could attend for the entire week, but many of them did, and almost all of them spent at least a full day at the Institute. The Institutes thus proved to be a living experience in interdisciplinary interchange and understanding, and the faculty who participated testify that they learned at least as much as they imparted at these sessions. Discussion after the formal papers has always been viewed as an important part of the Institutes, and conscious effort was made in the planning to provide adequate time for such discussion. Valuable as is discussion of this kind, its significance is almost entirely in terms of the face-to-face confrontation and the spontaneous interchange of opinions and viewpoints it provides. It is impossible to recapture this atmosphere afterwards, and the present volume, like its predecessors, makes no attempt to do so. This experience, which is a living one, is an added return to those who are able to spend the week required to attend the Institute as opposed to those who must be content with the reading of the published volume. We believe, however, that the published proceedings have a contribution to make to a far larger group than those who are able to attend the Institute sessions, and the success of the previous volumes in the Pastoral Psychology Series would attest to the validity of this conviction.

The 1965 Institute selected as its topic "Woman in the Modern World." When it was discovered that several books already bear the title which had been given to the Institute, the published volume was given the slightly altered title: *Woman in Modern Life*. The planning Committee decided to limit the Institute to a consideration of the lay woman, because it was felt that some restriction was necessary for satisfactory treatment in a single Institute, and because of the current focus on the lay person in the Church today, as a result of the emphasis provided by Vatican II. The woman in religious life is not treated in this volume, therefore, except incidentally and tangentially.

Some criticism had been voiced about prior Institutes because, although they were Pastoral Psychology Institutes, they gave little or no attention to the theological aspects of the topics under consideration, whereas theology has in recent years developed new and relevant insights into human nature. In planning the present Institute, the Committee tried to provide a better balance in this respect. It will be seen that Section I considers woman in theological perspective, and I believe that the reader will find this section informative and perhaps even surprising. The antifeminism of some of the Fathers of the Church will sound strange and perhaps offensive to modern ears, but as several of the contributors point out the Church, even today, continues to be antifeminist to a considerable degree. One of the great needs of the Church in our time is to discover how to bring woman into her decision-making processes—a recognition which women have never received, but which they have every right to achieve.

In the current Institute, the planning Committee made an effort to meet yet another criticism of earlier Institutes: the lack of any fresh empirical data. Two hitherto unpublished studies are reported in section II dealing with woman from the perspective of the behavioral sciences. One of these, presented by Sister Marie Augusta Neal, reports her findings on the attitudes of priests toward woman in a sample of Boston-area clergy. The second, a pilot-type study by Father Robert McNamara and Father Augustine Grady, focuses on the attitudes toward priests and nuns of two sub-samples of Catholic college women. The latter study is buttressed by sample data from a large study conducted at Mundelein College, Chicago, presented by the President of the College, Sister Mary Ann Ida.

Section III of the book moves to the consideration of the married woman. Here Dr. Paul Reiss presents the position paper dealing with Woman and Marriage Expectations, in which he points out that marriage is not only the normal but the invariable expectation of women, unrealistic as this expectation may be in substance, or in various of its features for the individual woman. The remainder of this section treats of the outcome of these marriage expectations in a selected critical instances: the Career Wife, the Childless Married Women, the Divorcée, and the Widow.

The fourth section concerns itself with the single woman in which, after a good-humored but probing paper by Dr. Robert Campbell on "Why Women do not Marry," certain salient features of the life of the single woman are considered: career, employment, sexuality, and spirituality in that order. The final section addresses itself to womanly perfection in terms of psychological fulfillment and the achievement to be found in service to the Church and the world.

All the previous Institutes had restricted attendance to members of the clergy. In the Institute on Woman, however, it seemed that this topic could be discussed appropriately only if a representative group of women was present, and registration for this Institute was consequently extended to women whose professional work related to the topic under discussion, such as, educators, teachers, social workers, and social scientists. The decision proved a happy one and made possible the interplay of viewpoints during the discussion period which the Institutes seek to provide.

It will be found, I think, that the volume is not only currently relevant but has a considerably forward thrust. Except in the case of formally appointed discussants, of which there were only three, the faculty members had no antecedent communication with one another so that the agreement in the volume, which is substantial, becomes impressive. What Father Hagmaier says, for instance, in his paper on "Sexuality and the Single Woman" as to why women do not marry convincingly corroborates what Dr. Campbell maintains in his formal treatment of this subject.

As editor, I am pleased to pay grateful tribute to the contributions of my fellow Committee members, all of whom are Fordham University faculty members and who shared with me the responsibility for the planning and conduct of this Institute: Rev. L. Augustine Grady, S.J., Assistant Professor of Theology; Rev. Joseph G. Keegan, S.J., Associate Professor of Psychology; Rev. Robert J. McNamara, S.J., Associate Professor of Sociology; and Rev. Edwin A. Quain, S.J., Professor of Classics and Director of the Fordham University Press. The Committee was much helped in its deliberations and planning by Dr. Dorothy Dohen who served as its consultant.

The delay in issuing these Proceedings is regretted by all concerned but is the fault of no one except an over-committed editor. The delay has been partially atoned for by updating, particularly in the references, in at least some of the papers. Owing to circumstances beyond the control of the planning Committee it was impossible to offer a Pastoral Psychology Institute when it would have been due in 1967 in virtue of the alternate-year basis on which the series had been conducted since 1955. The series will, however, be resumed again in 1969.

March, 1968   WILLIAM C. BIER, S.J.

I

WOMAN IN THEOLOGICAL PERSPECTIVE

Woman in the Old Testament

GEORGE S. GLANZMAN, S.J.

Father George S. Glanzman, S.J., holds a B.A. degree from Georgetown University, a Ph.L. and an S.T.L. from Woodstock College, and a licentiate in sacred scripture from the Pontifical Biblical Institute in Rome. From 1954 to 1963 he was Professor of Old Testament Scripture at Woodstock College, Woodstock, Maryland. In the latter year, Father Glanzman joined the faculty of the Theology Department at Fordham University, where he currently teaches courses in Hebrew, Biblical Aramaic, and other subjects related to the Old Testament. During the period 1958-1965 he was a visiting lecturer in the Oriental Seminary of the Johns Hopkins University, Baltimore. Father Glanzman is the author of Introductory Bibliography for the Study of Scripture.

This paper is not theological. Though occasionally the biblical books advance what might be called theological reasons for certain prescriptions or forms of conduct laid down for women, most of our Old Testament material gives us rather straightforward narrative or law from which the position of women may be deduced. This study, then, adhering closely to the biblical data, with some illustration from non-biblical sources, advances no "theology of woman"; it tries simply to reconstruct

1

in a very factual way some aspects of woman's place and role in the
Israelite-Jewish society of Old Testament times.

It would be a mistake to think that we can draw a complete picture of
the position of women in Israelite-Jewish society from the Old Testament
documents now available to us. Our documentation is fragmentary, and
we cannot even be sure that all legal prescriptions were actually put into
effect—in fact, we may guess that they probably were not. For example,
the various legal customs contained in the Book of Ruth, which may well
have been real living customs (Burrows, 1940), are not paralleled in the
Pentateuch. Again, there is no contemporary evidence "that the provisions of the Hammurabi Code were ever carried out" (Martin, 1958,
p. 28).

There is a further problem arising from the fact that our documentation spans well over a millennium of custom and law. It would be incorrect to conclude that the customs illustrated in the patriarchal narratives,
which have their best parallels among the Hurrians at Nuzu, were in
force during the period of the monarchy, or that monarchic practice
lasted on through post-exilic Judaism. We cannot, however, in this paper
delay over chronological details.

Whatever may be thought of the idea that in the Old Testament there
are scattered indications that Israelite society was at one time a fratriarch-
ate (Koschaker, 1933; Gordon, 1935), or that originally all Semitic
society was matriarchal (Smith, 1903; Aptowitzer, 1927, 1928), through
the period of Israel's settlement in Canaan and in the post-exilic period
its society was patriarchal. In this society the family was called "father's
house" (bêt 'āb). This does not, of course, mean that a father held
tyrannical sway over his household, though he was entitled to do many
things which would not be tolerated today (de Vaux, 1961, p. 20).
Genealogies were traced through the father; the relatives of the father
were the closest relatives of the children. The father was ba'al, "master,
lord, owner"; besides the usual verbs lqh and nś' employed to express
the idea "to marry," we find several examples of the root b'l used for
the same idea (v.g., Jer 31:32), i.e., when a man married, he could be
said to "become a master." Most commonly the husband was called 'iš,
"man"; but he was also called 'ādōn, "lord," of his wife, even though
this word is properly used of the relations of master to slave or king to
subject.

All this does not imply that the woman was a mere chattel. There are
two fundamental texts that indicate the role and importance of woman in
the life of man. The later of these texts, the P-teaching on the creation
(Gn 1:1–2:4a), differs considerably from the earlier J-story of the

making of man and woman (Gn 2:4b-25). According to P, God made man, that is mankind (*'ādām*), at once male and female (Gn 1:27). Mankind is a whole consisting of the two parts, man and woman; without the two of them, there is no mankind (Pedersen, 1926-1940, I, 61). They are equally an exact copy, a statue of God. The sexual role of the two is clearly expressed in the blessing: "Be fruitful and multiply" (Gn 1:28); that this is a blessing rather than a command is clear both from here and from Gn 9:2.

In the J-tradition on the other hand, God first makes the male who is again called *'ādām;* the word is explained after man's origin from the ground (*'ᵃdāmā*). It is only afterwards, when God realizes that it is not good for man to be alone and that he needs a help (*'ezer*), that God makes the female; she is called *'iššā*, "woman," and the popular etymology explains the term by saying that she is taken from *'îš*, "man." It should be noted that in this story the role of woman is to remedy the loneliness of man, though without her it is still possible to have mankind. Though the woman corresponds perfectly to the man (*kᵉnegdô*), there is nothing said about sexual relations to be had between them, and in fact it is quite probable that intercourse, a creative act, was not intended—at least according to this story—for mankind.

It has often been noticed that the remark in Gn 2:24 is rather hard to understand in a patriarchal society. Does it really mean that a man leaves his own father's house to go live in the family of his wife in the relationship of a *beena* marriage? This is possible, but other explanations appear much more likely. It is true that when a man marries he does leave his father's house to found his own house, though in historic Israel he does not become a member of his wife's clan and his ties with his father's house are by no means completely severed. Since the etiological character of Gn 2:4b–3:24 is so clear, I rather think that the author is simply stating a condition which he feels must have existed before the fall. The sin of the man and woman reverses everything, and in particular it is only after the fall that the woman has desire for the man and that the man rules over her (Gn 3:16); these are the actual human conditions that the author knows, and their explanation is to be found in the fall, so that before the fall things must have been different.

MARRIED WOMEN

We know a fair amount about the position of woman in the Israelite marital society. She is reckoned among man's possessions, together with his ox, ass, etc. (Ex 20:17; Dt 5:21). According to the laws of the

Pentateuch, a woman had no rights of inheritance, neither from her husband nor from her father, unless there was no male to inherit. The customs found in the Book of Ruth, however, stand in opposition to these laws; Naomi appears to have been her husband's heir since Boaz buys Elimelek's property from her, the widow. A man could divorce his wife and, if he did, she returned to her father's house; but a wife could not divorce her husband. If a wife had sexual relations with a man other than her husband, both would be guilty of adultery and could be put to death (Lv 20:10; Dt 22:22); but there was no prohibition of this type against a married man having intercourse with an unmarried woman, even if he had no intention of bringing her into his household as a concubine or secondary wife. Adultery was essentially a violation of the rights of one's male neighbor.

The woman's chief purpose was to be the mother of the man's children; it was her childbearing that won for her the closest attachment of her husband. Her children are commanded to honor her equally with their father, and in the Wisdom literature there are a number of passages enjoining respect for a mother. On the other hand, the childless wife was generally in a sorry state, and was usually the object of scorn on the part of her husband and his other wives. Yet there are stories telling of the deep affection of a man for his childless wife, v.g., Abraham and Sarah, Jacob and Rachel; Elkanah, the future father of Samuel, was truly in love with the childless Hannah: "Hannah why do you weep? . . . Am I not dearer to you than ten sons?" (1 Sam 1:9; cf. also v. 5).

The woman was expected to take care of the household chores: she had to tend the flocks, draw water from the well, cook, and work in the fields. Though some wealthy women might be able to avoid these tasks, it should not be thought that such work demeaned the woman. In the famous praise of the competent housewife (Prv 31: 10-31), it is precisely her ability at household work and her skill in managing the house that brings honor to herself and her husband: "Charm is deceitful, and beauty is a breath; the wise woman will be praised" (v. 30, corrected after LXX). The education of the young children—even of the boys— was in the hands of their mother (Prv 1:8; 6:20) or of a nurse.

In spite of her subordinate position in Israelite society, a wife was not a mere slave. Though a man might sell his own daughter into slavery, a husband could never sell his wife (Ex 21:7). Even a wife acquired as a war prisoner could never be sold.

WOMAN BEFORE MARRIAGE

Before her marriage, a woman belonged to her father. When the time came for her to be married—and we have no biblical information as to what that age must be—the prospective groom asked her hand from her parents; only after her father or guardian had agreed was her consent asked. This custom, however, did not mean that all marriages were devoid of love. A man might choose his wife even though he had not asked his own parents' approval or even though they disapproved. This would be rare in the case of the girl, though the story of Michal, Saul's daughter, falling in love with David (1 Sam 18:20) indicates that the girl might have some wider freedom of choice. In fact, there was probably a fair amount of opportunity for young women to make their own matches since they had a certain freedom while tending the sheep, drawing water, or gleaning in the fields (cf. the story of Ruth and Boaz). But given the conditions prevailing in the Israelite society, too much freedom could get a girl in trouble, and she might be exposed to the violence of the young men (cf. the rape of Dinah in Gn c. 34).

It was in no way an ideal in Israel for a girl to take up virginity as a state of life or profession; on the contrary, it was a great misfortune for a woman to die a virgin (Jgs 11:37; Is 47:8; 49:21). This is not to say, of course, that a girl's virginity was not prized. According to Lv 21:13-15, the high priest could marry no one but a virgin. It was the concern of the girl's father to protect her virginity, and anyone who violated it would be fined 50 shekels and would have to marry the girl (Dt 22:29); or, according to Ex 22:16, the violator would have to pay the marriage price (*mōhar*) and marry the girl. Even if the father refused to allow his daughter to marry, the fine would still have to be paid. Naturally it would be the desire of any man to wed a virgin, and for future proof that she was a virgin when married, the blood-stained linen used on the wedding night was preserved (Dt 22:13-21); any man who falsely accused a woman of not having been a virgin when they married would be fined 100 shekels of silver and punished, "because he slandered a virgin of Israel" (v. 19). Virgins captured in war were a great prize, and after the battle against the Midianites, the captive virgins were divided among the fighting men and the rest of the people (Nm 31:18, 27).

WIDOWS

The widow, together with the orphan, was a subject of great concern in the ancient Near East. From many biblical and non-biblical texts it is clear that the widow was generally in a poor financial position (cf., v.g., 1 Kings 17:8-12), and that she was liable to be unjustly treated in the law courts (cf. v.g., Is 1:23). Though the Book of Deuteronomy is particularly concerned to commend the widow to the charitable care of the community and to issue stern warnings to judges about their treatment of her, we gather, especially from the prophetic writings, that there were many abuses.

WOMEN IN PUBLIC AND RELIGIOUS LIFE

The biblical texts supply some information on the activity of women in public affairs. Deborah, who is called a prophetess and a "judge" (Jgs 4:4), and Jael were honored as heroines for their part in the defeat of a Canaanite army led by Sisera (Jgs cc. 4–5). During the struggles over the succession which broke out around David's deathbed, Bathsheba was instrumental in gaining the throne for her son, Solomon. To judge from the case of Maachah (1 Kings 15:13; 2 Chr 15:8-16), the role of queen-mother was a matter of importance (Albright, 1953, p. 158). Jezebel exercised a commanding influence over Ahab in public religious and non-religious affairs (1 Kings 18:4, 8, 19; c. 21). After the revolution of the northern general Jehu, Athaliah was able to usurp the throne of Judah and to hold it for about six years (2 Kings c. 11). Huldah, the prophetess, was consulted by Josiah in connection with his great public religious reform (2 Kings 22:14-20).

It is very likely that women shared in the festivities of the three great feast days, sc., Passover, Pentecost, and Booths; at least for the last named, a man's daughter and maidservant, and the widows, are specifically mentioned (Dt 16:14). Presumably the wives of Elkanah accompanied him to Shiloh when he went to sacrifice (1 Sam 1:3-5). Probably women went to the sanctuary to celebrate the festival of the New Moon or the Sabbath (2 Kings 4:23).

Because of her sex and ritual uncleanness, a woman could not function as a priest; though Israel's neighbors had priestesses, we never read in the Bible of such a practice in Israel, nor is there any feminine form of "priest" (kōhēn). It is a difficult problem to determine whether any women were employed among the personnel of the Temple (de Vaux,

1961, pp. 383-84). Though we know of singing and dancing women, we must not immediately conclude that they formed part of the personnel regularly employed in the cult. During periods of religious syncretism, it appears that male and female prostitutes took part in the worship, following the mode of the Canaanites; but for orthodox Yahwism this was an abomination.

EDUCATION OF WOMEN AND THEIR PLACE IN THE ARTS

The education of women was in the care of their mothers and was presumably limited to instruction in whatever would prepare them for their roles as wives and housewives. Some, however, may have been given further education since it is quite certain that women were engaged in the arts of playing, singing, and dancing, to a far greater extent than men. Whether any of the literature of the Old Testament was produced by women, it is impossible to say; the notices in Ex 15:21 and Jgs 5:1 concerning Miriam and Deborah singing songs are no guarantee that they composed the songs.

CONCLUSION

If we rely only on the data that can be gathered from the biblical texts, it becomes obvious that the social and legal status of woman in Israelite society was lower than that of the women of Egypt, who could often head a family with all the rights and privileges attached to this status, or of the women of Mesopotamia, who could make contracts on their own, acquire property for themselves, go to court of their own accord, and even be heirs of a share of a husband's property.

Whether in the charge of her father before marriage or under her husband after marriage, an Israelite woman belonged to a man. Her highest role in life was to bear children and to keep her husband's house. Though occasionally a woman might go beyond this role to break into public life, this would be the exception. But the place of the woman in Israelite society was not simply that of a menial—unless, of course, she were a slave; she was honored in her childbearing and by the efficient management of the household. There is sufficient evidence that at the basis of the man–woman relationship there was a genuine feeling of love.

REFERENCES

Albright, W. F. *Archaeology and the religion of Israel* (3rd ed.). Baltimore: Johns Hopkins Press, 1953.

Aptowitzer, V. Spuren des Matriarchats im jüdischen Schrifttum. *Hebrew Union Coll. Annu.,* 1927, *4,* 207-405; 1928, *5,* 261-297.

Burrows, M. The marriage of Ruth and Boaz. *J. Bibl. Lit.,* 1940, *59,* 445-454.

de Vaux, R. *Ancient Israel* (trans. by J. McHugh). New York: McGraw-Hill, 1961.

Gordon, C. H. Fratriarchy in the Old Testament. *J. Bibl. Lit.,* 1935, *54,* 223-231.

Koschaker, P. Fratriarchat, Hausgemeinschaft und Mutterrecht in Keilschriftrechten. *Zeitschrift für Assyriologie,* 1933, *41,* 1-89.

Martin, W. J. The law code of Hammurabi. In D. Winton Thomas (Ed.) *Documents from Old Testament Times.* London: Nelson, 1958. Pp. 27-37.

Pedersen, J. *Israel: its life and culture,* I-IV. London: Oxford University Press, 1926-1940.

Smith, W. Robertson. *Kinship and marriage in early Arabia* (2nd ed.). London: Cambridge University Press, 1903.

Woman in Traditional Theology

PAUL F. PALMER, S.J.

Father Paul F. Palmer, S.J., obtained all of his education at Woodstock College, receiving his bachelor's degree in 1931, his master's in 1932, and finally his doctorate in sacred theology in 1942. He taught dogmatic theology for almost twenty years at his alma mater, with a brief interlude from 1951 to 1955 at the Jesuit Theologate in Toronto, finally joining the Fordham University faculty in 1963. Father Palmer, in addition to various articles contributed to Theological Studies, *is the author of three books, all of them published by the Newman Press:* Mary in the Documents of the Church *(1952);* Sources of Christian Theology: I. Sacraments and Worship *(1955), and* Sources of Christian Theology: II. Sacraments and Forgiveness *(1959).*

Some years ago a book appeared with the title *What Men Know About Women.* The book was nicely bound but quite slim. There were but six pages and every page was blank. In the period we are to study, roughly the Patristic period, we do not find the same reticence on the subject of women. In fact, there seems to be no phase of woman's life that appears to be mysterious to the Fathers of the Church and early ecclesiastical writers. And yet I must stress from the beginning that their attitude towards women is rarely theological, as though the nature of woman differed essentially from that of man, or that woman needed a special theology to explain her existence as part of the human race redeemed by Christ. However, the Patristic attitude towards woman—and men have had all the lines—can be seen in a theological perspective. I would like to consider two dimensions of this theological perspective: (1) the essential equality of man and woman in nature and in grace; (2) the Christian emancipation of woman.

THE ESSENTIAL EQUALITY OF MAN AND WOMAN

It may seem strange to raise the question of Patristic teaching on the essential equality of man and woman. It is like asking the question whether Negroes have souls or whether they actually are part of the human race. The biblical foundation for the basic equality of the sexes is clear enough. Woman as well as man has been made to the image and likeness of God, as the priestly account of creation reminds us (Gen 1: 27). And even in the earlier, or Yahwist, account of the creation of man, where the woman is drawn from man, Yahweh declares his intention of making for Adam "a helper like unto himself" (Gen 2:18). And yet, as we shall see, this earlier account will create some ambiguity for Clement of Alexandria, writing in the early part of the fourth century. For the most part, however, it is the priestly description of man and woman as made into the image and likeness of God which founds the essential equality of man and woman. Oddly enough the passage is used time and again to prove that woman, in the excessive use of artificial adornments, is defacing the image of God in whose likeness she has been created.

The theme is set by Tertullian in his treatise *De cultu feminarum* and is given classic expression in the treatise *De habitu virginum* of St. Cyprian of Carthage in the middle of the third century.

Cyprian's treatise is concerned almost exclusively with the conduct of consecrated virgins who, at the time, lived at home rather than in communities. In the passage to be cited, however, Cyprian extends his remarks to include all women:

> . . . I think that not only virgins and widows but married women also, and all women in general, should be warned that the work of God and His creature and image should in no way be falsified by employing yellow coloring or black powder or rouge, or, finally, any cosmetic at all that spoils the natural features. God says: *Let us make man to our own image and likeness.* And someone dares to change and transform what God has made! They are laying hands on God when they strive to

remake what He has made, and to transform it, not knowing that everything that comes into existence is the work of God; that whatever is
changed, is the work of the devil [*De habitu virginum,* 15; Keenan,
1932, p. 59].

Cyprian's argument will not appeal to women today, although consecrated virgins for the most part do avoid the use of cosmetics. To suggest that nature cannot be improved upon may be true of the lilies of the
field that neither spin nor sew, but natural beauty can be enhanced and
the lack of it disguised, without running the risk mentioned by Cyprian,
that "when the day of resurrection comes your Maker may not recognize you" (*De habitu virginum,* 17; Keenan, 1932, p. 61).

Not only is woman made to the image and likeness of God, but, like
man, her body and her members are the temple of God, a theme introduced by St. Paul and developed by Tertullian and by Cyprian in their
respective treatises, *De cultu feminarum* and *De habitu virginum.* To
cite Cyprian:

> . . . reflecting as well as knowing that our members are the temple of
> God, cleansed from all impurity of the old corruption by the sanctifying
> waters of life, and that we are under obligation not to dishonor nor to
> defile them, since he who dishonors the body is himself dishonored.
> Of these temples we are the custodians and the high priests. . . . And,
> indeed, men as well as women, boys as well as girls, every sex and every
> age should give heed to this and be concerned about it, in keeping with
> the religious obligation and the faith which are due to God, lest what is
> received pure and holy through the benevolence of God be not guarded
> with anxious fear [*De habitu virginum,* 2; Keenan, 1932, pp. 43-45].

When we turn to the ecclesiastical writers of the East we find an antifeminist bias which is characteristic of every ancient culture, pagan,
Jewish, and Christian. Thus, Clement of Alexandria, a contemporary of
Tertullian, can conclude quite simply: "Males are better and first in
everything" (*Stromata,* 4, 8). And yet Clement, who is most harsh on
the vanity and conceit of women, simply takes it for granted that they
too have been fashioned to the image and likeness of God:

> It is absurdly out of place for women who have been made to the
> image and likeness of God, to dishonor the archetype by assuming a
> foreign embellishment, preferring the evil arts of men to the workman-
> ship of God [*Paedagogus* 3, 11; Burghardt, 1957, p. 138].

Cyril of Alexandria has hundreds of passages in which the theme of man
(*anthropos*) as made to the image and likeness of God is developed.
Rarely does he distinguish man from woman in the use of the text from
Genesis 1: 27. The rare exceptions are prompted by two considerations,

the first physiological and psychological, the second scriptural or Pauline.

According to Cyril, woman is not only physiologically or biologically inferior to man, she is inferior psychologically. Speaking of the purification of a woman after childbearing, Cyril remarks:

> The experts tell us that if it is a male child that is deposited in the womb, it just about receives its specific nature when forty days have elapsed; but if it is a female, the process is slower, since the female is weak and impotent. They say it needs twice forty days, that is eighty, for its specific nature to emerge clearly [*De Adoratione,* 15; Burghardt, 1957, p. 127].

The experts in question are the fathers of Greek medicine, Hippocrates, Galen and Empedocles, not to mention the great philosopher and scientist, Aristotle, who regarded woman as "an incomplete or mutilated man" (*De animalium generatione,* 2).

We should not be surprised that Cyril takes for granted the prejudiced and *a priori* views of these ancient *periti.* As late as the year 1771, the Sacred Congregation of the Council, in discussing the question of abortion, referred to the 40–80-day norm as the more common and accepted opinion on the time of animation (Burghardt, 1957, p. 127). And St. Thomas Aquinas is a faithful disciple of Aristotle in explaining the reason why a woman is an imperfect creature (*aliquid deficiens*) and the result of chance (*occasionatum*). Holding that the operative element (*virtus activa*) is resident in the male seed, and that it tends by nature to produce what is perfectly similar to itself, namely one of the male sex, St. Thomas concludes:

> But the fact that a female is generated is due to some weakness in the active power, or some indisposition [in the woman], or even some change induced from without, for example, South winds which are humid [*Sum. theol.,* 1, q. 92, a. 1].

What is surprising in Cyril of Alexandria is a deepseated antifemininism which goes beyond the physical or physiological deficiencies of woman. Woman is not only inferior to man in physical size and strength, but, to quote Father Burghardt's summary of Cyril's views:

> She has not the strength to achieve the virtue of which man is capable. She is of imperfect intelligence. Unlike her male complement, she is dull-witted, slow to learn, unprepared to grasp the difficult and the supernatural; for her mind is a soft, weak, delicate thing. Briefly, "the female sex is ever weak in mind and body" [Burghardt, 1957, pp. 127-128].

Given this antifeminine bias it is perhaps understandable why Cyril is more hesitant than his predecessors to admit without qualification that woman is made to the image of God. This hesitancy finds scriptural precedent in a rather cryptic passage from St. Paul in which women are admonished to cover their heads while present in the assembly. To quote Paul:

> A man indeed ought not to cover his head, because he is the image and glory of God. But woman is the glory of man. For man is not from woman, but woman from man. This is why the woman ought to have a sign of authority over her head because of the angels [1 Cor. 11: 7-10].

In his commentary on this passage from 1 Corinthians, Cyril insists that even though woman was made to the image and likeness of man, she is "by no means alien to him; on the contrary, [she is] of the same nature and species" (*In Epist. 1 ad Corinthios* 4: 4; Burghardt, 1957, p. 134). However, as Cyril continues in his commentary, he cannot resist concluding that

> since man is God's image and glory . . . let him maintain freedom fit for God and keep his head uncovered. . . . And seeing that woman is in man's likeness, image of an image, and glory of glory, and that nature legislates long hair for her, why does that which is first [man] emulate what is inferior in grace? Woman, too, is indeed in God's image, but as by means of the man, so that in some way she differs a little in nature [*In Epist. 1 ad Corinthios,* 4: 4; Burghardt, 1957, p. 134].

Fortunately, Cyril's psychological bias against woman and his theological ambiguity on the essential equality of man and woman in nature are not reflected in the Church's practical attitude towards woman. Christian teaching and practice has been based more on the statement of St. Paul: in Christ Jesus, "there is neither male nor female" (Gal 3: 28). Both have been redeemed by Christ, both are called equally to the heights of Christian perfection. Man and woman are incorporated into Christ and his Church by the same rites of initiation. And while it is true that women were not ordained for a strictly liturgical ministry, widows, deaconesses and consecrated virgins enjoyed a privileged position in the Christian assembly which was not shared by the ordinary layman. Again, in times of persecution, women of every status proved themselves as heroic as men in their witness to Christ. Admittedly, the Church in her prayer of the virgin and martyr reflects the common view of woman as the weaker sex, but only to marvel at the wonders that God can accomplish in and through her:

> O God, who, among the other marvels of your power, has granted the victory of martyrdom even to the weak sex, grant, we beseech you, that we who celebrate the birthday of your virgin and martyr, may through her example draw closer to you. Through Christ Jesus our Lord. Amen.

There is, perhaps, no way of comparing the number of women and men who gave the martyr's witness during the periods of persecution, but the Roman liturgy has composed an impressive litany of virgins and martyrs which is recited in the Canon of the Mass: Felicity and Perpetua, Agatha, Lucy and Agnes, Cecilia and Anastasia.

THE CHRISTIAN EMANCIPATION OF WOMAN

Thus far I have considered the attitude of the early Church towards women as such. Unquestionably, the emphasis has been on the privileged position of the consecrated virgin and the widow. In fact, there are some authors who find in the institution of virginity the basic emancipation of woman (cf. Rössler, 1912, p. 690). Until the coming of Christ, woman's sole function and her great ambition was to be of service to man, preferably in marriage. Her vocation was to satisfy her husband's desires, to be the mother of his children, and, as principal wife, the custodian of his household. In this latter capacity we have numerous examples of exemplary women, of whom the *mulier fortis* of Proverbs, Chapter 31 is the type. But even in Proverbs, the strong woman is proclaimed because she is a credit to her husband.

As a result of Christ's teaching on celibacy embraced for the sake of the kingdom of God (Mt 19: 12) and Paul's more explicit teaching on the preeminence of the virginal state (1 Cor 7), there is open to woman a vocation that is quite independent of a particular man, a vocation that has significance in itself, and which is not subordinate to the vocation of a husband. St. Paul stresses the freedom that the unmarried have from the cares of family life, a freedom that is at times overstressed by some authors in their zeal for promoting the religious life, an aspect of virginity which could apply equally to the unmarried career woman and the consecrated virgin. However, even the most zealous defenders of virginity stress that it is not physical virginity as such but the complete dedication to "the things of the Lord" that distinguishes the true virgin as the bride of Christ. Her vocation, like that of her patroness, Mary, will include the role of mother, not of a particular family, but of the larger family of God which is the Church. Such was the role of the consecrated virgin in the early Church and such it is today.

Granted that the institution of virginity played an important role in the emancipation of woman, I believe that the basic and more general emancipation stems from Christ's teaching on the question of divorce, and, by implication, his insistence on the marital rights of a woman, rights which will be made explicit by St. Paul.

All three synoptic writers record Christ's rejection of the presumed right of a Jewish male to divorce his wife for reasons tolerated by the Mosaic Law. In Mark's account, however, there is a significant variation which explains why divorce is wrong, and why, by implication, polygamy as well. Matthew and Luke record our Lord as saying "Whoever divorces his wife and marries another, commits adultery" (Mt 19: 9; Lk 16: 18). Mark adds: "Whoever divorces his wife and marries another, commits adultery against her" (Mk 10:12).

The conception of adultery against a woman is quite startling since it is completely incompatible with all polygamous codes of law. In all such codes, including the Mosaic Law, adultery was regarded as the violation of the rights of a male. For all practical purposes, the wife was regarded as the property of the man, much in the same way as was his home, his livestock, and his other goods. This concept is reflected even in the Code drawn up on Sinai, where our ninth and tenth commandments form a single command in justice: "Thou shalt not covet thy neighbor's wife. Thou shalt not covet thy neighbor's goods." Christ's teaching, as recorded by Mark, is distinctive in this, that woman is regarded as having marital rights which can be violated by her husband, that a man does in fact commit adultery against his wife either by divorcing her and marrying again or by bringing another woman into his home.

Without touching directly the question of polygamy, St. Paul furnishes the principle which underscores the basic equality of man and woman in marriage: "The wife has not authority over her body but the husband; the husband likewise has not authority over his body, but the wife" (1 Cor 7: 4). Marriage then is a mutual surrender; once that surrender is made neither the husband nor the wife has the right in justice to give oneself to another, either inside or outside of marriage.

This fundamental equality of man and woman in marriage is to my mind the distinctive contribution of Christianity not only to the ethics of marriage but to the rejection of the double standard of morality which allowed in a man what it condemned in a woman. So revolutionary is the concept of adultery against a woman that many non-Christians even today fail to grasp its significance. Thus, Louis Epstein, writing in the Harvard Semitic Series, advances the rather strange thesis that the early Church did not forbid polygamy except for a bishop or presbyter, concluding

> even if we should assume that the Apostles wished to prohibit polygamy, it is thoroughly impossible . . . to consider polygamy equal to adultery, unless we are ready to consider sex relations between a married man and a prostitute adultery on the part of a man [Epstein, 1942, p. 15].

Admittedly this concept was completely foreign to Jewish thinking and even to that of the monogamous Greeks and Romans. However, there are few Christians today who would agree with Epstein, and the reason is to be found in the Church's insistence on the teaching of Christ that a man can commit adultery against his wife, and Paul's principle that a husband has no authority over his body, but the wife.

True, even after the conversion of the Empire, public opinion and Roman law were as yet unprepared to admit in practice the consequences of Christian teaching. But public opinion was changed and new laws ultimately written as the direct result of the constant prodding of the Church Fathers of the East and the West. More often it was the conscience of the Christian congregation that was instructed. But there was one memorable occasion when Gregory Nazianzen (c. 380) challenged the double standard of morality in a sermon preached before the Emperor Constantius:

> I find that most men have a tendency to be most unreasonable and that their laws are both unfair and inconsistent. Why, for example, have they restrained the wife but have been indulgent to the husband? Why is the wife who violates the bed of her husband an adulteress—and the penalties of the law for this are most severe—while the husband who commits adultery against his wife [note the expression] is liable to no penalty? I do not accept this enactment; in no way do I approve this custom. Those who made the law are men and therefore their legislation is hard on women. . . . The two, Christ says, shall be one flesh; so let the one flesh have equal honor [*Oratio* 37, 6-7].

At a time when Milan was the seat of the Empire in the West, Ambrose the Bishop of that city preached a sermon which may well have come to the attention of the Emperor Theodosius:

> But I warn you, husbands, who walk in the grace of the Lord, not to unite yourself to an adulterous body—for one who joins himself to a harlot is one body with her—nor make this the occasion of your wives' divorcing you. And let no one be deluded by the laws of men. For every defilement is adultery, nor is the man permitted to do what the woman is not. The same chastity is demanded of the husband as of the wife. Whatever sin he commits with one who is not his wife is condemned as the crime of adultery. Accordingly, learn what you must avoid, lest one make himself unworthy of the sacraments [*De Abraham,* 1].

Rather than multiply passages from individual Fathers of the East and the West, let me confine myself to the teaching of St. John Chrysostom, to my mind the most eloquent and realistic defender of the rights of women in the Patristic age.

Basil the Great, the Father of Eastern Canon Law (c. 380), had yielded to custom and public opinion in assigning a lesser penance for a husband who had relations with a single woman than for a wife who had relations with a single man. In the wife's case, the penance was that of the adulteress, fifteen years in the graded penitential discipline. In the husband's case, the penance was that of the fornicator, seven years in the same discipline. However, Basil himself admits that he sees no reason for the distinction except that custom has had it so (cf. *Ad Amphilocium, epist.* 188, can. 21). Chrysostom is more forthright in challenging custom:

> We are quite aware that many people judge it to be adultery only when a man corrupts a woman wedded to a husband. For my part, if a man, so long as he is married, has illicit relations with a common harlot or with a servant girl or anyone not his wife, I contend that this is adultery. . . . Do not bring up against me outside laws which drag women who have committed adultery into court, and which demand that they be punished, but leave unpunished husbands who corrupt servant girls. Rather, I'll cite you the law of God which binds equally the husband and the wife, and which calls such conduct adultery [*Hom. in verba "Propter fornicationem"* 4].

Chrysostom spells out the law of God in two homilies: Paul's first Epistle to the Corinthians, Chapter 7, and his Epistle to the Ephesians, Chapter 5. Unfortunately, neither homily has received adequate notice in the books on marriage that I have read. Hence, you will pardon the rather extensive quotations that I shall make. In his homily on Corinthians, Chrysostom discusses what has come to be regarded as the "marriage debt": "Let the husband render the wife her due, and likewise the wife her husband" (1 Cor 7: 5). After delicately reminding the woman that she has no right to refuse her husband, and that Paul's qualification, "except for prayer," is not to be coupled with the expression, "Pray always," as Tertullian and Jerome would have it, Chrysostom offers the following advice to husbands and wives:

> When you, the husband, see a harlot tempting you, say "My body is not mine, but my wife's." And let the wife say the same to those who would undermine her chastity: "My body is not mine, but my husband's." . . . In other matters [Paul] says, let the husband have the prerogative; but not where there is a question of chastity. For "the husband has not authority over his own body, neither has the wife." Here, there is great equality, but no prerogative [*In 1 Cor. Hom. 19,* 1].

Returning to the question of the marriage debt, Chrysostom implies that the marriage act is not only demanded in justice but also in love:

Suppose, in the case of husband and wife, the wife is continent without the consent of her husband. If he commits fornication, or, abstaining
from fornication, he frets and grows restless and heated and quarrelsome
and gives all kinds of trouble to his wife, what is gained by fasting and
continence, when a breach has been made in love? [*In 1 Cor. Hom.
19, 1*].

In his homily on Ephesians, perhaps the greatest encomium of Christian
marriage in the Patristic age, Chrysostom stresses the role of love, both
human and divine. For Chrysostom "there is nothing that so welds life
together as the love of man and wife," a love which demands that a
husband be ready to lay down his life for his wife, as Christ gave his life
for his bride, the Church. With some regard for the spiritual attainments
of the wife, he asks both husband and wife to discuss together what they
have heard in the Sunday sermon, and concludes: "If anyone marries in
this way and with these ideals in mind, he will be but little inferior to
monks; the married will be but little below the unmarried." Chrysostom
might have ended on this note, but by way of epilogue, he returns to the
central theme developed in his homily on 1 Corinthians. True, there is
present in the passage a note of paternalism, but I believe that there are
few women today who would not welcome from their husbands the sentiments that Chrysostom counsels:

Above all, banish from her heart that notion of *mine and thine*. . . .
Say, "Even I am thine, my child dear"; this advice Paul gives me when he
says: "The husband has not authority over his own body, but the wife."
If I have no rights over my own body, but it is you who have, much
more have you rights over my possessions. . . . Thus by your language,
teach her never to speak of *mine and thine*. Again, never address her
simply by name, but add some terms of endearment, with honor and
much love. . . . Prefer her before all others, on every account, both for
her beauty and her discernment, and praise her. . . . Teach her the fear
of God, and all good things will flow as from a fountain and your home
will be full of ten thousand blessings [*In Epist. ad Ephesianos, Hom. 20*].

Unfortunately, Chrysostom's emphasis on the role of human love and
tenderness in marriage is not typical of the Church Fathers of the East,
nor did it influence to any degree the teaching of the scholastic doctors
of the West. Western thinking was more dependent on Augustine. From
Augustine the early scholastics inherited the view that concupiscence is
the operative element in the transmission of original sin, and that, as a
consequence, concupiscence is present in every marital embrace, an evil
which can be wholly excused only when the purpose of the act is procreation (Palmer, 1955, pp. 134-138). In this context the role of the
wife as mother was stressed but at the expense of her equally essential

role as loving companion of the husband. In one place Augustine does not hesitate to assert that the only reason why God created Eve as a helpmate to Adam was for the purpose of procreation (*De genesi ad litteram,* 9, 3). And Thomas Aquinas sums up the reason when he says: "In all other pursuits a man is helped better by another man than by a woman" (*Sum. theol.,* 1, q. 92, a.1).

Commenting on the cult of adulterous love in the early Middle Ages, C. S. Lewis is correct, at least in part, when he traces its rise to the reaction that set in to the more rigorous teaching of the Schoolmen. If every passionate lover is an adulterer, better that a man take a mistress than defile his own wife. If the marital act is blameless only when it is prompted by hope of offspring, then it becomes the mark of a true lover as the above-mentioned author observes in the words of the Canterbury Tales (Lewis, 1951, p. 18), to serve Venus

More for delyt than world to multiplye.

SUMMARY

Traditional theology has contributed much to the Christian emancipation of woman by insisting that a woman has rights which can be violated by her husband. In doing so it was successful in removing many of the more glaring inconsistencies in the double standard of morality as applied to husband and wife. Its chief failure was to overlook the role of the wife as lover as well as mother. For experience has proved that where procreation is divorced from human love and marital affection there is danger that a man will take a wife for childbearing and a mistress for lovemaking.

Perhaps one of the greatest contributions to the complete emancipation of woman has been the stress in contemporary theology on the so-called secondary values in marriage, love and companionship, values which safeguard the dignity of the wife as the perfect complement of her husband, values which will lead the husband, in the words of Chrysostom, "to prefer his wife before all others, on every account, both for her beauty and her discernment."

REFERENCES

Burghardt, W. J. (S.J.) *The image of God in man according to Cyril of Alexandria (Studies in Christian Antiquity,* No. 14). Washington: Catholic University Press, 1957.

Epstein, L. *Marriage laws in the Bible and the Talmud (Harvard Semitic Series).* Cambridge: Harvard University Press, 1942.

Keenan, Sister Angela Elizabeth. *Thasci Caecili Cypriani De Habitu Vir-ginum (Patristic Studies,* vol. 34). Washington: Catholic University Press, 1932.

Lewis, C.S. *The allegory of love.* New York: Oxford University Press, 1951.

Palmer, P. F. (S.J.) Mary and the flesh. In T. Burke (S.J.) (Ed.) *Mary and modern man.* New York: America Press, 1955. Pp. 110-140.

Rössler, A. Woman. *Cath. Encyc.,* 1912, *15,* 687-694.

Woman in Contemporary Theology

CHRISTOPHER F. MOONEY, S.J.

Christopher F. Mooney, S.J., Chairman of Fordham University's Theology Department, received his B.A. (1950) and his M.A. (1954) degrees from Loyola University, Chicago, and his doctoral degree from the Institut Catholique, Paris, in 1964. He has contributed to a number of theological journals, including Theological Studies, Harvard Theological Review, Downside Review, Scripture, *and* Religious Education. *Father Mooney is a foremost American authority on Father Teilhard de Chardin, as attested by his recently published and widely acclaimed* Teilhard de Chardin and the Mystery of Christ *(1966).*

In *The second sex,* one of her most controversial books, Simone de Beauvoir (1953) insists that in spite of all that Christianity has done for woman, it has nonetheless contributed in no small measure to keeping her in a state of dependence unworthy of her dignity as a human being. Such an accusation does in fact touch the nerve center of a problem area which has become the concern of a number of theologians in recent years. What precisely is woman's vocation in the Church, and how does it differ from that of man? As yet there are no satisfying answers to these questions. Several veins of though have been uncovered, however, which promise eventually to yield a more satisfying theology of woman than we have

21

today, and it is the purpose of this paper briefly to examine these and to
reflect upon the possible lines of their future development.

One of the chief reasons for the lack of any extensive theological reflection upon woman is that until 1945 the Church herself had made no
significant statement on the new status achieved by woman through the
great social, scientific, economic and political upheavals of the present
century (Rondet, 1957). This is not to say that the popes before Pius
XII were unconcerned about woman. They were indeed concerned, but
almost all their pronouncements concerned the duties of woman in marriage and family life (Faherty, 1950, pp. 10-108). Between 1945 and
his death, however, Pius XII faced for the first time the fact that, even
though the natural vocation of woman may be to maternity and the
home, the individual vocation of a modern woman in the Church may
well be to play a special role in social and even political life. God may
deliberately be placing modern woman in circumstances which force her
to work outside family life, precisely in order to accomplish through her
an influence upon society which she alone can exert. A woman with such
a vocation would have to possess the same professional training as that
of a man in any given area of influence. Hence the equality between man
and woman must be recognized not simply on the human level, but on
the social and political level as well (Pius XII, 1945).

The revolutionary nature of these early statements of Pius XII can
be judged by the fact that, when he made them, the official status of
woman in the Church still tended to reflect a mentality current in the
centuries when canon law was being elaborated: namely, a conviction of
woman's weakness and especially of her lack of skill. Church law consequently tried to protect her from a brutal and disorganized world by
providing her either with a husband or with a walled cloister (Soullard,
1959). But with Pius XII there came solicitude not for the weakness of
woman but for her mission in the Church. In later pronouncements his
emphasis falls on the fact that the Church needs woman just as much
as it does man, in order to promote on the various levels of human
culture the Christian ideals of peace, justice and human dignity (Pius
XII, 1956).

What must be insisted upon, however, is that the individual woman
is to accomplish this new role by cultivating those very qualities which
are characteristic of her as a person. There is to be no question, therefore, of modifying in any way her personal makeup, for it is precisely

by being what she is that she will help to offset that impersonalism which tends to impregnate the organizational structures of modern life. The common spiritual equality of men and women before God will thus tend to have very different modes of expression, not only in their interior attitudes but also in their exterior work as Christians in the world. Significantly enough, all these ideas were touched upon to some extent by Pope John XXIII in a 1960 address, though his purpose in doing so was clearly to leave their development to the theologians (John XXIII, 1960).

BIBLICAL CONCEPT OF COUPLE

What then have the theologians done with this problem of modern woman's mission in the Church? At the risk of oversimplification we can distinguish three main lines of development. The first is a strong emphasis upon the primitive biblical concept of the couple. Man and woman were created for each other, to love each other and to perpetuate each other. The plan of God is that there be neither man nor woman alone, but a community of the two, which is in fact an image of the divine community. God's unity in a trinity of Persons reflects itself in a human nature which is bisexual. It is Karl Barth who has in fact given this idea its most forceful formulation: only male and female together are man. To be created in God's image means to be created male and female; these are synonymous expressions in the book of Genesis and they designate the mystery of the free "I-Thou" relationship within God's own personal life in so far as it has been communicated to man. All that is feminine must somehow be present in God just as all that is masculine. The biblical concept of the couple thus shows human nature to be a third transcendent dimension, a completion perceptible only by the eye of faith (Barth, 1958, pp. 183-187; 313-316).

But this same concept likewise enables us to speak of masculine and feminine not as opposites but as complementary metaphysical principles which are in fact part of every man's and woman's life. Virility and femininity would thus be seen as two modes of being human, two modes of reflecting the nature and activity of God. There must be gentleness, sensitivity and compassion in man as well as in woman, since these qualities are somehow also divine; for the same reason woman must develop strength, initiative and firmness of will, and become the maker as well as the mother. Such a theological perspective has served to throw into strong relief the positive value of feminine qualities. Femininity can be treated as a good in itself; no longer simply a way of facing life with

feeble resources and the need of protection, but an original and autonomous mode of finite existence, present in man as well as woman,
though usually tending to dominate in the latter. Bisexuality therefore
points in two directions: backwards to the mystery of creation in God's
image, and forwards to human participation in the redemptive mission
of Christ. Whatever distinctive contribution woman must make to this
redemptive mission, it is absolutely necessary that she make it precisely
as woman (Tilliette, 1963, pp. 116-118; Arnold, 1963, pp. 20-23).

WOMAN'S ROLE IN CULTURE

This brings us to the second contemporary development regarding
woman's role in the Church, namely, the sporadic attempts which have
taken place to articulate what Gertrud von le Fort (1954) has called
"the nuptial character of culture." This does not mean that there are
to be no independent cultural achievements by women alone, but such
achievements will be the exception. What woman accomplishes in the
world she will almost always accomplish as a companion to man, for
it is as man's companion that she constitutes one of the polarities of
human nature. To see this relationship solely in terms of marriage and
generation is to grasp only half of its responsibility, for whatever applies
to new being in a biological sense applies also to new life produced by
artistic or spiritual creation. Man and woman together are needed to
build human society. Man can make no truly creative contribution to
human culture without a response from woman, an active response, for
woman's receptivity is not passive acceptance but an answer to man,
the answer of a companion who inspires, encourages and fructifies. The
receptivity of woman is therefore dependent upon her initiative as a
person. She will receive from man only if she wishes to receive and to
the extent that she freely chooses (von le Fort, 1954, pp. 33-46; Stein,
1959, pp. 1-15).

The necessity of this companionship and cooperation of woman in
man's cultural undertakings will be seen more clearly, perhaps, if we
reflect upon the importance of the religious element in all truly human
achievement. This element involves humility and a reverence for the
divine which is needed before man can participate fruitfully in the
creative activity of God. Such reverence and humility, say those who
write in this vein, would seem to be more characteristic of woman than
man. It is woman who symbolizes the free and loving submission of
creature to Creator and is able to inspire this surrender in those around
her. She tends to transcend the role she plays in events rather than to

overrate it, and can see more easily in the complex web of human action the creative presence of God. The feminine impetus thus means an impulse toward reverence. Woman's collaboration enables man to realize that his own creative impetus is in reality a movement toward cooperation with God, who usually chooses to remain silent in man's labor and in some sense anonymous. This creative anonymity of God tends to be reflected in the active receptivity of woman, and man must somehow participate in this receptivity if he is to have reverence for God in the midst of his human achievement (von le Fort, 1954, pp. 47-51; Henry, 1949, pp. 467-475).

WOMAN IN THE EVOLUTIONARY SYSTEM OF TEILHARD DE CHARDIN

A third development in contemporary theology has been suggested by the evolutionary system of Pierre Teilhard de Chardin. Teilhard was convinced that true revolutionary progress resides not in the forces of tangential energy, now moving inevitably toward an ever greater technical mastery of mind over matter, but rather in the forces of radial energy, which in man have become "psychosocial," urging him forward toward ever-higher forms of interpersonal communion. Because modern man has suddenly become conscious of what is taking place in him, it follows that the successful outcome of evolution now depends upon his free decision to cooperate with these forces of radial energy which, in Teilhard's system, reach their highest form in human love. Love is in fact the key to the whole evolutionary process, since it alone unites human beings in such a way as to complete and fulfill them by joining them to what is deepest in themselves. On the strictly phenomenological level this is a fact of daily experience, especially in the sexual love between husband and wife, and in several of his essays Teilhard goes out of his way to discuss this "sexual sense" in relationship to what he calls the growth of amorization in the noosphere. "The mutual attraction of the sexes is so fundamental a fact," he says, "that any explanation of the world which does not succeed in incorporating it structurally, as an essential part of its edifice, is virtually condemned" (Teilhard de Chardin, 1962, p. 91).

This love between man and woman, however, can have no lasting significance for the human race unless it conquer the temptation to create "a universe for two" and submit to a growth by which the "sexual sense" is gradually transformed into a human and cosmic sense. Teilhard's faith in Christian revelation, moreover, enabled him to link this growth of love-energy to the growth of Christian charity, since in the present supernatural order the real Omega of evolution is the Body-Person of Christ. Christ is the Center toward which all true love and charity must converge; in Him alone will the married couple find that equilibrium necessary for an unselfish expansion of their human love toward the community and the world. "Love is a function of three terms: man, woman and God. Its whole perfection and success is bound up with the balanced harmony of these three elements" (Teilhard de Chardin, 1962, p. 94).

We must recognize, therefore, that human love is still in process of development. As an energy it goes far beyond the needs of reproduction, and is searching ceaselessly for fuller and more meaningful forms of expression. Woman has not yet completely revealed man to himself, nor *vice versa*. It is not in isolation that man and woman move toward God; the evolving structure of the universe demands that these two modalities of human nature progress upward together. To divorce the spritual progress of mankind from relationships between the sexes, whether inside or outside marriage, is to forget that this duality must eventually be found even when human nature is completely divinized and united to Christ at the end of time. The spiritual life cannot be based on the human "monad," but only on the human "dyad."

Now, for Teilhard, woman is the key to this development of the human dyad, because she much more than man is eminently suitable to be a carrier of unselfish love, and hence the factor of balance and equilibrium. It is through her that the action of Christ will usually pass in sublimating sexual attraction. "For man, woman is the one term capable of launching this forward movement. Through woman and through woman alone is man able to escape the isolation in which he risks becoming imprisoned by reason of his own masculine perfection" (Teilhard de Chardin, 1962, p. 93; see also Mooney, 1965, and Devaux, 1963). Because the feminine influence tends to arouse and to nourish a love of the invisible, Teilhard sees this influence as the basis of woman's vocation in the world. "No man can do without the feminine, any more than he can do without light, oxygen or vitamins, and the evidence for this becomes more glaring every day" (Teilhard de Chardin, 1950, p. 33; see also 1962, pp. 40-42, and 131-134). Woman thus becomes in Teilhard's system the affective principle in cosmic development, the symbol of a world in evolution, the unifying impetus by which the human race is enabled to take the step toward universal love.

MARIOLOGY AND THE THEOLOGY OF WOMAN

The three veins of thought we have just examined show promise of yielding a more satisfying theology of woman than we have today, and it would not be out of place briefly to reflect upon possible lines of their future development. One of these may well come from the concerted theological effort today to bring Mariology closer to its Christological center and to present doctrine concerning Mary in the context of her relationship to the Church. The Constitution on the Church of Vatican II has in fact attempted to do this by making Mary's motherhood the fundamental fact in interpreting all statements concerning her role as mediatrix in the economy of salvation. Precisely because she is mother of Christ she cares for all the brethren of Christ. His unique office as Mediator, shared by all Christians in so far as they are helpers and mediators to each other, is shared in a special way by Mary, just as His unique office as Priest is shared at different levels by His ministers. Mary cooperates in the work of salvation, therefore, in the same way as every Christian does, namely through faith, charity and union with Christ; and if she is rightfully considered to be the type or image of the Church, this is because her cooperation was perfect and her union with Christ complete (Vatican Council II, 1966, Ch. 8).

This insistence today upon Mary's active role in the Church as a function of her motherhood may well become the starting point for some meaningful theological resolution of that dilemma so painful to modern woman—namely, the dichotomy between freedom and femininity. The clarification of doctrine is always in God's providence a response to definite religious dangers, and one of these is certainly the future of contemporary woman. In the past she has been faced with a vast historical heritage of prejudice and custom, which forced her to keep well outside the masculine world and made her quite incapable of cooperating in any meaningful way with man's decisions and achievements. The danger now is that, in order to possess that complete equality with man which seems at last within reach, she will want to become more and more like man and less and less like woman. Such a tendency is in fact just as destructive as its opposite extreme, which seeks to chain woman to an abstract "nature" or to imprison her in a highly elaborated set of "feminine" qualities which discourage her initiative and ignore her originality as a person. What is needed then is an equilibrium, and this could well come from a deeper understanding of Mary's relationship to Christ and the Church. For Mary is the eternal woman in a truly ontological sense, and every woman becomes more like her insofar as she fulfills her mission in life, whether she herself is psychologically conscious of this or not. Mary's cooperation with God's plan for the world today is an active mediatorial effort, for she shares this office of her Son at its highest level. Yet she is mediatrix always as mother, with that tenderness which motherhood brings, whether it be physical or spiritual. Woman has need for such tenderness today, certainly as much as she has for autonomy, and her new-found freedom may itself be a silent plea that the tenderness of Mary be not excluded from the mechanized world of tomorrow.

WOMAN'S EQUALITY IN ECCLESIASTICAL AFFAIRS

A second line of development in the theology of woman may come when Catholic women are eventually allowed greater voice in the decision-making of the Church. It has been said often enough, and not without reason, that in no institution in western civilization is there less equality to be found between the sexes than in the Catholic Church. To a large extent social and cultural reasons are responsible for this. Until modern times women have generally been thought incompetent in public affairs, and we have already seen to what extent canon law was influenced by this mentality. While always maintaining the equality of woman with man in their relationship with God (in accordance with Gal 3:28, "There is neither male nor female . . . in Christ Jesus"), ecclesiastical authority said almost nothing of woman's relationship with man in Catholic life. It is true that over the centuries great authority has been exercised by the women who have founded and governed various religious orders, but such authority has never extended beyond these groups into the hierarchical and parochial functioning of the Church. This brings us now to a much more fundamental reason for the exclusion of women from any kind of direction in Church affairs.

The various levels of Church government have always been associated historically with the priesthood. While there is no intrinsic doctrinal reason to prevent a woman from becoming a priest, the fact is that from the most primitive times women have been excluded from such ordination. The early Church did have the office of deaconess, but there is good reason to believe that this concerned not liturgy and cult but a teaching function, or perhaps some type of authority in charitable works. Rom 16:1-2 is an explicit reference to the deaconess Phoebe; I Tim 3:8-13 seems to be a list of the qualifications for the office of deaconess as well as deacon, and the Evodia and Syntyche of Phil 4:2-3 may well have been deaconesses at Philippi. A strong case has been made for the office of deaconess by Margaret Brackenbury Crook in her book, *Women and religion* (1964, pp. 122-125, 143-147). This office seems to have lasted up to the middle of the third century. At one time too women actually took part in liturgical functions, but no feminine clergy ever seems to have developed, and liturgical custom very soon excluded women altogether from any official function at Mass (Daniélou, 1960). Though by baptism women participate in the priesthood of Christ at the level common to all the faithful, only men are ordained to the official priesthood in the Church.

But must all future discussion of women's equality in ecclesiastical affairs center upon the priesthood? What modern woman wants is some official voice in the Church; there seems to be relatively little demand on her part for an official position in cult. Such an ecclesiastical voice could well be granted to her by reason of her participation not in Christ's priestly function but in His function as prophet and king. The primitive office of deaconess seems to have been just such a participation, recognized publicly and carrying with it a certain degree of ecclesiastical authority. Catholic women today do in fact exercise the teaching function very widely, and they influence to a greater or lesser extent many decisions on the parish and diocesan level. But the reasons for this are usually pragmatic, a question of sufferance, not of right. Until some public ecclesiastical position is actually conferred upon a good number of women, it is difficult to see how the Church can seriously claim that her male and female members enjoy the same equality which they possess today in civil society.

Nor can it be objected here that St. Paul did not favor such a place for women in the Church. One of the most saintly and erudite of modern Catholic women, Edith Stein, has vigorously attacked these appeals to St. Paul in matters concerning women's clothes and other social customs of the time. In the famous passage of I Cor 11:2-16, she says, divine instructions and purely human advice should be carefully distinguished. The context here is clearly one of woman's right to pray in the public assembly and also to "preach" under certain conditions. There is every reason to believe, she adds, that Paul would write quite differently about woman's place today.[1] The same would hold true also for the injunction of I Cor 14:34-35, that "women are to keep silence in the Churches." The occasion for this prohibition seems to have been

[1]Without any explanation, the editors of Edith Stein's published works have ommitted these comments from *Die Frau*, where they should appear on page 25 following her comments on I Cor 7:14-16. For the missing remarks see Hilda Graef's biography, *The scholar and the cross* (1955, pp. 83-84).

the custom at Corinth to have not only a discussion following the reading of Scripture, but also a question period. In 14:16-33 Paul gives rules of decorum to be observed at these times, and in verses 34-35 he goes on to silence women who, contrary to Jewish and Greek custom, wished to take part in these discussions. The women in question, however, are clearly ordinary members of the congregation and not the "preaching" women whose rights Paul has vindicated in Chapter 11. Once more, therefore, we have an appeal to customs generally observed at the time. No one can legitimately invoke such a prohibition today when women who speak in public shock no one at all.[2]

FEMININE MODES OF RELIGIOUS EXPRESSION

Finally we should underline a serious problem regarding this greater voice for women in ecclesiastical decision-making, one whose danger has been insisted upon most forcefully by Karl Rahner (1964). This concerns the fact that in the West Christianity has tended to take on many features which appeal more to feminine than to masculine piety. What Rahner objects to is not specifying Christianity either as masculine or feminine, which is both legitimate and necessary, but of making it "effeminate," that is to say, of putting a characteristically feminine stamp where it does not belong. The special danger today is that feminine modes of religious expression have become more widespread in the Church than masculine. The type of "holy picture" ordinarily circulated for religious ceremonies, the statues to be found in all too many churches, the style of prayers composed for novenas and acts of consecration, the overemphasis on "devotions," fulfillment of rules, external observances, all this tends to appeal on the popular level to women rather than men. This is not to say that women have been chiefly responsible for this state of affairs. On the contrary, it is precisely the male clergy who have perpetuated in the western Church forms of piety which were inherited from baroque Europe, but which still appeal today to large numbers of unreflecting women.

What is needed, then, in Christian piety is a development of the

---

[2] See the commentary of Jean Héring, *La Première épitre de Saint Paul aux Corinthians* (1949, p. 130). One modern theologian (Arnold, 1963, p. 62) does, however, invoke this text to justify excluding women from the priesthood. Exegetes have in general been puzzled by the inconsistency in Paul's statements on women in Chapters 11 and 14, some claiming that 14:34-35 are an interpolation in the text.

masculine preference for silence, simplicity and for religious ceremonial which stresses the transcendent rather than the sensible. This means that the woman who seeks some voice in the Church must be vividly aware of a paradox: the more she tends to promote her own official status, the more she must also tend to discourage modes of religious expression which have greater appeal to women than to men. We thus have an added reason for keeping completely separate the two questions of recognized responsibility and participation in cult. The Church must indeed become a Church where woman has true equality with man; the danger to be avoided at all costs is encouraging thereby a womanly Church (Rahner, 1964, pp. 65-67).

CONCLUSION

It would not be out of place to note by way of conclusion that most of what has been said in this paper is actually part of a much larger question, namely, the relationship in the Church between Christians who have received the sacrament of orders or have entered religious life and those who have not. The ultimate reason for the lack of a serious theology of woman is that up to now there has been no serious theology of the layman. Only when present efforts actually produce such a theology will it be possible to see in their proper perspective the distinctive roles of man and woman in the Church. Moreover, the lines of development outlined here are not the only ones possible. We have already suggested that one area of neglect has been the recognition of woman as a person. The present theological concern for freedom and interpersonal communion ought therefore make more meaningful all future discussion of woman. A thorough reevaluation of the current theology of sex and marriage would without doubt also bring rich insights (Jeannière, 1967, pp. 126-173). It might well be asked, too, whether anyone but a woman theologian will be able to make any original contribution to this area. One thing is certain: up to now Catholic theology has neglected woman. Outside of a concern for family life, the Church has paid little attention to woman's personal mission and showed scant interest in giving her a true equality with man in the affairs of the parish or diocese. Certain also is the fact that this neglect must end. All aspects of woman's Christian vocation must in the future be accounted for, and the divine idea of which she is the realization must be brought right to the surface of the Christian consciousness, so that its riches may be seen at last and all its depth understood.

REFERENCES

Arnold, F. X. *Woman and man.* New York: Herder & Herder, 1963.

Barth, K. *The doctrine of creation.* Edinburgh: Clark, 1958.

Crook, Margaret B. *Women and religion.* Boston: Beacon, 1964.

Daniélou, J. Le ministère des femmes dans l'Église ancienne. *La Maison-Dieu,* 1960, *61,* 70-96.

de Beauvoir, Simone. *The second sex* (trans. by H. M. Pashley). New York: Knopf, 1953.

Devaux, A. A. Le féminin selon Teilhard de Chardin. In F. Bedarida (Ed.) *La femme, nature et vocation. Recherches et Débates* cahier n° 45. Paris: Fayard, 1963. Pp. 120-138.

Faherty, W. B. (S.J.) *The destiny of modern woman in the light of papal teaching.* Westminster, Md.: Newman, 1950.

Graef, Hilda C. *The scholar and the cross.* Westminster, Md.: Newman, 1955.

Henry, A. M. (O.P.) Le mystère de l'homme et de la femme. *La Vie Spirituelle,* 1949, *80,* 463-490.

Héring, J. *La première épitre de saint Paul aux Corinthians.* Paris: Delachaux & Niestlé, 1949.

Jeannière, A. (S.J.) *The anthropology of sex* (trans. by Julie Kernan). New York: Harper & Row, 1967.

John XXIII. La femme au foyer et au travail (allocution of December 7, 1960). *Nouvelle revue théologique,* 1961, *83,* 295-297.

Mooney, C. F. (S.J.) Teilhard de Chardin and the Christological problem. *Harvard Theol. Rev.,* 1965, *58,* 91-126.

Pius XII. Allocution to working women (August 11, 1945). *Acta Apostolicae Sedis,* 1945, *37,* 213-217.

Pius XII. Allocution to Centre Feminin International de l'Action Catholique (October 14, 1956). *Acta Apostolicae Sedis,* 1956, *48,* 779-786.

Rahner, K. (S.J.) *Theology for renewal.* New York: Sheed & Ward, 1964.

Rondet, H. (S.J.) Éléments pour une theologie de la femme. *Nouvelle Revue Théologique,* 1957, *89,* 915-940.

Soullard, P. M. (O.P.) Le status de la femme dans l'Église. *Lumière et vie,* 1959, *8,* 53-64.

Stein, Edith, *Die Frau.* Freiburg: Herder, 1959.

Teilhard de Chardin, P. (S.J.) *L'énergie humain.* Paris: Seuil, 1962.

Teilhard de Chardin, P. (S.J.) Le coeur de la matière. Unpublished essay, 1950.

Tilliette, X. (S.J.) La femme et la féminité. In F. Bedarida (Ed.) *La femme, nature et vocation. Recherches et Débates* cahier n° 45. Paris: Fayard, 1963. Pp. 101-119.

Vatican Council II. Dogmatic constitution on the Church. In W. M. Abbott (S.J.) (Ed.) *The documents of Vatican II.* New York: Herder & Herder, 1966. Pp. 14-96.

von le Fort, Gertrud. *The eternal woman* (trans. by Marie Buehrie). Milwaukee: Bruce, 1954.

II

WOMAN FROM THE PERSPECTIVE
OF THE BEHAVIORAL SCIENCES

Woman in the Light of Modern Psychiatry

PAUL G. ECKER

*Paul Gerard Ecker received his M.D. de-
gree from the School of Medicine of Western
Reserve University in 1944. His residency
training in internal medicine was taken at the
Peter Bent Brigham Hospital in Boston. He
combined this training with a simultaneous
teaching fellowship at the Harvard Medical
School. His psychiatric residency was at the
New York State Psychiatric Institute at Columbia, subsequent to which he held a teaching
position at Columbia Medical School. Two
years were spent in research at the Rockefel-
ler Institute. Subsequent to his work in New
York, Dr. Ecker served as Chief of the Functional Disease Service at the Hospital of the
University of Pennsylvania. Currently, Dr.
Ecker, who is a diplomate, American Board of
Psychiatry and Neurology, is engaged in private psychiatric practice in Philadelphia, where
he is also an instructor in psychoanalysis at
the Institute of the Philadelphia Association
for Psychoanalysis.*

No topic could have been chosen which would have been as potentially
controversial or as subject to preconceptions as the one selected. It is a
safe assumption that the stubborn facts of one's own history and social
perspectives are certain to introduce a strong subjectivist bias to any
discussion.

The current writings on this subject span the entire spectrum from the conservative Victorian position limiting the activity of women to the home, to housewifely work, to the rearing of the children, and to seeing woman as the meek and compliant partner to her husband, whose commitment ought at least comply with the *obiter dictum* of St. Monica 1200 years ago that women "should look upon matrimony as a deed of sale . . . into servitude," to the opposite extreme of those obsessed with the current *furor reformandi,* who vigorously plead the ideology of a clear and progressive equality at all levels between the sexes. The latter would see the husband becoming more compliant, more passive towards his wife, more active in his participation in the physical details of the management of the home and care of the children, thus leaving his wife relatively free to follow her own interests in a career and life outside the house (Rossi, 1965). Where we are attempting a delineation of so elemental a factor of the human condition, a multitude of perspectives is necessary. The house is many-sided, and, before some sort of sense can be made of the larger issue, some attempt ought to be made at clarification of the vantage point from which the discussion is to proceed.

GENERAL PSYCHIATRIC APPROACH

To the physician and psychiatrist, then, what seems salient and essential lies in the attempt to define the basic differences in human biology between the male and the female, the biological individuality of the sexes. It seems to me upon reading and re-reading many of the current discussions on the problems of woman in modern society, that insufficient attention is being paid to the fundamental psychobiological differences between men and women. Freud once said that biology is destiny. This observation, at once trite, underscores in a profound sense the fact that we start with what is biologically given in human nature: namely, that woman is not and cannot be the same as man. Again, make no mistake, I am less concerned with any current stereotype of femininity which is a reflection of the cultural milieu of the moment, than I am with the delineation of those essential qualitative biological and psychological differences, which, by their very nature, distinguish the man from the woman, and about which much remains to be learned.

Psychoanalysis as an ontology of conflict, is at once a therapy, a theory, and a technique for the study of the interplay of forces within the mind and the individual historical and experiential data of growth and development. As it should be, psychoanalysis is still largely directed to the study of those ill by way of neurosis, and has led to profound illuminations of the nature of psychic conflict within the individual. Yet a perusal of the psychoanalytic writings will fail to provide adequate definitions as to the essential nature of what constitutes the feminine. It remains as much a riddle today as it always seems to have been. Insofar as psychoanalysis, or, in a more general sense, modern psychiatry and medicine are concerned, the focus which can be provided on the topic under discussion is limited. Freud never abandoned his fundamental position of the biological rootedness of the individuality of mind. His position was largely deterministic but not absolutely so. He saw the force in biological development reflected not only in the personality of the individual but in the social organization in a larger sense.

However, the general perspective of the Pastoral Psychology Institute on woman is not the study of mental illness in women, neither the woman suffering from psychoneurosis or from psychosis, nor, for that matter, the delinquent woman. Rather, it is the nature of the woman's place in the modern world.

I think we would all agree that in the United States at the present time there is indeed offered an almost unlimited opportunity for women. It is probably true that a woman has to work a little bit harder than a man to reach the same point and that there may be islands of bias, as, for instance, the individual professor who will not give her the same fair share as may be accorded the male student, but I think that these attitudes are largely of the past. Nor as one reviews the literature on this topic is one overly impressed with the considerations given to the plain Jane who works in a factory or in the store or in the shop. She is neither careerist nor a professional person, but simply a woman with a job, possibly working to get out of an unhappy home, possibly working, as I suspect most women do, to help supplement her husband's income. If we are to assume that we are not living in the best of all possible worlds, where then is the focus of conflict? For certainly today as in any other time we find discontent in many women. I would suggest that the focus of conflict at a social level, as far as woman is concerned, may in fact lie in the issue of the career woman and in the problem of creativity. Since the question of the career woman will be considered elsewhere,[1] I will limit myself to a consideration of the problem of creativity.

CREATIVITY IN THE WOMAN

It is probably not without reason that most women are aware of a deep and abiding sense of well-being during their pregnancies, a feeling likely to persist for some time after the birth of the child. No physician who has regularly delivered women is unaware of the poignancy, and the

[1] The career wife, p. 123; The career woman, p. 194; The employed woman, p. 210.

heightened narcissism which most women experience when they see
their new-born child. Is in fact birth not the true biological paradigm
for creativity even in man, at the same time as it is the most profoundly
masochistic of all experiences?

Two examples will suffice concerning the nature of mental activity as
experienced by men in their creative efforts. I can do no better than to
point to two men, creators of unmistakable genius—Henri Poincaré,
the great French mathematician of the 19th Century, and *il divino*
Michelangelo.

It seems very likely that the period of productivity at a truly original
creative level is limited in point of time in most scientists of genius. It
is a truism that most of the great and incisive theories in mathematics
and in physics have been arrived at by men under 40 years of age. The
same seems not to be as true of the brilliant historian or the great
artist, some of whom are apparently able to continue their productive
work through many years of their lifetime. Of course, I refer here to
those works of true and great originality, work that could be counted
as marking a turning-point in the successive scientific and political revo-
lutions that have taken place in history.

Michael Polanyi (1957) quotes Poincaré who gives us a beautiful
description of the successive stages in creativity as experienced by the
mathematician. The first he defines as the stage of preparation or the
formulation of the problem. The second, the long period of arduous and
intensive attempt at solution, Poincaré regards, at least in part, as an
unconscious activity of the mind which he defines as a period of incuba-
tion. Lastly comes the successful solution, the period of illumination.
It should be remembered that the scientist forces the hand of nature,
causing her to reveal her secrets. Paul Michel (1964) quotes Mario
Guiducci, the student of Galileo, from a lecture on Michelangelo to the
effect that *non sono novita in natura*—the scientist creates nothing but
only grasps the essence of what is already there.

So, too, did Michelangelo conceive of his genius at work in his artistic
creations. His labors gave birth to the form immanent in the Platonic
sense, in the marble itself, hidden, covered over, by the opacity of what
was superfluous and unnecessary in the stone, the *sorvechio*. It would
seem that the greatest artists and the greatest scientists who gave thought
to their own inner processes in the creative act regarded the process, in
essence, as one of bringing forth what was already there. How many of
the words seem to be metaphors for birth itself.

The world has known many individual women who have met and
competed successfully on the ground usually held by men. One senses

disappointment on the part of some women that their fellows are not more dedicated to the problems of the world, more desirous of expressing themselves in positions of political power and intellectual prestige. Is it possible that the conscious or unconscious narcissistic gratification in childbirth diminishes the drive to produce in either the material or intellectual sense? Every man seeks some small piece or vista of immortality for himself. Each struggles to achieve some degree of narcissistic gratification in work, in achievement, in success. If, indeed, women come to pursue careers in science, in medicine, in the arts, and in the humanities to a degree greater than they have in the past, we may indeed find that their contribution will be uniquely and qualitatively different from that of the man. It is commonplace to speak of women's intuitiveness, their greater emotional reactivity, their greater capacity for empathy, their minimal interest in abstraction—in sum, those attributes which Erikson encompassed under attention to the inside rather than the outside (Erikson, 1964). Will we not find as our ability to measure psychological phenomena is enhanced, as our comprehension of the mind is deepened and extended, that there will emerge true qualitative differences not only in the biological sense but in the psychological sense as well, between men and women even in the nature of their thought processes?

There has been a decline in the number of women obtaining doctoral degrees in the United States from a high of about 15 percent of all persons obtaining doctoral degrees in the 1920s to 10 percent in the 1950s (Degler, 1964). I suspect that the reason may be found in the essential nature of womanhood which turns inward to find her deepest sources of gratification in accord with the essential demands of her own biological constitution, and discovers these in motherhood, and in the mutuality and complementarity of her relationship to a man. There is no implication here that these goals may not be realized by any individual woman, who may, in addition, successfully and actively pursue some aspect of intellectual endeavor.

PSYCHOANALYTIC VIEWPOINTS WITH RESPECT TO WOMAN

Psychoanalysis has been able, within limits, to chart the stages of psychosexual development and to shed new and valuable light on the nature of intrapsychic conflict. Certain key formulations have been arrived at which are fundamental to our understanding of the genesis of intrapsychic conflict in women (Bonaparte, 1953; Deutsch, 1944; Freud, 1933), with reference particularly to the classical neuroses:

anxiety hysteria, the phobias, and obsessional states. However, we should fall heir to what Whitehead referred to as the fallacy of misplaced concreteness if we attempted to explain away the essential differences between women and men only in the light of knowledge arrived at in the study of conflict. As Freud pointed out so clearly at the end of his lecture on the psychology of woman in the *New Introductory Lectures on Psychoanalysis,* ". . . we must remember that an individual woman may be a human being apart from [her femininity]" (Freud, 1933, pp. 184-185). Depending on the shifts in the balance of psychic forces within the individual, conflict may emerge in a woman's life at any particular stage of her development. Most commonly the three periods associated with the greatest stress and turmoil are those of early childhood, adolescence, and the menopause.

Many years ago Freud pointed to the essential bisexuality innately present in both men and women. What has long been known to be true embryonically and anatomically has now been confirmed by the increasing number of endocrine studies demonstrating the presence in the normal individual of one sex of the hormones of the other. Similar dispositions are evident at a psychological level and any stereotypes equating femininity with passivity, or masculinity with activity, except in the final and ultimate biological aspect of the sexual relationship, are simplistic. Psychoanalysis has demonstrated parallels in the early phases of development in both the boy and the girl.

As has been demonstrated amply in psychoanalytic study, the early attachment to the mother is decisive in the development of the young girl in that period defined as the pre-Oedipal stage of psychosexual development. Psychoanalysis of adult neurotic women, as well as the observation and analysis of young children, has clarified the successive stages of psychosexual development as reflected in the ambivalent oral, sadistic, and phallic wishes towards the mother, the role of phantasy, and the nature of the castration complex in bringing about the turning away of the young girl from the mother to the father at the height of the Oedipal stage in development (Freud, 1933). It is both inevitable and necessary that even in an ideal relationship between the mother and child, the mother should at times be a frustrating and denying object to the child.

As is regularly demonstrable in the setting of the psychoanalytic situation, the anatomical distinction between the sexes gives rise to the castration complex in the girl as a psychical consequence. The intense preoccupation with the body and the struggle for the mastery of physical sensations almost invariably result in a shock when the little girl becomes aware of the difference between her body and that of the boy; she then to some degree develops envy of the phallus.

Small children perceive the difference between the sexes very early, and as little boys and girls become aware of the essential anatomical differences there is the struggle on the part of some to account for these differences at a phantasy level. As Lillian Malcove* observed, one of the persistent and universal phantasies denies any physical difference between the boy and the girl or the man and the woman; maintains that each sex is equally endowed physically, and what observable apparent differences do exist are to be accounted for in the light of the individual solution in phantasy. Is it possible, as Malcove has suggested, that the persistence of this unconscious phantasy, unresolved according to reality by the age of four or five and continuing to exist in the unconscious, accounts for the implicit assumption of the equality of the sexes throughout the later years of life? Do we, indeed, as Malcove intimates, confront two groups of individuals, the majority on the side of reality who accept the biological difference between the sexes in its essential and real sense, and those, on the other side, for whom the phantasy is the reality, and who apparently persist in the denial throughout their lives of the differences between men and women in a physical or biological sense?

In the mature woman, analysis regularly uncovers as one of the prime factors leading to analysis the unconscious wish to achieve the longed-for organ which she felt deprived of early in life, although the wish has long since been repressed and remains active only in the unconscious mind. Freud felt that this fact accounted for the relatively greater degree of envy and jealousy in women as compared to men (Freud, 1933). The lack of a phallus regularly accounts for the sense of inferiority so often found in women. The little girl may then turn to her father, the wish for the penis being transformed to the wish for a baby by him. The hostility towards the mother at this phase may be evidence of the wish to replace the mother as the exclusive object of her father's love. The complete resolution of this conflict may only finally be achieved in marriage and subsequent motherhood. A less successful solution to the castration complex is the emergence of strong aggressive masculine trends in the little girl at this stage. Homosexuality in women generally is evidence of regressive reaction of the early relationship to the mother, the paradigm for female homosexuality generally being the mother-child relationship.

* Personal communication.

Much less clarification has occurred in relation to the further development of the girl in adolescence. This period, a time of intense emotional upheaval in both sexes, is accompanied by a regressive reactivation of the earlier infantile conflict as well as the whole spectrum of conflict in the salient aspects of emergent socialization, in the development of values and ideals in the transition from youth to adulthood. Ample confirmation of Freud's theses has emerged from a careful study of woman's reactions to sexuality, the problems of frigidity, the reactions to the birth of a child in the form of post-partum depressions and, lastly, the emotional upheaval which so regularly accompanies the menopause, with its consequent involution of the capacity for reproduction.

Psychoanalysis as a technique is the most powerful that we have available today for the microscopic study of the psychological development of the individual woman. It has adumbrated the decisive aspects of infantile neurosis, infantile sexuality, and the essentially intrapsychic nature of conflict in the classical psychoneuroses in women as well as in men. As is true in medicine in the larger sense, the study of the normal has only emerged out of the study of the disordered and the abnormal. The larger problem of how successful adjustment is achieved in the face of overwhelming conflict still remains as much of a problem in psychiatry and in psychoanalysis as it does in medicine, in relation to the problems of successful development of natural immunity. Even less is known concerning the aspects of the prevention of neuroses. Psychoanalysis has never abandoned the position originally formulated by Freud that the psychic fate of the individual lies in the interplay of the forces of the constitution, the biological make-up of the individual, and the forces operative in his environment coupled with the salient problem-solving role of phantasy in mental life. It seems clear that there is as yet little scientific understanding of factors relating to the strength of the instincts, the biological predisposition to anxiety, and the capacity for the development of adequate and viable defensive functions in mental life.

CONCLUSION

In our society, in which the rate of change in economic growth is so rapid, in which the struggle for the essential animal necessities in the form of food and shelter is nearly completely overcome by modern technology, there is almost unlimited social mobility possible to the individual with an almost total absence of caste, so that, dependent only on his own resources, drive and potential, the individual is subject to greater stress on the one hand, and, on the other, the possibility of an almost limitless material success. We see a progressive breakdown in religion and in those traditions which have always provided man with meaning and value for life. In confronting these aspects of modern life with the implicit and ever-present possibility of frustration, modern woman, like modern man, is exposed to an increasingly greater degree of uncertainty. This uncertainty, which has heretofore existed in relation to life expectancy, to illness, and death, which has, in others words, been related to the problems of staying alive, seems to have shifted now to another center of gravity—the constellation of success, status, and achievement.

In one, and, I suspect, fundamental sense, the problem of woman in society at large may not be materially different from the problems faced by man. Different ages and different times have offered their own distinctive solutions to the riddle of man's place in this universe. From the time of the Middle Ages, with its closed world, but with its expectation of a better world to come, through the Renaissance, with its open universe, and ever-widening scope of human aspiration, to our own day with our Utopian expectancy of a world infinitely perfectable in the extension of knowledge and the control of nature, man has sought to find and to define values out of which some essential meaning could be found for the struggle of his existence.

As Freud (1930) stated in his *Civilization and its discontents*, some measure of discontent will always remain. For this reason more than any other, it may be that the problem posed in this Institute is in a sense an insoluble one. Women act as individuals, not as members of a sex, and so they have continued to act, I suspect, through all of time.

REFERENCES

Bonaparte, Marie. *Female sexuality*. New York: International Universities, 1953.

Degler, C. N. Revolution without ideology: the changing place of women in America. *Daedalus,* 1964, *93,* 653-670.

Deutsch, Helene. *The psychology of women*. New York: Grune & Stratton, 1944.

Erickson, E. H. Inner and outer space: reflections on womanhood. *Daedalus,* 1964, *93,* 582-606.

Freud, S. *Civilization and its discontents*. London: Hogarth, 1930.

Freud, S. *New introductory lectures on psychoanalysis*. New York: Norton, 1933.

Michel, P. H. Problems of artistic creation. *Diogenes,* 1964, No. 46, 25-53.

Polanyi, M. Problem solving. *Brit. J. Phil. Sci.,* 1957, *8,* 89-103.

Rossi, Alice S. Equality between the sexes: an immodest proposal. *Daedalus,* 1964, *93,* 607-652.

Rossi, Alice S. Women in science: why so few? *Science,* 1965, *148,* 1196-1202.

Psychological Differences Between Men and Women

ANNE ANASTASI

Anne Anastasi received her A.B. from Barnard College in 1928, and her Ph.D. from Columbia University in 1930. She taught at Barnard College and Queens College prior to joining the Fordham University faculty in 1947. She is currently professor of psychology at Fordham University. Dr. Anastasi is the author of more than 100 journal articles, monographs, and contributed papers, and is, in addition, the author of the following books: Differential Psychology *(1937, 1949, 1958),* Psychological Testing *(1954, 1961, 1968),* Fields of Applied Psychology *(1964), and* Individual Differences *(1965). Dr. Anastasi is a fellow of the American Psychological Association, which organization she has served both as recording secretary and president of the Divisions of General Psychology and of Evaluation and Measurement. She has likewise served as president of the Eastern Psychological Association and the American Psychological Foundation.*

There is certainly no dearth of data on sex differences in psychological traits. Nearly every available psychological test, whether concerned with abilities or personality traits, has been administered to male and female samples and the results compared. In addition, a variety of other observational procedures have been employed to compare the behavior, attitudes, and self concepts of the two sexes from infancy to old age.

For our present purpose, I plan first to identify major differences found between men and women in aptitudes and in personality. I shall then examine more specifically the attitudes of men and women toward each other and the concepts of masculinity and femininity prevailing within each sex in our culture. Finally, I shall consider certain basic questions regarding the origins and interpretations of the observed sex differences. We cannot stop with a descriptive survey of how women differ psychologically from men. We must also ask what the differences mean.

APTITUDES

With regard to ability, we may begin with a look at those familar but widely misunderstood instruments known as "intelligence tests." First, it should be noted that certain intelligence tests have been deliberately constructed so as to eliminate sex differences in total scores. This procedure is well illustrated by the Stanford-Binet scale, which introduced the IQ into mental testing. In the development of this test, items showing a large difference between the percentage of boys and girls who answered them correctly were excluded, on the assumption that they might reflect specific sex differences in training and experience. Among the remaining items, those slightly favoring girls were balanced against others favoring boys to an equal degree. Thus the fact that no significant sex differences in IQ are found with the Stanford-Binet is an indication of the care with which this procedure was followed and has no bearing on sex differences in ability.

A more general problem pertains to the use of such global scores as the IQ. Group differences may be completely obscured when we compare total scores on a test that combines different aptitudes, as is true of most intelligence tests. If, for example, boys excel in numerical aptitude and girls in verbal aptitude, an intelligence scale containing an equal number of verbal and numerical items will yield no significant sex difference in total score. Should the scale be overweighted with items of one type, on the other hand, it will favor the sex excelling in that trait and will show an apparent difference in general intelligence. With increasing knowledge about the distinctness of the traits making up intelligence, psychologists now recognize that global scores on intelligence tests must be interpreted with considerable care. IQ's derived from different intelligence tests may measure different combinations of abilities. For all these reasons, then, it is more meaningful to investigate sex differences in separate aptitudes rather than in the varying composites of traits covered by intelligence tests.

In specific aptitudes, several significant differences have been established between the average performance of men and women in our culture (Anastasi, 1958, Ch. 14; Terman & Tyler, 1954; Tyler, 1965, Ch. 10). Males as a group excel in speed and coordination of gross bodily movements, spatial orientation, mechanical comprehension, and arithmetic reasoning. Females excel in manual dexterity, perceptual speed and accuracy, numerical computation, verbal fluency, and other tasks involving the mechanics of language. Many of these sex differences are manifested from infancy or early childhood. For example, observations of preschool children (Gesell *et al.*, 1940) show that boys are faster and make fewer errors than girls in walking a series of narrow boards, and also achieve more accuracy and distance in throwing a ball. Girls, on the other hand, show superior control of finger and wrist movements in such tasks as dressing, buttoning, tying a bowknot, washing their hands, and turning doorknobs.

That adult women can carry out many manipulatory activities more quickly and accurately than men has been widely recognized in industry. This fact was especially apparent during World War II, when women were often assigned to assembly, inspection, and similar industrial operations. Such observations are corroborated by performance on aptitude tests in which small objects must be assembled with fingers or tweezers. Also of vocational significance is woman's superiority in perceptual speed and accuracy, particularly in tasks requiring rapid shifting of attention. These are the principal functions measured by clerical aptitude tests, in which women make a consistently better showing than men at all ages (Andrew & Paterson, 1959; Schneidler & Paterson, 1942).

Sex differences in language development also appear early in life (McCarthy, 1954). On the average, girls begin to talk earlier than boys; and during the preschool years they use a larger vocabularly and more mature sentence structure than do boys. Girls also make more rapid progress in learning to read. On most verbal tests, girls surpass boys during the elementary school period. At the high school and college levels, however, females excel only in the more mechanical aspects of language, as illustrated by word fluency, spelling, and grammatical usage. At these age levels, tests of verbal comprehension and verbal reasoning show either no sex differences or small differences in favor of boys (Anastasi, 1958, Ch. 14; Wesman, 1949).

On tests of spatial and mechanical aptitudes, males excel by large and significant amounts. This sex difference, however, does not appear until late childhood. Among preschool children, no sex difference has been noted in such tasks as block-building, fitting differently shaped pieces into form boards, and recognizing shapes (Gesell *et al.,* 1940). At the elementary school level, boys are clearly superior on tests involving form boards, puzzle boxes, mazes, directional orientation, and estimating the number of blocks in piles (Anastasi, 1958, Ch. 14). Although males tend to excel on all tests requiring spatial visualization, the differences in their favor are still larger on tests calling also for mechanical comprehension. The latter is illustrated by questions about the use of tools or the operation of common mechanical objects (Bennett, Seashore, & Wesman, 1963).

A highly consistent sex difference has been found in spatial orientation. This difference can be illustrated in experiments with the subject seated in a chair that can be tilted at different angles, within a room that can itself be independently tilted (Witkin *et al.*, 1954). When visual and bodily cues conflict in this situation, women tend to rely more on visual cues, men more on bodily cues. As a result, women make larger errors than men in judging their own bodily position. Women also perform more poorly on tests in which visual stimuli must be judged independently of their surroundings, as when the position of a rod must be determined independently of the position of the frame around it, or when a simple geometric figure must be identified within a more complex design. In all these situations, women tend to be more often misled by the surrounding visual field. These sex differences have obvious implications for the performance of certain occupational activities. It has also been suggested that they may be related to personality differences.

In the numerical area, sex differences again fail to appear until children are well along in the elementary school period (Anastasi, 1958; Terman & Tyler, 1954). From that stage on, girls tend to perform better than boys on computation tests. In the solution of arithmetic problems and on other numerical reasoning tests, on the other hand, boys excel consistently. There is also some evidence that males are superior in problem solving generally, especially when the problem requires a change in approach and a reorganization of facts in new ways (Sweeney, 1953). Of particular interest is the finding that performance in problem solving is related to sex differences in attitudes toward problem solving (Carey, 1958) and to the degree of sex-role identification (Milton, 1957). Within each sex, closer identification with the masculine sex role, as indicated on a personality inventory, was found to be associated with superior problem-solving skill. These findings open up interesting possibilities regarding the part that sex differences in attitudes may play in the development of abilities.

PERSONALITY

Among the principal personality differences found between the sexes are the greater aggressiveness, achievement drive, and emotional stability of the male and the stronger social orientation of the female (Anastasi, 1958, Ch. 14; Bennett & Cohen, 1959; Terman & Tyler, 1954). Sex differences in aggression are manifested from early childhood. Investigations of nursery and preschool children utilizing teachers' reports, direct observation of spontaneous activities, or psychological tests have repeatedly shown that boys manifest more anger, aggression, destructiveness, and quarrelsome behavior than do girls. This sex difference may also help to explain the much higher incidence of behavior problems among boys than among girls of school age. In standardized self-report inventories administered to high school, college, and miscellaneous adult samples, males score significantly higher than females on both aggression and dominance scales (Edwards, 1959; Gordon, 1953; Guilford & Zimmerman, 1949).

There is evidence from a variety of sources pointing to sex differences in achievement motivation. In our culture, males exhibit a stronger drive to achieve and to advance than do females. Data in support of this difference are provided by vocational choices of high school students, personality inventory responses, performance on projective tests of personality, and results of specially designed experiments on level of aspiration (Antatasi, 1958, Ch. 14; Edwards, 1959).

Another area in which large sex differences have been found is that of emotional adjustment. At the preschool and elementary school levels, girls report more fears and worries than do boys and also manifest more so-called nervous habits, such as nail-biting and thumb-sucking. Behavior problems, on the other hand, are more common among boys. The total amount of maladjustment or instability may thus be no different in the two sexes at these age levels. Girls may simply develop less overt or less aggressive symptoms of maladjustment than boys, owing to differences in sex roles and socially imposed restrictions. This interpretation was supported by the results of a longitudinal study of California children between the ages of 3 and 13 (Macfarlane, Allen, & Honzik, 1954). In this study, significant sex differences were found in the frequency of different *kinds* of problem behavior. Boys more often exhibited overactivity, attention-demanding behavior, jealousy, competitiveness, selfishness in sharing, temper tantrums, and stealing. Girls were more likely to suck their thumbs; be excessively reserved; fuss about their food; be timid, shy, fearful, oversensitive, and somber; and have mood swings.

On self-report personality inventories, clear-cut sex differences in overall extent of emotional instability begin to appear in adolescence. Among adults, large and significant differences on adjustment inventories have been found, women as a group reporting more evidence of maladjustment (Gordon, 1953; Guilford & Zimmerman, 1949). That such differences cannot be attributed entirely to women's greater willingness to report emotional difficulties is suggested by a study of a college group (Darley, 1937). Students who had taken a personality inventory were subsequently interviewed by two experienced counselors. The excess of maladjustment among the women, as revealed by the interviews, was even greater than that indicated by the test scores.

Many sex differences in interests, attitudes, and interpersonal relations center on the greater social orientation of women (Johnson & Terman, 1940; Terman & Tyler, 1954). This sex difference appears early in life and continues into old age. Throughout childhood, sex differences in social orientation have been observed in a variety of ways. In the play activities of nursery school children, for example, boys show more concern with things, girls with personal relationships. At all ages, girls engage more often in "social" games involving cooperative activities with other children; they read more books about people and more often express an interest in occupations dealing with people. Parents' records of the questions children ask show that girls ask a significantly larger proportion of questions about social relations than do boys. Girls' wishes, fears, daydreams, and pleasant and unpleasant memories more often concern people. Even studies of childrens' dreams have indicated that girls more often than boys dream about people in general, as well as about their own family.

Surveys of adults by means of personality inventories reveal similar sex differences. Women report more social interests, concern about social welfare, loyalty to group and friends, tendency to analyze the motives of oneself and others, desire to do what is expected, willingness to accept blame and to give in to others, need for sympathy, and readiness to help others (Allport, Vernon, & Lindsay, 1960; Edwards, 1959).

CONCEPTS OF MASCULINITY AND FEMININITY

Another major area of sex differences pertains to the attitudes of men and women toward each other. What are the beliefs, opinions, expectations, and ideals of men and women in our culture regarding members of their own and of the opposite sex?

Some investigators have approached this problem by asking men what traits they would most value in a wife and asking women the corresponding question about husbands. In general, men reply that they want a partner who is physically attractive, socially adept, sexually responsive, and a good homemaker. Women do not stress good looks in a man, but want a husband who is industrious, ambitious, has good occupational prospects, is considerate, and conforms to moral and social standards (Baber, 1939; Christensen, 1958; Hewitt, 1958; Langhorne & Secord, 1955). Women usually want a husband who is more intelligent than they are; men rarely want their wife to be the more intelligent partner (Baber, 1939; Beigel, 1957). There is also evidence that many women still structure their lives on the premise that men are repelled by intellectual women and that consequently the development and use of intelligence by a woman reduces her chances of marriage (Matthews, 1960; Matthews & Tiedeman, 1962).

In a survey concerned with the personality needs to be fulfilled by the marital partner, men more often said they wanted a wife who "respects my ideals," "appreciates what I want to achieve," and "stimulates my ambition." Women more often wanted as a husband "someone who shows me a lot of affection," "someone who helps me in making important decisions," and "someone I can look up to very much" (Strauss, 1947). Corroboration of some of the reported differences in marital preferences is to be found in a comparison of the domestic grievances cited by husbands and wives (Terman, 1938, Ch. 5). Among the grievances rated high in seriousness, husbands listed slovenly appearance of the wife, while wives listed lack of business success of the husband.

Underlying many of the attitudes expressed by men and women toward each other is the different relation that vocational career bears to marriage for the two sexes in our culture. For men, career plans are virtually a prerequisite to marriage. For women, on the other hand, such plans usually represent a potential source of conflict with marriage (Matthews & Tiedeman, 1962).

Another type of investigation has concentrated on defining contemporary concepts of masculinity and femininity in our culture. In one such study (Vroegh, Jenkin, & Black, 1966), adult men and women were given adjective checklists and rating scales to be used in describing the following six concepts: (1) most masculine person you can imagine; (2) most feminine person you can imagine; (3) least masculine person you can imagine; (4) least feminine person you can imagine; (5) most males are; and (6) most females are. The response of male and female raters proved to be quite similar and could therefore be combined. The specific adjectives endorsed revealed both similarities and differences between the contemporary concepts of masculinity and femininity. Among the terms most descriptive of Most Masculine Imaginable and unique to this concept were: athletic, capable, confident, energetic, humane, and vigorous. Among those most descriptive of Most Feminine Imaginable and unique to it were: charming, graceful, gracious, warm, and understanding. It is interesting to note that a number of items were common to the descriptions of both Most Masculine Imaginable and Most Feminine Imaginable. Some of these items were: attractive, cooperative, emotionally stable, good natured, healthy, intelligent, sexually attractive, and well-groomed.

The most descriptive words for Least Masculine Imaginable were: effeminate, emotionally unstable, and apologetic voice. For Least Feminine Imaginable, the most descriptive terms were: argumentative, arrogant, bossy, and sexually unattractive. It is apparent from these examples that the traits associated with the most masculine and those associated with the most feminine persons were socially desirable, while the traits associated with the least masculine and those associated with the least feminine persons were socially undesirable.

The findings also suggest that the concepts of masculinity and femininty are not opposite ends of a continuum but represent two distinct variables in terms of which men and women in our culture are evaluated. Thus when frequencies of item endorsement were correlated between Most Masculine Imginable and Most Feminine Imaginable, the correlations were positive rather than negative. The correlations between Least Masculine Imaginable and Least Feminine Imaginable were likewise positive. In other words, the raters tended to choose many of the same traits to characterize individuals of either sex who fitted the sex stereotype of the culture. Apart from those few items that differentiated between the two concepts, any item that was socially desirable was generally endorsed equally often for both Most Masculine Imaginable and Most Feminine Imaginable. A related finding is that Most Masculine Imaginable was not equivalent to Least Feminine Imaginable, nor was Most Feminine Imaginable equivalent to Least Masculine Imaginable. In fact, the two concepts were negatively correlated.

The concepts represented by Most Males Are and Most Females Are elicited descriptions that were less distinctive or differentiating than those associated with the more extreme concepts. These findings support the investigators' contention that the frequency of traits among men or women in general is not a satisfactory basis for defining the concepts of masculinity or femininity. It should be noted, of course, that this investigation was only exploratory and its results, although suggestive, need further corroboration.

CAUSAL MECHANISMS

After this brief overview of descriptive data on existing sex differences, we must now inquire about the causes of such differences. The fact that men and women differ in any particular aptitude or personality trait does not, of course, imply that the difference stems from a hereditary, biological characteristic associated with sex. We need to look into the cultural influences that act differentially upon the two sexes and to inquire into the specific ways in which cultural and biological factors interact in the psychological development of men and women.

Although living in the same homes, boys and girls in most societies are reared in different subcultures. In countless ways, they receive differential treatment from parents, other adults, and playmates. They are dressed differently, given different toys, taught different games, and expected to behave differently in many situations of daily life. The personalities of mother and father are themselves important factors in the child's developing concept of sex roles, providing models of what is expected of each sex in the particular culture. Until quite recently, available opportunities for schooling differed for the two sexes, especially at higher educational levels. Even now, insofar as boys and girls may attend separate schools, it is likely that there are differences in curricular content, teaching methods, and emphases on different subjects for the two sexes. Although today women have entered nearly all vocational fields, there are still conspicuous differences in their relative acceptance and opportunities for advancement in several occupations. Ultimate vocational goals undoubtedly influence the individual's general life orientation, attitudes, motivation, and interests. These factors may in turn affect the development of abilities along different lines.

Even the biological differences between the sexes, moreover, interact with cultural conditions in the development of aptitudes and personality traits. The different roles men and women play in the reproductive functions undoubtedly contribute to sex differentiation in psychological development. Thus the long period of childbearing and child-rearing, biologically associated with the female partner, has far-reaching implications for sex differences in interests, attitudes, emotional traits, vocational goals, and achievement.

Sex differences in aggressiveness and dominance result partly from the greater body size, strength, and physical endurance of the male, and partly from the presence of male sex hormones. In this connection, it should be noted that greater male aggressiveness has been observed in animal as well as in human behavior. Fighting, restlessness, and resistance to control have been commonly reported as more characteristic of male than of female animals. That this difference is probably related to the presence of male sex hormones is indicated by experiments involving the removal of gonads, as well as the injection of sex hormones.

Another significant sex difference is to be found in the developmental acceleration of girls. Not only do girls reach puberty earlier than boys, but throughout childhood they are also further advanced toward their own adult status in all physical traits. The psychological effects of this sex difference in developmental rate probably vary widely from trait to trait. In infancy, the developmental acceleration of girls may be an important factor in their more rapid acquisition of language and may give them a head start in verbal development as a whole. Another possible implication of girls' developmental acceleration is a social one. Because of their physical acceleration, girls tend to associate with boys older than themselves. Since the girl is usually younger than the boys with whom she associates socially—and younger than the man she marries—she is likely to be surpassed by most of her male associates in education, intellectual level, and general experience. Such a situation may be at the root of many social attitudes toward the sexes. A younger person is likely to have less wisdom, knowledge, and sense of responsibility than an older one, and such an age difference may have been traditionally perceived as a sex difference.

Still another biological difference between the sexes pertains to the greater viability of the female, or the higher death rate of males at all ages, from the prenatal period on. We could speculate at length regarding the possible social implications and indirect psychological effects of this difference. One consequence is an excess of women, which increases with age. This condition obviously influences the relative opportunity of men and women for marriage. A proportional scarcity of males makes marriage more competitive for the female than for the male and may in turn affect the attitudes of men and women toward marriage.

These examples will suffice to illustrate the varied and intricate mechanisms whereby biological differences between men and women may lead to differential development of aptitudes, interests, and personality. It is the social implications of such physical differences, rather than the biological sex differences themselves, that lead to divergent psychological development. Moreover, because of the important part that cultural factors play in the development of all psychological traits, we must recognize that sex differences in these traits are neither universal nor fixed and immutable. Cultural variations in sex differences are amply illustrated by the findings of anthropology and by the history of our own society (Anastasi, 1958, Ch. 14; Barry, Bacon, & Child, 1957). As cultural conditions change, sex roles and the psychological traits associated with them will change accordingly.

SIMILARITIES VERSUS DIFFERENCES

So far we have been examining and trying to explain psychological differences between men and women. But in focusing upon differences, we must not lose sight of similarities. We can readily find traits that yield no significant mean differences between the sexes. This is true of many of the items in the Stanford-Binet Scale (McNemar, 1942, Ch. 5), as was mentioned previously. It is also true of three of the eleven subtests of the Wechsler Adult Intelligence Scale (Weschsler, 1958, Ch. 10), to cite another example.

With regard to attitudes, the same surveys that provide data on sex differences contain even more striking evidence of similarities. In one previously cited investigation of the emotional needs that men and women want their spouses to fulfill, the two needs that ranked highest for *both* sexes were: "someone who loves me" and "someone to confide in" (Strauss, 1947). The same general theme emerged in another study of needs, in which both men and women assigned a very high value to a marital partner who is thoughtful, kind-hearted, affectionate, sympathetic, loving, faithful, loyal, and patient (Langhorne & Secord, 1955). These requirements, of course, are what anyone would recognize as a basis for a successful and satisfying interpersonal relationship. Such a relationship is what both men and women seek from each other. Similarly, in a survey of domestic grievances that interfere with marital adjustment, both husbands and wives ranked as most serious several personality weaknesses of their partner of the type that disrupts interpersonal relations. Examples include being selfish and inconsiderate and complaining too much (Terman, 1938, pp. 98-100).

There is still another sense in which similarities between the sexes must be taken into account. Ultimately it is with *individuals,* not with groups, that we are concerned. It is the individual who must make decisions and plan his life. And for individuals, the group differences we have been considering are often a poor guide. When Samuel Johnson was asked which is more intelligent, man or woman, he is reported to have replied, "Which man, which woman?" This remark highlights an important fact about *all* group comparisons, namely, the wide individual differences existing within each group, with the resulting overlapping between groups. Even when the average of one group excels that of another by a large and significant amount, individuals can be found in the poorer group who surpass individuals in the better group. Because of the wide range of individual differences within any one group, as contrasted with the relatively small differences between group averages, an individual's group membership is a very unreliable basis for predicting his standing in most psychological traits.

REFERENCES

Allport, G. W., Vernon, P. E., & Lindzey, G. *Study of values* (3rd ed.). Boston: Houghton Mifflin, 1960.

Anastasi, Anne. *Differential psychology* (3rd ed.). New York: Macmillan, 1958.

Andrew, Dorothy M., & Paterson, D. G. *Minnesota Clerical Test: Manual.* New York: Psychological Corp., 1959.

Baber, R. E. *Marriage and the family.* New York: McGraw-Hill, 1939.

Barry, H., III, Bacon, Margaret K., & Child, I. L. A cross-cultural survey of some sex differences in socialization. *J. abnorm. soc. Psychol.,* 1957, *55,* 327-332.

Beigel, H. G. The evaluation of intelligence in the heterosexual relationship. *J. soc. Psychol.,* 1957, *46,* 65-80.

Bennett, E. M., & Cohen, L. R. Men and women: personality patterns and contrasts. *Genet. Psychol. Monogr.,* 1959, *59,* 101-155.

Bennett, G. K., Seashore, H. G., & Wesman, A. G. *Differential Aptitude Tests* (1963 edition), *Forms L and M.* New York: Psychological Corp., 1963.

Carey, Gloria L. Sex differences in problem-solving performance as a function of attitude differences. *J. abnorm. soc. Psychol.,* 1958, *56,* 256-260.

Christensen, H. T. *Marriage analysis. Foundations for successful family life* (2nd ed.). New York: Ronald, 1958.

Darley, J. G. Tested maladjustment related to clinically diagnosed maladjustment. *J. appl. Psychol.,* 1937, *21,* 632-642.

Edwards, A. L. *Edwards Personal Preference Schedule: Manual.* New York: Psychological Corp., 1959.

Gesell, A., et al. *The first five years of life.* New York: Harper, 1940.

Gordon, L. V. *Gordon Personal Profile: Manual.* New York: Harcourt, Brace & World, 1953.

Guilford, J. P., & Zimmerman, W. S. *The Guilford-Zimmerman Temperament Survey: Manual.* Beverly Hills, Calif.: Sheridan Supply Co., 1949.

Hewitt, L. E. Student perceptions of traits desired in themselves as dating and marriage partners. *Marriage fam. Living,* 1958, *20,* 344-349.

Johnson, Winifred B., & Terman, L. M. Some highlights in the literature of psychological sex differences published since 1920. *J. Psychol.,* 1940, *9,* 327-336.

Langhorne, M. C., & Secord, P. F. Variations in marital needs with age, sex, marital status, and regional location. *J. soc. Psychol.,* 1955, *41,* 19-37.

Macfarlane, Jean W., Allen, Lucile, & Honzik, Marjorie P. A developmental study of the behavior problems of normal children between twenty-one months and fourteen years. *Univ. Calif. Publ. Child Develpm.,* 1954, *2,* 1-122.

Matthews, Esther. The marriage-career conflict in the career development of girls and young women. Unpublished doctoral dissertation, Harvard Grad. Sch. Educ., 1960.

Matthews, Esther, & Tiedeman, D. V. The imprinting of attitudes towards career and marriage upon life styles of young women. *Harvard Stud. Career Developm., No. 18,* 1962.

McCarthy, Dorothea. Language development in children. In L. Carmichael (Ed.), *Manual of child psychology* (2nd ed.). New York: Wiley, 1954. Pp. 492-630.

McNemar, Q. *The revision of the Stanford-Binet Scale: an analysis of the standardization data.* Boston: Houghton Mifflin, 1942.

Milton, G. A. The effects of sex-role identification upon problem-solving skill. *J. abnorm. soc. Psychol.,* 1957, *55,* 208-212.

Schneidler, Gwendolen R., & Paterson, D. G. Sex differences in clerical aptitude. *J. educ. Psychol.,* 1942, *33,* 303-309.

Strauss, A. Personality needs and marital choice. *Soc. Forces,* 1947, *25,* 332-335.

Sweeney, E. J. Sex differences in problem solving. *Stanford Univer., Dept. Psychol. Tech. Rep. No. 1,* Dec. 1, 1953.

Terman, L. M. *Psychological factors in marital happiness.* New York: McGraw-Hill, 1938.

Terman, L. M., & Tyler, Leona E. Psychological sex differences. In L. Carmichael (Ed.), *Manual of child psychology* (2nd ed.). New York: Wiley, 1954. Pp. 1064-1114.

Tyler, Leona E. *The psychology of human differences* (3rd ed.). New York: Appleton-Century-Croft, 1965.

Vroegh, K., Jenkin, N., & Black, M. A new approach to the study of masculinity and femininity. *Amer. Psychologist,* 1966, *21,* 635.

Wechsler, D. *The measurement and appraisal of adult intelligence* (4th ed.). Baltimore: Williams & Wilkins, 1958.

Wesman, A. G. Separation of sex groups in test reporting. *J. educ. Psychol.,* 1949, *40,* 223-229.

Witkin, H. A., *et al. Personality through perception.* New York: Harper, 1954.

Priests' Attitudes Toward Women

SISTER MARIE AUGUSTA NEAL, S.N.D. and
SISTER MIRIAM ST. JOHN CLASBY, S.N.D.

*Sister Marie Augusta Neal, S.N.D., the
senior author, is associate professor of sociology and Chairman of the Sociology Department at Emmanuel College, Boston. She received her A.B. degree from Emmanual College in 1942, her M.A. from Boston College
in 1953, and her Ph.D. from Harvard University in 1963. Sister Marie Augusta is a frequent contributor to sociological and religious
periodicals and is the author of* Values and
Interests in Social Change *(1965). During
1964-65 she was a member of the Massachusetts Governor's Committee for the Status of
Women.*

*Sister Marie Augusta's collaborator, Sister
Miriam St. John Clasby, S.N.D., is an assistant professor at Emmanuel College.*

The findings of this paper suggest that there is a strongly embedded
tradition among priests to so stress the male-female differences as related to mother-father roles that this emphasis has resulted in an in-
capacity on the part of some priests to perceive women as persons beyond
a certain stereotyped tendency to appreciate women in service roles
which idealize male dominance and reinforce cultural traditions charac-

55

teristic of primitive and peasant societies. It is further suggested that this stereotype shows up in striking form in the writings of priest-counselors for religious women. Such writings today cause strain for the religious woman who is making necessary adaptations to spiritual life in the modern world. In turn her response to the priest generates for him a major crisis in his own conception of his function as a spiritual advisor and particularly as a giver of retreats.

The first part of this paper will be a brief discussion of a sociological and psychological process that seems to be a part of the background from which the problem under examination springs. Part two will be the report of a rather systematic examination of spiritual treatises written recently by priests for religious women, juxtaposed with writings by women on women, and those by scientists on actual findings of sex differences in individual performances. The purpose of this juxtaposition is to try to demonstrate the mechanisms operating to reinforce patterns of behavior which all recognize as changing under the press of modern exigencies. The final section of the paper will present an analysis of a survey of a random sample of the priests of the Boston Archdiocese, responding to the queries: what woman active in the world today do you most admire? and, what man active in the world today do you most admire?

SOCIOLOGICAL AND PSYCHOLOGICAL BACKGROUND

The most striking sociological difference between modern industrial societies and those of primitive and peasant periods is the process of structural differentiation and specialization of function. When we describe the division of labor in a primitive tribe, we speak of two main divisions: by age and by sex. Jobs were divided between the old and the young on the one hand, and between men and women on the other. In the primitive tribe the division of labor was ascribed, not achieved. One did certain jobs in certain ways because he was young or old, man or woman. It would be defined as demeaning or temerarious for one to attempt a job outside his age or sex categories.

There was a second simplified pattern in the primitive society that distinguished it from modern society—the limited number of different institutional areas within which the process of living was carried out. Family and religion were the dominant institutional areas. The extended family, the tribe, took care of the production and distribution of goods and services (which today is done in a highly complex economic system quite independent of the family). It kept community order and punished deviants (tasks now done by governments and judicial systems); it trained the young in the ways of society (again, a job shared by the schools and mass media today).

The religious system, itself embedded in the family system of this primitive society, was not only a way of relating man to God, but was also the health and welfare service, the source of art, literature, dance, and all the cultural disciplines that today stand independent, as science, art, and philosophy. Even in the peasant societies characteristic of the Middle Ages, although government had by then been differentiated from family and religion, and had an independent set of role players and a philosophy related to its own specific function and era, still, much of the functioning of society in its economy, polity, education, class structure, and recreational activities was embedded in family and religious roles and normative patterns.

What distinguishes modern society more and more today is expressed graphically in Harvey Cox's (1965) provocative book *The secular city*— the fact that these overlapping functions are no longer characteristic of the structure of society. Whereas formerly being a man or a woman, being young or old, were the major determinants of roles in all areas of society, the division of labor today is becoming more and more determined by competence, achievement, personal capacity, and opportunity. This clear and striking change so familiar to the sociologist is still in many respects not explicit in the considerations of the strains of modern adult-role-playing, even though the source of many modern problems of role identity are immediately related to this structural difference from earlier societal forms.

If we consider the functional problems of social systems, as adaptation, goal attainment, integration, and pattern maintenance, we can readily see how in an earlier era adaptation and goal attainment, which are functions of the economy and polity in a total society, were perceived as male roles (Parsons, 1961). Wresting a livelihood from the wilderness or repulsing an enemy to preserve social order required sheer body force; physical strength was functionally necessary for survival against the elements. But today, it can very well be that finger dexterity is more necessary for operating a space ship or an electronic device than huge size or large muscles. Woman's body structure and social manner then become quite functional for adaptation when the object of exploration is the moon, and for goal attainment when capability to continue the dialogue is the requisite for maintaining world peace.

If adaptation and goal attainment are considered to be instrumental in the sense of getting things done, and the other two social functions (integration and pattern maintenance) are considered as expressive—in the sense of giving meaning and motivation to the doing, then we can see how the division of labor left the training of children and the inculcation of tradition predominantly to the women of the little community. The roles not requiring as much physical prowess came in time to be classified with all expressive functions as feminine roles. The emotional patterns of love and obedience learned in the family as legitimate reactions between parents and children were useful in the same form for all the other role relations. They carried over, for instance, to economic, political, and educational functions, when age determined excellence and only the older males moved into decision-making and initiating roles. And as long as the economy, the polity, and the educational system were simple extensions of the family, the mother came to be the prototype for all the expressive functions of the society. The kind of love, respect, and obedience that made one a good family member made one, then, a good community and organization member, since the dominance roles were played by fathers and the nutrient roles by mothers, and the expected response was that of a son or a daughter.

Today, however, an expressive response modeled on family role relations would be most dysfunctional in a world of eclectic values, wherein a simple directive to obey one's superiors would lead, as it did tragically not long ago, to the attempt to justify the behavior of an Eichmann, and would also lead, as it has in a number of ethnic adjustments, to generating dependent adults incapable of moving easily in and out of decision-making roles as one's expertise requires such moves to be made. In short, the resiliency of role change required of a society built on competence rather than ascription makes quite dysfunctional an identification of command with one sex and affection with the other. To define the expressive functions as feminine and the instrumental functions as masculine today is simply to impose the role distribution of the family on a highly differentiated social system. A lack of understanding of the structural changes that characterize modern societies is one major reason for the current confusion of young people in the choice of vocation. The competent female chemist and the male social worker, even though they themselves may be quite aware of their own adequacies, still have problems with their self-identities and the legitimation of their choices, when faced with other role players who are still defining the world in its tribal or peasant context.

It is a long time since the world has been a world of little communities structured as extended family systems. It is shorter time but an ended era in which the symbol of father and mother is appropriate for governors, bosses, teachers, and nurses. A simple command-obedience system or childlike affection applied indiscriminately to all the elders can in today's world lead to the disaster of an Eichmann who innocently claimed that he did only what he was told, or to the tragedy of momism that made many a boy in World War II an incompetent soldier (Strecker, 1951). In a world of eclectic values and specialized roles, men and women alike must be adult and whole, expressive and instrumental, trained to move with resiliency from command to obedience when their competencies call for the relinquishing or acceptance of power, and from service to reception of service when the situation calls for the exchange. Instrumental and expressive functions are requisite for the functioning of any group irrespective of whether it has an even balance of men and women. If modern society is to survive effectively, it must be able to draw on well-developed personalities capable of using with balance the head or the heart—whichever the situation calls for—with the assurance that the developed personality is capable of instrumental and expressive modes irrespective of sex.

Our increasing knowledge of personality development leads us today to be concerned with the development of persons capable of doing and being, using heads and hearts, thinking and emoting, achieving and serving, giving and receiving, so that it is no longer useful to continue the artificial stress on these as male and female competencies. When the family worked as a team in the economy we could afford to specialize with respect to intellect and emotion. When the individual goes forth as he does in modern society as a person in his own right, responsible for his own choices, rather than as a family member facing the world within the extended family, then it becomes functionally necessary to reorient our training and expectations to allow both women and men to develop their adult potentialities.

This need of adults for an adult world has brought to the forefront the thinking of the social psychologist, Jean Piaget (1932). Clear thinking, moral judgment, perception, capacity to reach beyond the self to the other with full acceptance of the self as person, emotional expressiveness as well as stability—all required for adaptation to a rapidly changing environment—make it peculiarly necessary that each man and each woman have within his or her childhood experience ample opportunity to move from dependency to independency at the rate and in the manner peculiar to each one's unique constitution and environment, rather than in some global form of male-female division of technique. The differences Piaget notes in capacities of children and adolescents are clear-cut: adolescents think beyond the present, begin to build systems and theories, while children have no second thought reflecting on their own thoughts—the requisite for theory-building. Adolescents begin the decentering process from the self to the other when they enter the world of work and become achievers rather than idealist reformers. Deductive thinking begins earlier than inductive in persons as it does in societies. Children relate to small groups and specific individuals while adolescents begin to relate to institutions and values as such. Even moral sentiments for the child are felt in the interindividual context; the child's only ideals are people who are actually part of his surroundings. In adolescents ideals become autonomous (Inhelder & Piaget, 1958, p. 339).

Perhaps we have given sufficient taste of Piaget's mode of analysis to present our second hypothesis. The dichotomies of male-female characteristics so familiar in spiritual instructions are strikingly similar to Piaget's description of child-adult differences. It is, then, highly probable that what is clearly recognized by the counselor, both priest and clinician, as male and female differences are, in fact, the culturally conditioned results of the over-protectedness of the female role player with respect to expectation, sanction, and reward, and actually the differences, rather than being male-female, are child-adult.

PRIESTS WRITING ON WOMEN

In journals devoted specifically to religious women and in others devoted to discussion of marriage, priests frequently write articles on what is called feminine spirituality (*Review for Religious, Sponsa Regis, Marriage*). These articles are intended as guides for the direction of women trying to achieve a higher level of union with God and a richer capacity to serve the neighbor according to the directive of the two great commandments. The themes of these articles easily sort into categories following the expressive-instrumental dichotomy discussed earlier, or into the adult-child dichotomy handled above in the Piaget reference. The more familiar of these dichotomies includes the following: Men are egocentric, women, alterocentric (Browning 1962, p. 20; Gallen, 1961, p. 242); men are devoted to things, women, to people (Gallen, 1961, p. 242; Dubay, 1963, p. 11; Rahner, 1964, p. 6); men use their intellects more, women, their emotions (Provera, 1959, p. 66); men work in an objective, detached manner, women work for the love of the other (Gallen, 1961, p. 245); men develop a spirituality based on principle, women, on love (Gallen, 1961, p. 245; Dubay, 1963, p. 11; Rahner, 1964, p. 7); women are concerned with the past, men with the future (Vann, 1954, p. 135; Rahner 1964, p. 10); women are passive, men are active (Vann, 1954, p. 139; Provera, 1959, p. 146); men focus on doing, women on being (Guitton, 1951, p. 224; Sattler, 1965, p. 8); men are concerned about achieving, women about serving (Vann, 1959, p. 220); men are analytic, women intuitive (Rahner, 1964, p. 6); men are the prophets, women, the mystics (Rahner, 1964, p. 6). All these differences are presented as embedded in the nature of women and the nature of men (see here Evoy & Christoph, 1963, 1965). Clear statements are made that these differences are natural to one or the other and this is claimed to mean that these differences come easily to them and that succumbing to these natural traits is more excusable when there are deficiencies. As an example of the first, Father Welsh says of women that they "have all the attitudes towards God and others that men must learn, sometimes with great difficulty" (Welsh, 1963, p. 636). And on the excusing side: "That is why a woman who is selfish in a self-centered kind of way is an anomaly more distressing to encounter than a selfish man" (Gallen, 1961, p. 245).

A few more quotations in context will suggest why these differences are emphasized. Father Vann says: "If, normally speaking, it is natural for man to have the last word in major questions of policy, in economic matters, and so forth, it is equally natural for the wife to have the last word in matters concerning her own domain as housewife and mother of her babies" (Vann, 1959, p. 220). In what sense is the baby the possession of the wife only? In what sense is wife juxtaposed to man? It is only in the old society that all women are mothers. The alternate concept to man is woman; to wife, husband. To cross these categories is to deny the structure of the world in which we now live.

Father Browning, elaborating a traditional theme of papal exhortations, states: "Every woman is destined to be a mother, a mother in the physical sense, or in the spiritual but no less real sense." (Browning, 1962, p. 20). To the degree that every woman is destined to be a mother, every man is destined to be a father, but this is not stressed. Since it is quite obvious that many women, especially the nuns to whom Father Browning is speaking, are not mothers, it seems evident that he is making a plea for these women to play the expressive roles, the service roles, and to do it because it is their nature.

Dubay observes: "While a number of women possess psychological characteristics more commonly found in men, for example, leadership, ambition, idea-interest, intrepidity, yet the majority are understandably enough *endowed* [emphasis added] with the feminine traits of loving, person-interest, timidity" (Dubay, 1963, p. 10). And again: "A woman's life is wrapped around by love. She yearns to bestow it, and yearns to receive it. We often find men who are substantially contented with pursuing their ambition, their project, their ideas, but rarely do we meet a woman who does not want before all else to love and be loved" (Dubay, 1963, pp. 10-11).

Provera claims: "Women, on account of the sensitivity of their sex, are more exposed to the danger of giving and accepting sensible affection than men" (Provera, 1959, p. 113), and again: "The feminine character is more suited to passivity, and there is sometimes a remnant of the infantile mentality still present which is regarded and developed as a virtue" (Provera, 1959, pp. 146-147).

Vann maintains: "Woman is by nature not activist, but contemplative. In primitive society it is the man who goes out to hunt, who ventures, who makes war; it is the woman who is the conserver, who stays to guard the home" (Vann, 1954, pp. 133-134); "The role of woman is to suggest and to inspire; not to act but to inspire man to act; not to command and take the initiative . . ." (Vann, 1954, p. 139). Over and over again come the characterizations of what is natural to women: sensitivity, emotionality, global thinking, situational specificity, and other pre-adolescent emphases, while physical prowess, intellectual superiority, emotional neutrality, and creativity are attributed to men with the concomitant and less-than-subtle request that woman supply for man as he moves in the instrumental direction the expressive services that he needs to sustain this venture.

WOMEN WRITING ON WOMEN

When women speak to women about feminine traits in this same traditional dichotomy of the expressive and the instrumental, and the child and adult, the polarities are there, but with one difference. Where the priest speaks of the ease and naturalness with which a woman assumes these characteristics and roles and implies that there is no effort involved, just a passive acceptance of her nature, the tradition-oriented woman, speaking of woman's role today, is urging her peers to strive to develop these "essentially feminine" characteristics. Dorothy Dohen says: "She [woman] has to give conscious consideration to these passive virtues, evaluate them in the presence of God, and make positive effort to integrate them into her own life" (Dohen, 1960, p. 253); "Woman today needs to learn to wait and to be passive, and patient in suffering, to be cheerful of heart in sacrifice" (Dohen, 1960, p. 254); "she must learn to accept" (Dohen, 1960, p. 255). In 1964 Sister Mary Eva wrote an article entitled: "Femininity can be Taught" (Sister Mary

Eva, 1964). While many women like Gertrude von le Fort (1962), Solange Hertz (1963), Marie Robinson (1961) and others outdo the priests in their agreement that women are essentially altruistic and have more receptive psyches, others like Rosemary Lauer (1963) protest these biological absolutes and moral imperatives as indoctrination.

Eleanor Maccoby, a substantial social psychologist and participant in the 1963 symposium on "The potential of woman," held at the San Francisco Medical Center, clearly recognizes these differences in ways of thinking and functioning (such as, less frequent use of analysis, and the greater concern with preservation), but she hypothesizes something quite different from nature, biology, or constitutional inclination as causal. Gene Marine, who reports the symposium, quotes Dr. Maccoby as follows: "There are consistent differences in the average performance of the two sexes. The key to the matter seems to be in when and how soon a child is encouraged to assume initiative, to take responsibility for himself, rather than relying upon others for direction of his activity" (Marine, 1963, p. 23). Dr. Maccoby refers to testing results in which overprotected boys were shown to have higher verbal skills, and the more independently trained girls were more analytic.

Witkin's findings on sex differences in perception and thinking point to the greater capacity of boys to overcome an embedding context, and he presents an impressive array of evidence for the sex differences he finds. Yet he makes a cautious conclusion. With regard to his findings on individual differences in perception—wherein women tend to be more field dependent than men—he says: "The results of these studies contribute to a picture of small but persistent differences in style of field approach. They also raise interesting questions concerning sex differences in differentiation, as well as the role of cultural and constitutional factors in the origins of sex differences" (Witkin, 1962, p. 215). Witkin still concludes that, at the present stage of evidence, we cannot interpret these findings with confidence. He also presents evidence that shows poorer long-range memory, but better short-range memory in girls, and that girls are more field dependent than boys; that boys show a more analytic and girls a more global approach; that men are superior to women in set-breaking capacity, but not in susceptibility to set. All of these relate to a capacity to overcome an embedding context. In general, they add up to evidence that women tend to be more global than men in their perceptual and intellectual functioning as distinct from analytic, and more dependent on others in their social functioning. These researchers are only now delving into the cause of these differences between men and women. Items in their hypothesis which

postulate a multiple base are these: sex organ differences; the encouragement of a more dependent role for women in our culture; an emphasis
placed on self-reliance and achievement in the training of boys and on
nurturant roles for girls; the positive value placed on differentiation of
boys from girls in our society, and well-defined views in our culture of
personality differences between men and women (Witkin, 1962, p.
220-221). The caution with which these hypotheses are stated suggests
the reluctance of the scientist to make any absolute assertions about
cause of differences. If the cultural factors are major determinants, then
the very explicit claim for natural differences and the moral imperative
mode of communicating found in the priests' positions are probably
major factors in generating and preserving the differences found. The
priests are in this way the culture carriers who preserve the model and
reinforce it in the child-training process.

The scientific evidence points to the existence of differences, small,
but persistent. The lack of clear knowledge as to which factors are
determiners of the differences—nature or nurture—presents us now
with a relevant issue: Is it a good thing for the evident differences to be
developed and sustained by the conscious urging, rewarding, criticism,
and direction of women to preserve and further develop these differences, and by the sustaining of man in the preservation of the intellectual and action-oriented opposites by the rationalizations often
being used? Or is this the moment to critically reevaluate the function
of these directives in view of the need of two major personality developments: (1) the development by men and women of more balanced
expressive-instrumental modes of response within their self-systems
rather than leaning toward some tandem effect with another person; (2)
the need of generating in childhood for both boys and girls an environment wherein opportunity for growth to maturity is consistently open
to both sexes without the ambivalence built in by these dichotomous
expectations?

THE SURVEY

In the spring of 1961, as part of a larger problem, I included in a
survey of 25 percent of the priests of the Boston Archdiocese in urban
parish work and 25 percent in suburban parish work the following two
questions: (1) What women active in the world today do you most
admire?; (2) What men active in the world today do you most admire?

The larger problem was reported in *Values and interests in social
change* (Neal, 1965), but the question considered here has not been

used in any earlier report. I was seeking to find out if priests tend to perceive women in ways differently from their perceptions of men when responding to a general stimulus that leaves the definition of the situation unstructured. The findings are, in several cases, significantly different from what could be expected by chance. These differences fall into three main groups: (1) use of general catagories rather than reference to specific individuals; (2) the use of non-response; (3) the number and types of women chosen in contrast to the number and types of men chosen. Although the question asked for and expected a listing of specific individuals, 20 percent of the priest-respondents used general categories in referring to men and 32 percent used them in referring to women. This means that rather than naming names, they said they admired statesmen, doctors, missionaries, etc., when speaking of men, and nurses, teachers, sisters, etc., when speaking of women. These categorical responses took the following forms: "good Catholic mothers with six or more children," "holy nuns," "many in CFM," "housewives," "women fulfilling the function of mothers in some way," for women, and for men: "someone that will get things done," "educators," "obscure priests," "intelligent people."

There were some striking differences within the sample of priests when the sample is broken down into the categories which I call value-change, interest-change, value-nonchange, and interest-nonchange. These categories need some clarification. In the study of which this material is a segment (Neal, 1965), I was examining the responses of priests to pressures for change which were facing the Church in the 1950s and early 1960s. These pressures are still as relevant today as they were at that time. The reaction of Church members during the '50s to the new thinking of theologians like Yves Congar, Henri DeLubac, M. Chenu, Karl Rahner, Bernard Häring and others, ranged from enthusiastic acceptance and recognition of what they were saying, on the one hand, to outright rejection of them as persons, on the other. This division of opinion easily fell into that liberal-conservative pattern familiar today during this period of rapid change as a typical response continuum to much that is occurring in the political, social, and economic domain.

In many cases, however, although the above-mentioned dichotomy seems relevant, its use misses some of the differences within the classification of liberal or conservative that distinguish the responses of individuals. Thinking through the reason why this categorization is so evident and yet deficient, I hypothesized that there is another dimension to the liberal-conservative dichotomy which, when added to this division, explains a great deal of the difference in response patterns. That dimension is a value-interest continuum. Besides a characteristic resistance to or acceptance of change-oriented stimuli, many people have an equally characteristic response in terms of a commitment to values that are deeper than the situation in which the behavior takes place and so meaningful that it becomes a determinant of whether a person will or will not accept change-oriented stimuli. Other people to the same degree have a deep commitment to the special interests of the groups with which they identify which likewise becomes the determinant of whether they will accept or reject stimuli to change. (One could argue that these two orientations are not mutually exclusive and that the dichotomy in consequence is not logically valid. At the behavioral level, however, the division seems to be sufficiently dichotomous to justify examination.)

On the basis of the above assumptions, common categories of response could fall into a four-dimensional pattern in a richer explanatory model than the two-dimensional liberal-conservative dichotomy. In this four-fold model, value-change men are opened to change for value reasons, interest-change men for interest reasons, while value-nonchange men are at the same time closed to change for value reasons and interest-nonchange men for interest reasons. This typology is not an arbitrary division of the world into logical sets, but rather an expression of modes of identification with the social system, or at least so my hypothesis goes, so that value-change men are those whose concerns focus on adaptation to current conditions, and interest-change men are those seeking the goals of the system as it is now institutionalized and in the most expedient mode. On the other hand, value-nonchange men are those concerned with maintaining the already institutionalized value system rooted in institutions with a long tradition; and interest-nonchange men are those mainly concerned with integrating the new members of social systems to customs as they are now patterned. These types of people are responding not only to functionally necessary dimensions of social structure, but to dimensions whose purposes are often served at the expense of a loss to one of the other functions, so that the behavior of the committed person is frequently at cross purposes.

The testing of the above hypothesis was the content of the earlier work, *Values and interests in social change* (Neal, 1965), and the findings of that study suggest the usefulness of considering the four-fold categorization for investigating further patterns of behavior observed in social interaction like the one here under consideration. In

TABLE I
Distribution by Orientation Group of Responses
of Priests to Admiration of Men and Women Question

Orientation		Used categorization				Refused to respond				Named specific people			
Score *	N	Men Admired		Women Admired		Men Admired		Women Admired		Men Admired		Women Admired	
		N	%	N	%	N	%	N	%	N	%	N	%
VC	91	10	9	21	23	15	16	43	47	66	73	27	30
IC	28	4	14	6	21	5	18	13	46	19	68	9	22
VNC	55	14	25	21	38	8	15	25	45	33	60	9	16
INC	73	21	29	30	41	19	26	34	47	33	45	9	12
0 score	12 †	4	33	5	42	1	8	4	33	7	58	3	25

* Value-change, interest-change, value-nonchange, interest-nonchange.
† Twelve priests with 0 scores could not be classified.

the Boston diocesan sample, thirty-five percent of the priests responded as value-change men; eleven percent as interest-change men; twenty-one percent as value-nonchange men, and twenty-eight percent as interest-nonchange men. Twelve men or five percent of the sample on the instrument used to determine these divisions chose items equally in both directions and hence could not be categorized into any one of these groupings. These men would correspond to those in Berelson's (1954) voting study whose commitment is determined by the mode of the stimulus, since they could accept contradictory positions on the attitude items. Persons of this type are found in most attitude studies and often respond as highly suggestible to stimuli that are well phrased and attractive in format. Their responses are sometimes analyzed as *Yea* saying and *Nay* saying. As in this group, they are usually but a small percentage of all respondents.

When these categories are used to sort the responses of priests on the question of women and men admired, it can be seen from Table 1 that priests open to change used categories only half as many times as the priests opposed to change. But even these priests used categories twice as often when referring to women as when referring to men. (This categorization was chosen in the content analysis because it suggests, when used, that the respondent tends to perceive other individuals more as role players than as persons.)

The same table is even more interesting in the use of non-response. Here all four groups of priests have practically the same percent of non-response, forty-six percent when referring to women. The highest non-response when referring to men is twenty-six percent for the interest-nonchange group, those most resistant to new ideas; while all the other groups refused to choose men only sixteen percent of the time. This means that the priests most open to change that is value-based were just as closed to choice of women as those most resistant to change. This finding poses the question: Is this typical of all men or just of priests, i.e., this reluctance to respond with a choice of women admired in contrast to men admired? This question will be considered presently, but to complete the examination of Table I, the last column shows that among those who actually name names, the value-change men do it seventy-three percent of the time for men but only thirty percent for women, while among the interest-nonchange men, the naming of women is as low as twelve percent while men are chosen forty-five percent of the time. Obviously there are differences in response to this kind of stimulus in terms of the categories employed.

In comparison with the priests' responses a sample of parents of

TABLE II

*Comparison of Responses of Priests with those of Married
Couples on Admiration of Men and Women*

		Used categorization				Refused to respond				Named specific people			
		Men Admired		Women Admired		Men Admired		Women Admired		Men Admired		Women Admired	
N		N	%	N	%	N	%	N	%	N	%	N	%
259	Priests	52	20	83	32	48	19	119	46	159	61	57	22
53	Fathers	1	2	5	9	8	15	12	23	43	81	28	53
59	Mothers	1	2	5	8	5	9	5	8	51	86	42	71

By Chi square test, these priest-laity differences are significant beyond the .01 level.

social psychology students when asked the same questions responded in categories only two percent of the time for men and nine percent for women admired. (There were 112 in this sample.) This small pilot study suggests that categorizing is more characteristic of the priests than of other adults.

Similar differences are revealed in the use of non-response. The priests failed to answer the question on women forty-six percent of the time and on men nineteen percent. In the case of both men and women, the fathers failed to name men they admired fifteen percent of the time and women twenty-three percent. But only nine percent of the mothers failed to name both men and women they admired. These findings are not definitive since the circumstances under which the parents were studied were different from those obtaining with the priests, but they are interesting in that the priests consistently rank higher in evading this question. One might seek the difference in the conditions of the presentation of the stimulus. The priests were responding to this question as part of a larger questionnaire. One might assume that this had something to do with the reluctance to respond. On the contrary, however, although the question does appear on the seventh page of the schedule, on the eighth page was a check list of what magazines, journals, and newspapers were read and the non-response level of the priests to this portion of the questionnaire was only two percent. Throughout the questionnaire, items which could be answered by a check were responded to with a higher frequency than open-ended questions, but even here there was a wide variation in the amount of response. Questions of the type "Where have you traveled and how long did you stay?" had a non-response level of twelve percent, while the question "What priestly training needs new methods?" was omitted only twenty-three percent of the time. Even the question "Where would you initiate change if you had the opportunity?" was omitted only thirty-four percent of the time although a good percentage of the priests (forty-nine percent) were non-change oriented.

TABLE III

Number of Different Men and Women Chosen
by Each Group

N	No. of Different Men	No. of Different Women
259 Priests	64	22
53 Fathers	39	21
59 Mothers	46	24

In the third area of difference presented in Table III, the type of person selected, a further pattern emerges. The priests chose 64 different men; the fathers, 39; the mothers, 46. It should be remembered that five times more priests were choosing than men and women in the parent sample. From the sheer variety of choice, it is clear that priests tend to differentiate men more than they do women.

Because of the difference in choices made, the only way we can compare them meaningfully is to compare the types of people chosen. Of the men chosen by the priests, thirty-six percent are Catholic heads of state or Catholic Church leaders, while nineteen percent more are heads of state or other political leaders, and only four percent fall into the diffuse category of non-power roles. The fathers chose Catholic Church leaders about as often as the priests (eight percent, as compared with six percent for the latter); but they chose other political figures only thirty-five percent of the time, leaving forty percent of their choices for men outstanding in a variety of professional and service roles. Mothers chose political figures only twenty-three percent of the time, and a variety of men in the different professions, in service, and in entertainment roles forty-nine percent of the time. Among the choice of women, the most frequent choice of the priests is Claire Boothe Luce (17 choices), a Catholic woman in politics. Barbara Ward, the internationally famous economist, is chosen but five times. Eleanor Roosevelt had five choices (although she had died prior to the survey). The priests' choices for women in the performing arts included Loretta Young, Marian Anderson, Irene Dunne, Helen Hayes, and Grace Kelly. Authors were the next most popular choice, and these were limited to Sister Madeleva, Moira Walsh, Phyllis McGinley, and Jean Kerr. There is a clear Catholic preference in the choices. (This was also true for the men chosen: Kennedy, DeGaulle, Adenauer, being the most frequent choices along with the pope and the cardinal.) Just three wives of famous men drew choices: Mrs. Jacqueline Kennedy, Mrs. Lyndon Johnson, and Mrs. William McNamara, each of whom received but one choice. Queen Elizabeth was chosen twice. This was, of course, in the summer of 1961, before Jacqueline Kennedy had risen to fame. The rest of the choices, all individual, included Catherine de Hueck, Helen Keller, Mary Newland, and three local women. Thirteen priests stated that they admired no women.

Among the parents, choices of women are more unique, but the largest cluster are wives of political leaders, women in politics, and women in the performing arts. The priests chose many more Catholics than did any other choosers. In fact, only seven of these choices went to non-Catholic women, and 38 of them to 23 different non-Catholic men. On the whole, however, the major differences were their reluctance to choose at all, and their higher tendency to choose women's roles rather than specific women.

The findings of this study are significant only to indicate hypotheses that ought to be investigated further in view of the larger discussion included in this report. These hypotheses are three: (1) Pastoral counseling tends to present and consider women more in the role of mothers, than as individual persons; (2) The definition of the woman's role as a mother role encourages a kind of over-dependency that works against adjustment to the changing expectations of women as adults living in the modern world; (3) There is a tendency for priests to perceive women as categories of service workers rather than as individual persons requiring a unique personal response.

In an age in which the person is a central concern, ought there not to be some serious consideration of methods of dealing with women on a more individual basis as persons rather than as categories, even if the category be such an important role as that of mother? We end with the question: In view of the changes in social structure and the rapid development of even further differentiation, along with the need of emotional and intellectual development of adults as persons as well as parents, ought the image and the role of women be left so undifferentiated in the perceptions and the choices of priests?

REFERENCES

Berelson, B. *Voting*. Chicago: University of Chicago Press, 1954.

Browning, C. (C.P.) Woman's highest fulfillment. *Rev. Religious,* 1962, *21,* 19-27.

Cox, H. *The secular city*. New York: Macmillan, 1965.

Dohen, Dorothy. *Women in wonderland*. New York: Sheed & Ward, 1960.

Dubay, T. (S.H.) Psychological needs in the religious context. *Rev. Religious,* 1963, *22,* 3-13.

Evoy, J. J. (S.J.) & Christoph, V. F. (S.J.) *Personality development in religious life*. New York: Sheed & Ward, 1963.

Evoy, J. J. (S.J.) & Christoph, V. F. (S.J.) *Maturity in the religious life*. New York: Sheed & Ward, 1965.

Gallen, J. F. (S.J.) Femininity and spirituality. *Rev. Religious,* 1961, *20,* 237-256.

Guitton, J. *An essay on human love*. New York: Philosophical library, 1951.

Hertz, Solange, *Searcher of majesty*. Westminster, Md.: Newman, 1963.

Inhelder, B. & Piaget, J. *The growth of logical thinking from childhood to adolescence* (trans. by Anne Parsons & Stanley Milgram). New York: Basic Books, 1958.

Lauer, Rosemary. Women and the Church. *Commonweal,* 1963, *89,* 365-368.

Marine, Gene. The mental differences between the sexes. *Sci. Dig.,* 1963, *53,* 21-25.

Neal, Sr. Marie Augusta (S.N.D.) *Values and interests in social change.* Englewood Cliffs, N. J.: Prentice-Hall, 1965.

Parsons, T. An outline of the social system. In T. Parsons, E. Shils, K. D. Maejele & J. Pitts (Eds.) *Theories of Society.* New York: Free Press, 1961. Pp. 30-79.

Piaget, J. *The moral judgment of the child.* London: Paul, Trench, Trubner, 1932.

Provera, P. (C.M.) *Live your vocation* (trans. By Rev. Thomas F. Murray). St. Louis: Herder, 1959.

Rahner, K. (S.J.) Religions and the man. *Marriage,* 1964, *46,* No. 1, 6-12.

Robinson, Marie. The mature woman. *Marriage,* 1961, *43,* No. 2, 7-10.

Sattler, H. V. (C.S.R.) Why female? *Marriage,* 1965, *47,* No. 5, 6-10.

Sister Mary Eva (O.S.U.) Femininity can be taught. *Marriage,* 1964, *46,* No. 9, 24-28.

Strecker, E. A. *Their mother's sons* (new ed.). Philadelphia: Lippincott, 1951.

Thibon, G. *What God has joined together.* Chicago: Regenery, 1952.

Vann, G. (O.P.) *The water and the fire.* New York: Sheed & Ward, 1954.

Vann, G. (O.P.) *The paradise tree.* London: Collins, 1959.

von le Fort, Gertrud. *The eternal woman* (trans. by Marie Buehrie). Milwaukee: Bruce, 1962.

Welsh, R. (O. Carm.) Sensitivity. *Rev. Religious,* 1963, *22,* 662-667.

Witkin, H. A. *et al. Psychological differentiation.* New York: Wiley, 1962.

DISCUSSION

Rev. Joseph P. Fitzpatrick, S.J.
Professor of Sociology and Anthropology, Fordham University

I would like to make a comment about each of the major divisions of Sister Marie Augusta's paper: 1) her theory that priests represent women to themselves according to a set of qualities which are not natural to women, but which characterize women in a primitive or a folk society and which are no longer functional in our society; 2) her findings in a study of Boston priests that a large percentage of them do not discriminate between women according to individual personality traits, but represent them according to an undifferentiated image in which the qualities of the mother role predominate. The plea that

Sister makes as a consequence of her theory and her findings, that priests must learn to deal with women as individual personalities in the highly complicated social organization of the 1960s, is a plea to which we all shout an enthusiastic "brava." But the problem requires more than the shouting. We have to know more precisely what the problem is in order to know how to solve it.

THE ORIGIN OF FEMININE CHARACTERISTICS

At the heart of the first part of Sister's paper is the implication that what we have generally considered to be natural feminine characteristics are really not natural at all; they are functional to particular types of economic activity or social organization. These feminine characteristics, Sister suggests, developed as "functional requisites" in primitive or peasant societies because the "expressive needs" of those societies (those needs involving love, feeling, tenderness, meaning) had to be filled by women. The instrumental needs (hunting, plowing, fighting) could be done only by men. Our contemporary industrial and technological society has created a situation in which both instrumental and expressive needs can be filled indifferently by men or women. Therefore personal qualities related to expressive needs or instrumental needs can no longer be logically or reasonably based on differences of sex. Presumably these should be based on differences of roles, roles moreover which can be filled equally by man or woman.

This is a provocative analysis. From one point of view, it is extremely valuable in emphasizing again that many of the qualities which we have considered to be "natural" to women are not natural at all; they are cultural. Certainly one of the great contributions of the social sciences to contemporary life has been their success in revealing how unfounded and how dangerous is the universal tendency of men to project their particular cultural characteristics onto the plan of a divine or natural law. American girls think it is natural to fall in love and select their own marriage partner; girls in India think it is natural to do quite the opposite. The more light we can get, therefore, about what is cultural in the personality and behavior of women in our society and in every other society, the farther we will have advanced toward the possibility of mature spiritual direction. We will be able to distinguish between education and counsel which are helping a girl to relate herself effectively to a particular culture in a particular age, and the kind of education and counsel which is helping her to fulfill her nature. The confusion between nature and culture has been at the root of much of our difficulty in adjusting to our rapidly emerging world, and Sister has done a great service by emphasizing this once again. The Soviet Union has gone far beyond us in this regard in demonstrating that the practice of medicine, business management and even the exploration of space are tasks that are quite as natural to women as they are to men.

The problem I find with Sister's analysis is the basic problem I find with the nature-culture inquiry in general. Granted that personality development is the assimilation of a culture, and that culture intimately forms the personality—we still have the question: How far? Sister briefly summarized some recent scientific findings that there appear to be recognizable differences between men and women which go far beyond the physiological differences of their sex. But there is still some doubt that these may be cultural. It is true that we have created a society in which many expressive needs can be filled by men as well as by women. But are there some that cannot? And if so, what are they? How do we determine them? If personality is to be functionally related to social and economic organization—and if, in our contemporary social organization, men and women stand equally capable of filling instrumental and expressive needs—what will be the basis for differentiation, and by what norms will we differentiate? Can we not expect that the personalities of men and women in this situation will become increasingly similar? What then will be the basis of heterosexual relationships, since most of these are based not on physiological characteristics but on characteristics of personality? To be extreme about it, does this mean that we are moving toward one vast homosexual universe? If sex is no longer to be the basis of differentiation, what will be?

In practical terms, it seems to me that this comes down to the basic decision of roles. What roles will a man fulfill in a society; what roles will a woman fulfill? and evidently this decision will emerge from a growing consensus about values. And you all are aware that this problem of roles is one of the most difficult ones of our society and culture.

A second difficulty I find is the danger (which Sister seeks to avoid) of identifying "feminine characteristics" with immaturity. This can become a kind of ethnocentrism in reverse. I think the evidence of history and experience makes it quite clear that maturity is not a matter of the role you fill; but of the relation of the person to the role he is filling. In other words, a man in a patriarchal society can be very immature in the fulfillment of the dominant role, and a woman can be remarkably mature in the fulfillment of her subordinate role. Maturity, it seems to me, is a matter of the person's perception of his role, of its significance, of his motivation in fulfilling it; of his relationship to others as they fulfill it.

For example, in Sister's reference to Dorothy Dohen's (1960) book, I do not think Miss Dohen was supporting the traditional role as the ideal feminine role. Her entire book is a challenge to the concept of naturally differentiated personalities. She is very much in Sister Marie Augusta's corner. What Dorothy Dohen was getting at was this: when women fulfill the mother role, for example, they are compelled to accept the consequences of this role. It requires a good deal of passivity, patience, feeling. In a folk society, the culture would have automatically formed the woman's personality according to these qualities; but in our society these qualities needed for the fulfillment of this role must be formally and consciously taught, and formally and consciously learned. It is this reflective, self-conscious response to a role which is the mark of maturity.

THE PRIESTS' SURVEY

The second point for comment is the reaction of the priests to the question about identifying women and men whom they admire. I do not quite know what to make of the results of this inquiry. They certainly indicate that, within the limits of the study, the attitude of priests toward women is significantly different from that of the parents of college women. I was disappointed that Sister did not give more attention to the major difference which emerged from her larger study (Neal, 1965), the difference between the priests who were value-oriented and open to change, in contrast to those who were interest-oriented and closed to change. In her larger study Sister found that this personality difference was positively correlated to a whole series of questions or problems which the priests had to face. Furthermore, it is unfortunate that Sister did not have more opportunity to study the attitudes of the priests in contrast to the attitude of a better-matched sample of laymen. It is difficult as it stands to know to what extent the attitude of the priests is related to factors in their priestly life or training or to qualities which they share with laymen of similar personality. The conclusion Sister draws—and it is a disturbing one—that priests do not discriminate the individual personality of the one whom they counsel; that their counsel is presented to an undifferentiated type of woman with characteristics primarily suited for the mother role, is obviously a situation seriously in need of correction. But what must we correct? I think Sister's research has defined more sharply the

nature of the problem. I hope she or others will continue to seek to
determine what factors in the training or life of a priest are related to
this character of priests (or of some priests); whether the factors are
really factors in the priestly life or training or whether they are found
in unmarried men in general; or even in married men for that matter.
For example, if a study were done of a sample of laymen who are
interest-oriented and closed to change, would their attitudes toward
women be similar to that of the priests? Before we have some clarification on these points, it will not be easy to plan a strategy for reform-
ing those most irreformable of people, the Catholic clergy.

REFERENCES

Dohen, Dorothy. *Women in wonderland.* New York: Sheed & Ward, 1960.
Neal, Sr. Marie Augusta (S.N.D.) *Values and interests in social change.*
    Englewood Cliffs, N. J.: Prentice-Hall, 1965.

Girls' Attitudes Toward Priests and Nuns

REV. L. AUGUSTINE GRADY, S.J. and
REV. ROBERT J. McNAMARA, S.J.

Father L. Augustine Grady, S.J., received his A.B. degree from Georgetown University in 1939 and his M.A. degree in the field of counseling and guidance from Fordham University in 1953. For more than ten years he was Director of Student Counseling at St. Peter's College in Jersey City. In 1962 Father Grady came to Fordham University to begin a distinguished career in the Theology Department. For the academic year 1967-68 he was on leave, taking courses at Union Theological Seminary.

Father Robert J. McNamara, S.J. received his A.B. (1949) and M.A. (1953) degrees from St. Louis University, and his Ph.D. from Cornell University in 1963. He is a contributor to sociological journals, and is co-author of a Glossary of Sociological Terms (1957). Currently, Father McNamara is an associate professor in the Sociology Department at Fordham University. During the academic year 1966-67 he was on leave from the University, spending this time as a Senior Study Director at the National Opinion Research Center of the University of Chicago.

The purpose of this paper is not to open a can of worms, but simply to probe for the attitudes, favorable and unfavorable, which college girls have toward priests and nuns. We claim to have done only two things: first, get an indication of what in fact these attitudes are; second, try and discover whether or not the attitudes are related to a general mind-set found, frequently enough, among members of religious groups.

What we found can best be expressed if we proceed in the following fashion: first, describe the groups of girls who filled out our questionnaire; second, give an account of the attitudes we found; third, show the connection between these attitudes and attitude of mind which we shall call "restrictive"; last, discuss the implications of our findings.

THE SAMPLE OF GIRLS

We suspected that girls attending an all-girls' college would react differently to our questions than girls at a coeducational college. So we secured the cooperation of two teachers, both religious-order priests: one taught sociology at a Roman Catholic liberal arts college for women in New York City's metropolitan area; the other was a theology professor teaching undergraduates at a coeducational liberal arts college, part of a large Roman Catholic university in the same area. The woman's college group was composed of 60 girls, 83 percent of whom were juniors and seniors—the rest were sophomores; the coed college group had 58 members, all of whom were freshmen. Among the former, almost all were boarding at the college; this was true of only one-quarter of the latter.

The questionnaire was administered to the woman's college group shortly after Easter, 1965, in two sociology classes. Only two girls refused to fill it out. As for the coeds, the questionnaire was passed out to them at roughly the same time during their next-to-last class, and they were asked to return it on the last day of class. Of the 85 questionnaires passed out, 58 were returned. Among those who failed to return their questionnaires, some simply forgot, and some "cut" the last class. None refused because she opposed the study.

Obviously, then, we did not have a random sample of Catholic college girls. We cannot generalize from our results to the general population of such girls. We have a "convenience" sample—i.e., two groups of girls whom we could reach with our questionnaires and who are not obviously untypical of their general population. Small as the groups are, we think that a report on their attitudes is worthwhile, and hope it will spark a study which would include a great many more subjects drawn on a probability model to represent the whole population of college girls across the nation.

THE GIRLS' ATTITUDES

Every human being takes on a variety of roles as he goes through life; sometimes two roles conflict with each other, sometimes they all blend beautifully. The nuns with whom the college girls have come into contact have been playing at least two roles in their regard, however blurred the perception—by girls or nuns—of the content of the two roles and of the distinction between them. Quite obviously, the two roles are the educational and the pastoral. They are analytically distinct, no matter how muddled they get in real life.

This is not to say that the nun or priest cannot be an authentic educator, but must always muddy the mathematical or literary or psychological waters with apologetics or, at the very least, with Roman Catholic values. It always means, however, that the presence of nun or priest in the classroom is a sign of the Church's commitment to authentic education; it usually means, for the individual priest or nun, an opportunity to attract the student to his own basic values. Ideally the attraction occurs because the teacher teaches mathematics or English or psychology very well, and because his or her own personality is persuasively Christian.

This small study attempts to get at this second aspect of the pastoral role—i.e., the personal attraction exerted by the priest or nun in the classroom and counseling situation. We have made no attempt to get the girls' opinions about how well priests and nuns teach class (or run parishes), nor have we tried to find out whether the girls have even the dimmest idea of the Church's commitment to authentic education (or authentically human community life).

The method we used was as simple as we could make it. We simply asked the girls to whom they would go for help if they found themselves in real trouble over a problem of faith and a problem of love. We also asked them with whom they "would definitely *NOT* like to discuss such a problem." Then we asked them what "most important quality" they would look for in their advisor in such problems, giving them one choice among "devotion to the faith," "knowledge of Christian teaching," and "human understanding." Finally, this section of the questionnaire asked them how frequently they found this "most important quality" among nuns, among parish priests, and among priest-teachers or counselors. Tables I through IV summarize the answers to all these questions.

We must note right here that virtually all the girls (90 percent) had gone to Catholic primary and secondary schools. So they are responding from a background of at least thirteen years of Catholic education. Again, 90 percent come from homes in which both parents are Catholic; only five girls (four percent) say that they do not go to religious services at least weekly. In general, then, we can say that the background and environment of these girls are about as formally Catholic as they can be.

The question on the problem of faith was posed this way:

Suppose, right now, that you were deeply worried because you think that the bottom has fallen out of your religious faith. To whom among the following people do you feel that you would *FIRST* turn for help?

They were given the checklist which appears on the left-hand side of Table I, after being asked to exclude people of their own age "with whom you might well discuss the problem first."

TABLE I
Counseling and a Problem of Faith:
The First-Chosen and the Excluded Counselor

(Percent)

Counselor	To whom would you FIRST turn for help?		With whom would you NOT like to discuss the problem?	
	Woman's College	Coed College	Woman's College	Coed College
Father	5	3	33	31
Mother	9	5	30	36
Parish Priest	14	7	12	53
Older relatives	2	0	47	40
A Nun	17	7	23	59
Priest: Teacher or Counselor	47	72	6	2
Other	7	5	0	2
Total Percent	101	99	—*	—*
N	58	58	52	52
† NA	2	0	8	6
Total	60	58	60	58

* The figures do not add to 100 percent because the respondents were not restricted to only one choice.

† NA (No Answer): in this and subsequent tables the actual number of respondents not answering is given, and they are not included in the percentages. In the third and fourth columns of the table, the girls who do not answer are probably refusing to exclude anybody. The percentages in these two columns are based on total, not N (number responding).

Table I shows that the college girls, whether attending the woman's college or the coeducational one, do not bring up problems of faith around the house. Virtually none would talk first to her parents about such a problem, and about one-third would prefer never to discuss it with their parents. The same pattern, only more so, applies to other older relatives. The person to whom half of the woman's college group (47 percent) and three-quarters of the coed group (72 percent) would go for help first, and the person whom virtually no one would exclude as a counselor is the same: the priest-teacher or counselor. This, of course, surprises no one, for this is the way things are "supposed" to be in the general Catholic pattern.

Table I's story does not stop there, however. Just over half of the coeds (53 percent) would exclude the parish priest as counselor in a problem of faith and very few from either group would go to him *first* (14 and seven percent). One-quarter of the woman's college group (23 percent) and three-fifths of the coeds (59 percent) would exclude the nun as counselor. This is the beginning of a pattern which will continue through these tables: the coed group is very "hard" on nuns and parish priests, and the woman's college group is not exactly "easy" on them.

When the girls were asked which of the three qualities enumerated above was "most important" in an advisor, virtually all chose "human understanding" for both problems (faith: 89 percent; love: 97 percent). This makes the analysis of their responses much simpler, for we can eliminate the other two qualities and just ask this question of the girls: "In your experience, how frequently have you found [human understanding] to be present in the following groups of people?" The groups presented were nuns, parish priests, and priest-teachers or counselors. The possible answer categories were: never, rarely, half the time, usually, always—and these categories are combined in the left-hand side of Table II.

One-third of the woman's college group and two-thirds of the coeds find human understanding "never or rarely" present among nuns when their focus is on the problem of faith; very few find it "usually or always" present among the nuns. The exact opposite is the case for the priest-teachers or counselors: three-quarters and three-fifths (77 and 59 percent) of the groups find it usually or always present among them, and almost literally none finds it never or rarely present (zero and two percent). The parish priests fall in between these two extremes. Without exception, however, the coed group is *always* either proportionately more critical or proportionately less favorable to each of the three types of possible advisors.

TABLE II

Understanding Related to Faith Problem:
How Often the Girls Find Understanding Among Priests and Nuns

(Percent)

How often the girls find understanding in Priests and Nuns	Nuns		Parish Priests		Priest-Teacher or Counselor	
	Woman's College	Coed College	Woman's College	Coed College	Woman's College	Coed College
Never or rarely	34	66	14	27	0	2
Half the time	45	22	36	50	19	26
Usually or always	17	9	41	23	77	59
No opinion	4	3	9	0	4	13
Total Percent	100	100	100	100	100	100
N	59	58	58	57	58	57
NA	1	0	2	1	2	1
Total	60	58	60	58	60	58

TABLE III

Counseling and a Problem of Love:
The First Chosen and the Excluded Counselor

(Percent)

Counselor	To whom would you FIRST turn for help?		With whom would you NOT like to discuss the problem?	
	Woman's College	Coed College	Woman's College	Coed College
Father	5	4	25	33
Mother	31	29	22	29
Parish Priest	7	2	25	40
Older relatives	7	4	43	50
A Nun	3	5	42	71
Priest: Teacher or Counselor	39	51	10	3
Other	8	5	0	0
Total Percent	100	100	—*	—*
N	59	55	51	52
† NA	1	3	9†	6†
Total	60	58	60	58

* The figures do not add to 100 percent because the respondents were not restricted to only one choice.

† Most of these girls are probably refusing to exclude anybody. The percentages in the column are based on total, not N.

Table III presents the same general pattern as Table I. The question about the problem of love was posed this way:

Suppose, right now, your relationship with a particular boy has become a serious problem for you: you are both very much in love, but marriage is impossible for several years.

The girls were given the same checklist as for the problem of faith, and were again asked to whom they would go for help first, and whom they would exclude completely.

In this case, mother almost shares honors with the priest-teacher or counselor as a first choice. But she is excluded by considerably more girls than is the latter. Even more girls (42 and 71 percent) exclude the nun as advisor in this case than did so in the problem of faith. The parish priest again falls in between the two extremes. And again, the coeds are more critical than the other group, for proportionately more of them exclude every sort of possible counselor (except priest-teacher) than do the other girls.

TABLE IV

Understanding Related to Love Problem:
How Often the Girls Find Understanding Among Priests and Nuns

(Percent)

How often the girls find understanding in Priests and Nuns	Nuns		Parish Priests		Priest-Teacher or Counselor	
	Woman's College	Coed College	Woman's College	Coed College	Woman's College	Coed College
Never or rarely	47	71	16	29	2	2
Half the time	34	20	38	44	21	24
Usually or always	10	7	40	27	72	62
No opinion	9	2	7	0	5	13
Total Percent	100	100	101	100	100	101
N	58	55	58	55	58	55
NA	2	3	2	3	2	3
Total	60	58	60	58	60	58

Table IV shows what happens when the girls are asked—now in the context of the problem of love—how frequently they find "human understanding" among nuns, parish priests, and priest-teachers and counselors. The pattern is exactly the pattern of Table II. The only change in any way significant is that the proportions who feel that nuns never or rarely have the quality in the second context grow from 34 to 47 percent in the woman's college group and from 66 to 71 percent among the coeds.

RESTRICTIVENESS

Favorable and unfavorable attitudes do not, like Topsy, just grow. But it is difficult to trace their genesis, especially when they are related to as many different factors as the ones we have been examining. However, there are standard variables which must always be checked in a case like this one: academic attainment, socio-economic status, and ethnic origin. We can report here—without inflicting more tables on the reader—that the attitudes of the girls in both the woman's college group and the coed college group are *not* correlated with their academic attainment, as measured by their college grade-point indices. Neither are they related to the socio-economic status of the girls' families, as measured by the income and occupation of the father of the family. Nor does ethnic origin provide a clue for the etiology of the attitudes with which we are concerned. So we may say either that none of these standard sociological referents is related to attitude formation in the present case, or that the smallness of the two groups involved did not permit any small but statistically significant differences to emerge.

The questionnaire contained a series of statements, however, which can be used to shed some light on the types of girls who have more or less favorable or unfavorable attitudes toward priests and nuns. They are all items which have been used in other studies for purposes which we shall not detail here (Stouffer, 1955; Goldsen, 1960; McNamara, 1963; Greeley & Rossi, 1966). Agreement with these statements implies a readiness to restrict one's own range of future choice or to restrict the liberty of others. The statements are:

(1) Religions which preach unwholesome ideas should be suppressed.
(2) I would never marry a non-Catholic.
(3) If an admitted Communist wanted to make a speech in my community, I would be against allowing him to do so.
(4) Books by living Americans who are admitted Communists should be removed from the shelves of public libraries.
(5) An admitted American Communist should not be allowed to take any principal role in the entertainment industry.

All these statements have to do with religion in some way. The statements dealing with Communists touch religion indirectly, to be sure, but they are not unrelated to what we might call a formal position strongly supported by some groups within Catholicism. We are not concerned with whether or not these statements are "right" or "wrong" from any particular point of view. We are simply noting that each of

TABLE V

Restrictiveness and Attitudes Toward Priests and Nuns

(Percent)

I find the "most important" quality to be present among nuns	Restrictive Score	
	Not Restrictive	Restrictive
......rarely or never	66%	37%
.......half the time	20	37
....usually or always	8	9
no opinion	5	16
	99%	99%
N	(75)	(43)
I find the "most important" quality to be present among parish priests		
......rarely or never	27%	12%
.......half the time	41	35
....usually or always	28	37
no opinion	4	14
	100%	98%
N	(75)	(43)
I find the "most important" quality to be present among priest-teachers or counselors ...		
......rarely or never	3%	0%
.......half the time	26	12
....usually or always	64	65
no opinion	7	23
	100%	100%
N	(75)	(43)
I would definitely *NOT* like to discuss a problem of faith with		
..............a nun	49%	26%
.......a parish priest	36	26
I would definitely *NOT* like to discuss a problem of love with		
..............a nun	65%	40%
.......a parish priest	35	26
N	(75)	(43)

these statements would restrict behavior in one way or another, and are not concerned here about the wisdom or prudence of the restriction.

When we examined the responses to these statements, it was clear that agreement with them was related to less unfavorable attitudes to nuns and parish priests, although it did not affect attitudes towards priest-teachers or counselors.

To demonstrate this relationship, we constructed a crude score based upon the responses to these questions. If a girl agreed with none, she received a score of zero and was called "not restrictive"; if she agreed with only one of them, she received a score of "1"; with two of them a score of "2," and so on down the line. After having compiled this crude score, we cross-tabulated the results with the data on attitudes which we have already presented. The results are summarized in Table V. Because of the small numbers involved in the study, and because our analysis of the data showed us where the striking division of the respondents' opinions occurred, we divided the girls into only two groups instead of six. The first group we called "not restrictive": these 75 girls gave not one affirmative reply in the five chances they had to do so; the second group we are calling "restrictive": these 43 girls gave one or more affirmative replies. Notice that the names given to the two groups mean nothing more than the score upon which the names have been based.

What is intriguing about the resulting correlation is that there is a large proportional difference in the reactions of the two groups to priests and nuns. The "not restrictive" group is much more critical of nuns than is the "restrictive" group, for two-thirds of the former and only one-third of the latter think that the quality which they consider most important in an advisor—human understanding—is present rarely or never among the nuns. As regards the parish priests, considerably fewer hold the same opinions, although the differences between the "restrictive" and the "not restrictive" groups persist. As regards the priest-teacher or counselor, almost no one holds the same opinion, and the difference between the two groups vanishes.

The same sort of story is told in the last two items of Table V. Half of the not restrictive group say they would not talk to a nun about a problem of faith, and two-thirds say the same about a personal problem regarding love. But a far smaller proportion of the restrictive group makes the same statements (26 and 40 percent). In the case of the parish priests, whether the problem is one of faith or of love makes no difference, although the relatively small proportional difference between the restrictive and the not restrictive group remains in each case.

DISCUSSION AND EVALUATION

The patterns formed by the girls' attitudes, favorable and unfavorable, toward nuns, parish priests and priest-teachers or counselors are quite clear. The meaning behind the patterns is not. So we must address ourselves to the problem of meaning.

The sharply more critical attitude found among the coeds toward nuns is not completely surprising: they chose to go to a college which is not run by nuns; the others are attending a college run by a religious order of nuns, and, to a greater or less degree, chose to attend it. This obviously means that many among the coeds are breaking with a tradition for Catholic girls in New York—namely, that Catholic girls go to a Catholic woman's college. There have been very few other possibilities.

Two other factors lie beneath the surface, each of which most probably accounts for some of the relatively greater critical spirit manifested by the coeds. If we can judge by the admission policies of the two schools, the coed group almost certainly contains a higher proportion of very bright students; and very bright Catholic students have been found to be generally more critical of their Catholic schools than the less brilliant (Greeley, 1965). Secondly, three-fifths of the coed group, but only two-fifths of the woman's college group, say that they expect to get great satisfaction out of a career after graduating from college. (Virtually all from both groups expect to get even greater satisfaction from their future families; but more coeds add on the notion of career.)

It is highly probable that these three tradition-breaking factors—which, of course, are not unrelated to each other—explain all or most of the differences in critical attitudes toward nuns and priests found to exist between the two groups of girls. Only a much larger study, done on a national-sample basis, could tell the exact story. The sad fact remains, however, that an uncomfortably high proportion of girls, even at the woman's college, tend to be rather critical of the nuns, especially. It would indeed be silly to say that the nuns are all wrong and the girls are all right or *vice versa*; but, whatever the rights and wrongs may be, the fact that many girls feel that most nuns lack human understanding calls for reflection on both the educational and teaching role. Perhaps the particular woman's college is atypical of women's colleges across the nation, and perhaps not. We do not think so; at most we hope it is *becoming* atypical. But we need a far more extensive study before we can be certain.

The restrictive score shows that there is yet another factor at work, a personality factor. When we ignore the variable which we have already shown to be strongly associated with critical attitudes, lump all the girls together and then redivide them on the basis of the restrictive score, the same old pattern emerges all over again—i.e., restrictiveness is associated with being less critical. It is true that proportionately more of the coeds are classified as "not restrictive," but a considerable proportion of the woman's college girls are also not restrictive. If the numbers involved in our two groups were larger, and thus divisible into four groups large enough to give percentages some meaning, we suspect that the most critical group would be the coed "not restrictives," followed by the woman's college "not restrictives," and so on down the line. Some force is given to this argument by the proportionally large number of girls among the 43 classified as "restrictive" who have "no opinion" when asked how frequently they find "human understanding" among priests and nuns. They probably are in the position where they *could* answer, but do not think it proper to criticize religious figures.

This personality factor does not exist all by itself as the result of some distant childhood trauma. It is apparently internalized by the person because he exists in a cultural milieu which *both* inhibits criticism of one's elders and *also* expects a rather automatic agreement with propositions which seem to evoke the institutionally traditional "religious" response. There is doubtless a tendency for girls who fight this pattern to go to the coed college if they can. Once there, they will find reinforcement for their budding criticisms; for example, the *dis*agreement with the propositions we used for the restrictive score was somewhat more pervasive on the coed campus, and far more *intense*— i.e., proportionately more coeds disagreed *strongly* than did the girls at the woman's college.

In the last analysis, what we have probably done in the little survey is to snap a brownie picture of the past. The brightest of the students in Catholic colleges have been critical, and they have been moving away from institutional religious values (McNamara, 1964). In the DISCUSSION immediately following this paper, the ferment and change going on at a Catholic woman's college (Chicago's Mundelein College) is described. We suspect that Mundelein will become typical of women's colleges and that the rather grim picture prescribed in this paper will be only a relic of those tired old days before the spirit of Vatican II hit the Catholic colleges and the secondary and elementary schools. If it does not, role conflict for religious educators and teachers will grow unbearably bitter.

REFERENCES

Greeley, A. M. Criticism of undergraduate faculty by graduates of Catholic colleges. *Rev. relig. Res.,* 1965, *6,* 96-106.

Greeley, A. M. & Rossi, P. H. *The education of Catholic Americans.* Chicago: Aldine, 1966.

Goldsen, Rose K. *et al. What college students think.* Princeton, N. J.: Van Nostrand, 1960.

McNamara, R. J. (S.J.) The interplay of intellectual and religious values. Unpublished doctoral dissertation, Cornell Univer., 1963.

McNamara, R. J. (S.J.) Intellectual values and instrumental religion. *Sociol. Anal.,* 1964, *25,* 99-107.

Stouffer, S. A. *Communism, conformity and civil liberties.* New York: Doubleday, 1955.

DISCUSSION

Sister Mary Ann Ida, B.V.M.
President, Mundelein College, Chicago

The Grady-McNamara paper, based upon the attitudes of 118 young college women, provides certain interesting results which the authors' view as "so alarming" that they justify a large scale inquiry into the values and attitudes of Catholic college women towards their teachers and counselors. The study, which is strictly exploratory, attempted to discover the answer to three questions: do these young women have favorable attitudes toward their teachers and priests; how much influence upon these young women do their teachers and priests have; do the latter have the qualities which the young women value in teachers and counselors?

The report is divided into four parts: the description of the groups and the purpose of the study; the raw questionnaire data; the relationships of attitudes to other variables, and the evaluation of results. The findings are reported in five tables. I shall base my comments on a similar pattern.

DESCRIPTION OF THE GROUPS

My comments upon the Grady-McNamara study are based upon a survey carried out by Mundelein College in 1963. Over 1100 women students (over 99 percent of the student body) answered an extensive questionnaire which included the College Activities Index and 500 items prepared by faculty committees and tabulated and cross-tabulated by machine. Similar questionnaires were answered by the faculty and the alumnae and over 2000 cross-tabulations were made from the results of all the questionnaires. Thus there is available an extensive, professional tabulation on many points which parallel the present study. Its weakness is similar to that of the Grady-McNamara study, however, in that it represents students from only a single institution. Its strength lies in the fact that it is not a sampling but an almost complete response of a student body of over 1100 young women. The questionnaire also differed from the one under discussion in that its range of inquiry was far wider than the Grady-McNamara study, and attitudes toward the faculty (which is made up of lay men and lay women, sisters and priests) were only one of many points under consideration.

RAW QUESTIONING DATA

The New York study referred to problems of faith and morals and asked to whom the student would first turn for help. Certain questions in the Mundelein questionnaire represent similar inquiries and are here presented without comment. *All* numbers in the following tables represent *Percentages* and since there are differences in the various classes the responses are listed according to freshman, sophomore, junior, or senior answers in every case. Not all of the possible responses are listed here; I have selected those which seem most relevant to the questions asked in the first part of the Grady-McNamara summary: Do these young women have favorable attitudes towards their teachers and priests; how much influence upon these young women do their teachers and priests have; do they appear to have the qualities which young women value?

From Table III it is clear that theoretically a younger priest ranks as first choice with three out of four classes, the older priest ranks first with the seniors, sixth with the freshmen (other choices are not listed here). The older married woman ranks second in three classes, fifth with the sophomores and the younger sister ranks third with three classes, but sixth with the seniors. Of the choices here listed (the lowest five were omitted from this table) the older sister ranks in 4th, 5th, or 6th place each time. However, the range in percentages in many cases is very small and in no way compares with the great variation in the Grady-McNamara study.

TABLE I

Question: Whose Advice Have You Made Use of at Mundelein?

	Fr.	So.	Jr.	Sr.
Sister faculty member	61	56	54	61
Priest at Mundelein	5	10	12	27
Priest elsewhere	17	27	23	19
Departmental advisor	19	41	60	55

TABLE II

Question: What Kinds of Counseling Did You Receive and How Would You Evaluate Them?

	very inadequate				somewhat inadequate				satisfactory				very good			
	Fr.	So.	Jr.	Sr.	Fr.	So.	Jr.	Sr.	Fr.	So.	Jr.	Sr.	Fr.	So.	Jr.	Sr.
Academic	11	11	10	10	16	19	20	14	47	39	42	52	18	25	21	17
Personal	7	11	14	3	11	15	11	15	30	30	31	35	17	18	14	18
Spiritual	1	10	12	7	12	15	7	11	20	26	26	29	14	14	15	14
Vocational	7	9	9	11	17	16	19	14	26	34	34	34	15	19	16	19

TABLE III

Question: Assuming the Individual Were Well-Qualified, What Type of Counselor Do You Feel Would Be Most Understanding of Your Problems?

	Fr.	So.	Jr.	Sr.
Younger priest	25	31	26	16
Older priest	10	15	16	25
Younger nun	18	15	17	5
Older nun	14	7	8	15
Younger married woman	17	19	12	12
Older married woman	19	14	19	21

In the practical order as revealed by the data in Table I, the counselors most sought at Mundelein were the sister faculty members (61, 56, 54 and 61 percent of the time for freshmen, sophomores, juniors and seniors respectively). The priests at Mundelein (five, ten, twelve and 27 percent of the time) and elsewhere (17, 27, 23 and 19 percent of the time) ranked far lower.

Certain specific personal problems were identified in the Mundelein study. In regard to careers (Table V) the students' answers differ con-

TABLE IV

Question: If You Found Yourself in a Situation With Serious Moral and Emotional Implications What Expectations Would You Have of Receiving Help from the Following?

	a great deal				some				little				none			
	Fr.	So.	Jr.	Sr.	Fr.	So.	Jr.	Sr.	Fr.	So.	Jr.	Sr.	Fr.	So.	Jr.	Sr.
Retreat	38	54	41	42	39	30	31	34	17	10	16	15	3	3	9	6
Confessor	55	54	56	53	32	34	30	35	8	5	9	7	1	4	3	4
Private prayer	48	40	43	45	40	47	43	42	9	9	11	10	–	2	1	2
Consulting nun	19	15	11	11	44	43	45	35	20	26	27	29	10	12	15	23

TABLE V

Question: In Making Decisions About Their Careers Students Often Take Advice of Various Other Persons. For Each of the Persons Below Indicate Whether You Are Likely to Follow This Advice Frequently or Occasionally.

Person	frequently				occasionally			
	Fr.	So.	Jr.	Sr.	Fr.	So.	Jr.	Sr.
Mother	62	50	54	54	27	35	30	36
Father	49	38	38	39	30	36	34	32
Priest	33	28	33	32	40	45	42	40
Mundelein nun	33	36	37	41	48	42	38	40

siderably from that of the Grady-McNamara study. Advice would be *frequently* sought from mothers by 50 to 62 percent of the students; from priests by about 33 percent of them; and from sisters by 33 to 41 percent of them. The pattern changes when it is a question of serious moral or emotional problems (Table IV). Expecting to receive a great deal or some help from retreats were over 77 percent, from confessors over 80 percent, and from sisters over 53 percent, but from private prayer a consistent high of 87 percent. The kind of counseling actually received at the college (Table II) was rated as satisfactory or very good by over 68 percent of the students for the academic area, in the 50s for the personal, and a low in the 30s and 40s for the spiritual.

In the Mundelein study the most favorable image was undoubtedly presented to the students by a woman in a successful marriage (see Table VI), a less favorable image was the successful unmarried woman, and in between, the woman well-established in religious life (whom 93 to 95 percent of the students characterized as happy). All other choices were rated lower.

TABLE VI

Question: Below Is a List of Adjectives Descriptive of Personality Traits. Indicate by a Check Mark All of These Adjectives Which You Think Generally Apply to Each of the Women Identified in the Right-Hand Columns [Only 3 Are Listed Here as Most Significant]:

| | Woman with children in successful marriage | | | | Successful unmarried career woman | | | | Woman well-established in religion | | | |
	Fr.	So.	Jr.	Sr.	Fr.	So.	Jr.	Sr.	Fr.	So.	Jr.	Sr.
Happy	96	96	97	98	63	62	62	69	93	95	93	95
Complete	93	93	91	95	21	14	22	18	71	81	77	75
Aggressive	7	7	11	7	73	80	73	75	9	8	13	6
Neurotic	2	4	2	2	18	30	24	30	3	5	7	7
Independent	5	5	7	6	87	93	94	91	16	18	21	16
Feminine	85	91	88	90	49	42	47	52	59	57	66	68
Exciting	41	45	39	46	52	60	55	58	26	21	23	24
Dependent	59	60	58	56	2	3	2	5	54	60	54	54
Mature	88	92	92	90	64	66	69	68	75	79	83	83
Challenging	45	53	50	48	57	63	64	61	45	51	54	49

In general, it is clear that at Mundelein the nun is not a "poor last choice" in the case of a problem of faith or a personal matter. In practice, she is the first choice of many; in theory, she would be the first choice of 32 percent of the freshmen (as compared with 35 percent of the freshmen who would choose a priest). Many of the variations in choice from class to class reflect the actual personnel involved and are choices of persons rather than of "priest" or "sisters"—the seniors had an older priest teaching them, the sophomores had had a popular young priest give a retreat, the freshmen an older priest whom they did not like, etc. From our study we learned that our counseling system must be strengthened and that there must be greater opportunity for all faculty members to have closer contact with the students, but there was no alarming difference between the rapport of sisters and students and priests and students; it was surprising to find that the men teachers almost consistently fell at the lower end of the rating as counselors; while both the older and the younger married women ranked well, the single women as a whole did not.

RELATIONSHIP OF ATTITUDES TO OTHER VARIABLES

With the help of the College Activities Index and the Marquette Scale it was possibly to identify the type of student who answered the questionnaire even while keeping the answers anonymous. Thus various types of students—independent, sociable, impulsive, controlled, intellectual—were identified and the types of religious attitudes—moralistic, intellectualistic, apostolic and humanistic—were also tabulated. A highly complex set of cross-tabulations were obtained as a result, so that it was possible for us to identify what type of student sought help primarily from confessors, retreats, sisters, etc., in the various kinds of problems presented in the questionnaire. Certain questions were also established to test the liberal and conservative positions of the faculty, students and alumnae on basic issues such as those listed in the third part of the Grady-McNamara study. Because this paper is already too long, I can only indicate that on nearly every issue the sister faculty members were at the most liberal position followed by the seniors and/or the lay faculty in most cases. In one case at least, the cross-tabulation agrees with the Grady-McNamara study. The "controlled student" ranks very high in seeking the advice of confessors and sisters; the "independent student" ranks relatively high in seeking the help of the confessor and is average in regard to asking sisters' help; the "intellectual student" is relatively low in seeking the help of a confessor, average in seeking sisters' help.

Some two thousand cross-tabulations provide further material for this type of discussion!

EVALUATION OF THE RESULTS

One hypothesis of the authors of the study is that the coed college group is composed of young ladies who are more "in revolt" against what is called the traditional Catholic institution, are more critical of nuns, somewhat critical of parish priests and less inclined to praise the religious order of priests. Our study does not touch coeds so that this hypothesis does not fall under my observation. I agree that a study of the reasons why these girls chose a coed college would be rewarding. A Jesuit graduate student at the University of Minnesota utilized part of the Mundelein questionnaire for coeds at St. Louis University and the results of his study might provide a basis for some comparative conclusions.

The authors' suggestion that a personality factor is involved in the selection of the coed college can be contested, since, in the Mundelein group alone, there was as great a range of disagreement on similar questions as is represented in the two small groups under discussion. In our observation, it would seem that girls who have attended a highly satisfactory Catholic highschool are likely to choose a Catholic women's college; those that have been discontented in highschool are more anxious to seek a coeducational education in a Catholic or non-Catholic environment. Variations in types of Catholic women's colleges also account for varying types of students. An accurate study should cover a cross section of coeds in Catholic and non-Catholic institutions and girls in the many kinds of women's colleges.

The Mundelein study uncovered many areas of weakness in the college and in the relationship of faculty and students; it uncovered the fact that sisters did indeed have less influence than they thought they had, and that, in the mind of the students, there was a need for closer student-faculty relationship outside of classes. But this weakness was reflected not in regard to sisters alone but in regard to the whole faculty: priests, married and unmarried lay men and women as well as the sisters and, in the overall view, the sisters ranked most favorably in many instances. Further, we do not feel that the adverse criticism is much stronger than that which would be found in any honest study of any institution of higher learning in the country today. Were we to fail to develop the critical faculties of our students, were we to find that in a study as far reaching as our institutional analysis we had uncovered only content and complacency, we would have questioned either the validity of the questionnaire or the integrity of the student responses.

In the eyes of the faculty, the study revealed that for any academic advisor a load of thirty students is too great to provide a true personal relationship with each. Our answer has been to reduce the load of every advisor—lay or religious—to fifteen wherever possible, to provide the opportunity and the atmosphere for more informal contacts, to adjust the curriculum to provide for more intellectual exchange and to respond to the criticism of the students by an honest effort to change those areas of the college which needed improvement. It is impossible to generalize from our situation to that of the country as a whole; nor can a study such as the Grady-McNamara study support the hypotheses suggested. It can, however, highlight the great need that there is for a comprehensive study of Catholic education—women's colleges, coed institutions, and men's colleges—to discover strengths and weaknesses that are there and the manner in which we must improve if we are to continue to serve the cause of higher education in America.

III

THE MARRIED WOMAN

Woman and Marriage Expectations

PAUL J. REISS

Paul J. Reiss received his B.S. from Holy Cross College in 1952 and his M.A. in sociology from Fordham University in 1954. His Ph.D. in sociology was earned at Harvard University in 1960. From 1957 to 1961, Dr. Reiss was on the faculty of Marquette University, moving from instructor to chairman of the department in that time. Currently he is an associate professor and chairman of the Sociology Department at Fordham University. Dr. Reiss is a member of many professional organizations, among them the American Sociological Association, the American Catholic Sociological Society, the Society for the Study of Social Problems, and the National Council on Family Relations. He has contributed to various professional journals and has been editor since 1960 of Sociological Analysis, *the quarterly publication of the American Catholic Sociological Society.*

Sociologists and others have long recognized that one of the problems of marriage adjustment is that men and women frequently are not able to perceive and understand the expectations of each other with respect to marriage. Recognition of this fact renders very dubious indeed any claim I might have to speak, as a man, about women's marriage expectations. That I am a sociologist who is expected to take an unbiased scientific view of the subject does not fully compensate for my failure to be able to discuss this topic as an "insider." Two procedures, however, have, fortunately, been employed which should help to remedy this deficiency. In the first place, I have had my thoughts for this paper thoroughly scrutinized and augmented by my wife (though any of its deficiencies can hardly be assigned to her). Secondly, we have the advantage of having Mrs. Shattuck's comments on these ideas.[1]

Women's marriage expectations will be approached by discussing first the meaning, significance, formation and dynamics of marriage expectations as well as some of the major differences in marriage expectations among various segments of society. This discussion, it is hoped, will provide the necessary perspectives and context within which some of the major issues and problems of the marriage expectations of women in modern life may be treated in the concluding part of the paper.

THE MEANING AND SIGNIFICANCE OF MARRIAGE EXPECTATIONS

Human behavior in marriage as in other areas of society is normally patterned according to expectations which people have for their own behavior and that of others with whom they interact. There are very few instances in marriage where a woman does not have some set of expectations as to what her behavior will be and what she might expect in the behavior of her husband, children, or others. This, of course, does not mean that these expectations are always fulfilled. In this sense expectations are the norms which people have for their own behavior and that of others, norms which are most commonly followed in actual behavior but which may be violated. The expectations for marriage, about which we are speaking, are not the prescriptive norms concerning how people should act but rather expectations as to how in fact they will act. Thus a woman may expect that her husband should act in a certain way but believes that he will act in another way; she predicates her own actions on the latter.

It should be pointed out, also, that the expectations which women have with respect to marriage are not, and indeed, can not, be confined only to expectations concerning their own behavior, responses and states of feeling. They must also involve the behavior and responses of others. Women's expectations for marriage involve a whole set of expectations as to the behavior of husband, children, relatives, and friends, their

[1] P. 116.

responses to her actions and her responses to theirs. Marriage expectations may be likened to those in a chess game in which each player moves in accordance with a whole set of expectations as to the behavior and responses that both he and his opponent will make. The expectations which a women may have as to her roles and feelings as a wife or mother implicitly includes expectations as to the roles of husband and children.

These expectations which both men and women have for marriage are very important subjects of study for three reasons. In the first place, since marriage is so basic and pervasive, these expectations are expressions of the values and goals of people—what they consider to be important or unimportant with respect to human life and society. Secondly, these expectations are in themselves major determinants of behavior. It is, for example, because a woman may expect that her husband will react favorably to her seeking a job that she begins looking for one. Thirdly, the marriage expectations which women have are important because they frequently become the norms against which the actual marital experience is judged. Satisfaction, happiness or fulfillment in marriage is determined not only by the experiences in marriage, but just as much by the expectations which women have for marriage in the first place. Marriage expectations are significant then as reflectors of goals and values, as determinants of behavior, and as standards of performance or satisfaction.

THE FORMATION OF MARRIAGE EXPECTATIONS

Marriage expectations are the consequence of a wide variety of forces to which a woman is subject from almost the beginning of her life. The little girl is not very old before she begins to perceive the role which her mother has in the family. In learning the roles of a child she at the same time acquires the reciprocal roles of mother. Thus the first major source of marriage expectations is the woman's own family, a family which in its patterns of behavior reflects the culture of the society in which it is situated. This family may also reflect the subcultures of various segments of the society such as the working class, ethnic or racial groups, religious groups, etc. It is through interacting with those who possess this composite culture that the woman acquires the cultural expectations as to marriage; since every family develops its own culture, these expectations differ from family to family. It is clear, however, that today the family is not the sole source of cultural expectations. Peer group, school or church may reinforce, modify or reject the expectations acquired in one's own family. These agencies serve to mitigate some of the differences in expectations which result from family differences, although churches, schools and peer groups may introduce new variations.

Today one must also recognize the influence of the popular culture as expressed in the mass media of communication. From movies, television, magazines, and books women receive impressions which help formulate their own marriage expectations. While marriage expectations are a by-product, a latent function, of these agencies, we now have various marriage-preparation and marriage-counseling programs which directly intend to influence marriage expectations.

While these sources of marriage expectations are generally recognized (home, school and church are usually recognized as good influences, peer group and popular culture as bad influences, and marriage-preparation programs as necessary to correct the imbalances), one source of marriage expectations, often overlooked, perhaps because it is too obvious, is the husband. Marriage expectations are only abstract expectations before mate selection takes place. After that they become specific, i.e., expectations as to marriage with this specific man. The particular attributes, behavior and expectations of the husband or husband-to-be are important influences on the marriage expectations of any woman. Particularly in our contemporary society which permits a wide variation in marital roles rather than prescribing a rigid pattern, interaction before marriage with the husband-to-be is a major source of marriage expectations. Especially is this the case when the husband comes from a different social class, religious, or ethnic group wherein the marriage expectations are different. This is one of the reasons why selection by the parents of a marriage partner unknown to their daughter works in a society with definite marriage expectations, but would not work in the United States where marriage expectations are formed to a great extent from the husband's and wife's interactions with each other. It is for this reason also that general guides for couples preparing for marriage can go just so far if they are to be applicable to all.

THE DYNAMICS OF MARRIAGE EXPECTATIONS

While a woman enters marriage with a set of expectations derived from the sources we have mentioned, these expectations are continually being revised and elaborated throughout marriage. A woman celebrating her fiftieth wedding anniversary with her husband has marriage expectations for the future which may or may not be fulfilled. It is a distortion of reality to think of marriage expectations as being formed prior to marriage and then to consider only the fulfillment or frustration of these expectations previously formed. Unfortunately we tend to think of the pre-marriage years alone when we speak of marriage expectations. Marriage expectations are dynamic, frequently changing. These changes are partly the consequence of the continuing effect of the factors mentioned above, but they are brought about especially by both a woman's experiences in marriage and by new situations developing in her marriage.

As a consequence of her experiences with her husband, children, and others, the woman is continually reformulating her marriage expectations. They may be quite different after ten years and five children from what they were at the beginning of marriage. This reformulation is particularly extensive during the earlier years of marriage. The whole process of marriage adjustment is, for the most part, the process of redefinition of marriage expectations as a consequence of experience in marriage. Studies of marital adjustment also indicate that it is usually the wife who makes greater adjustments in expectations (Goode, 1956).

Marriage expectations are also subject to change as a consequence of changing situations which force the adoption of new and modified roles. Most marriages pass through phases which could be described as the pre-natal phase, the child-bearing phase, the post-parental phase, and a phase of widow- or widowerhood. Marriage is thus dynamic, not static, and expectations change to accommodate to the new situations. It would be impossible for a woman at marrying to have expectations concerning these aspects of marriage which she can neither predict nor foresee. Women may have to develop a set of expectations as to the role of the wife of a successful business or professional man, the wife of an unemployed man, the role of mother of a large family, mother of a teenager, "mother-in-law," "grandmother," "working wife," "wife of a retired man," "head of the family," "widow," "divorcée," etc. Marriage expectations change, sometimes dramatically, with these new situations. Although there may be a period, such as after the sudden death of a husband, when expectations are very unstructured, it is not long before a new set of expectations as to the roles and satisfactions of the woman emerge. It is as important for us to consider these expectations as it is to consider the expectations of those entering marriage.

DIFFERENCES IN MARRIAGE EXPECTATIONS

There are, of course, differences in marriage expectations between any two women. While cultural factors may be similar, a woman's unique personality and life experiences, as well as her interactions with her husband, insure that her marriage expectations are going to be to some extent unlike those of any other woman. In addition to this, as we have already pointed out, American society allows for a wide range of marriage patterns rather than prescribing a rigid pattern for all. There are, however, some systematic differences in marriage expectations which are associated with sub-cultural differences among various segments of American society. We might expect differences in marriage expectations between Catholic and Protestant women, between children of immigrants and children of native-born parents, between women raised in rural areas and those raised in cities, between women who did and those who did not attend college, between those from the upper, middle, working and lower classes, and, as we have already inferred, between those married for many years and those about to be married. Significant differences in marriage expectations are related to two variables which are of particular importance for the future and for pastoral work, i.e., differences relating to socio-economic class and those relating to age or length of marriage. These variables deserve added attention because there has been a tendency among those dealing with marriage to be concerned only with the young, college-educated woman. Perhaps we need a reminder that the majority of women are not college graduates, that about half of the population identify themselves as in the working class, that almost half the married women at any given time do not have any children living in the home, that about 30 percent of all women are over 45 and about ten percent are over 65 years of age. Pastoral work necessitates a recognition of these women and a realization of differences in their marriage expectations.

MAJOR ISSUES CONCERNING MARRIAGE EXPECTATIONS

Marriage is a complex institution, including a wide range of human behavior. There are, therefore, numerous expectations which women have about marriage. In order to focus our discussion on some of the more important aspects, some which appear to present problems for women in modern life, we will discuss eight statements about the marriage expectations of women. These could even be considered hypotheses to be tested; they may be supported, rejected, supported in part, or supported for only some segments of the society.

1. *Virtually all young women expect to get married—and stay married for life.* At least one definite statement can be made about women's marriage expectations: They do have such expectations. Several studies

of young women have indicated that over 95 percent include marriage in their life plans (Turner, 1964). In so doing, women are meeting the expectations in American society that women should be married. Wanting to be married is never looked upon as a deviant desire for a woman while rejection of marriage is often so judged. Conformity to this cultural norm which specifies marriage for women does bring with it the problems on the one hand of society forcing marriage on women who may for some reason not be fitted, physically or psychologically, for marriage, and on the other hand labeling as deviants those who remain single.

These expectations for marrige are generally fulfilled with over 95 percent of the women who reach teenage eventually marrying (Jacobson, 1959). Here, however, we can perceive the first instance of the modification, with age, of marriage expectations. Of those who have not married by the age of 30, only one-half will eventually marry. If the expectation of marriage is to be realistic, it must be radically revised by single women in the span of a very few years.

The second part of the statement indicates that women expect to stay married for life. By this we mean that the young woman expects that her marriage will last, that she will spend the rest of her life married to her chosen, or to-be-chosen, husband. This expectation flies in the face of reality—approximately one out of four marriages ends in divorce—but it is maintained as part of the optimistic orientation of American culture. One might say that the woman who has not yet selected a husband intends, of course, to marry only a very suitable one when he comes along and the woman who has fallen in love with a man cannot but believe that they will be happily married for life. It is not true that young couples enter marriage frivolously because of the expectation that they can easily break the marriage if it does not work out. They firmly believe (often on weak grounds) that their marriage will succeed. Divorce or separation is almost always, then, a failure with respect to original marriage expectations. Both social class and age are important variables here, however. The chances of a marriage of five or ten years' duration ending in divorce is much reduced (Jacobson, 1959). Also those in the middle class (those with more education) are also more unlikely to have a divorce (Jacobson, 1959). A woman in the lower class who marries at a young age a man like herself without much education could, but does not, perceive a high possibility of divorce or desertion. A middle-class woman, married for ten years to a college graduate like herself, can more realistically expect that her marriage will not end in divorce.

Women today, despite higher divorce rates, can look forward to longer periods of married life than ever before. On the average a woman marrying at 20 years of age can expect approximately 43 years of married life. However, of those marriages which survive divorce, about two-thirds will be broken by the death of the husband, leaving the woman a widow for an average of 14 years. One-half will be widows for at least 15 years; one-third for 20 years (Jacobson, 1959). Now, the expectations which young women have for marriage normally do not include a long period of widowhood. The prospects are too far in the distance to be of concern to the young woman. Such expectations are not so remote for the middle-aged wife whose husband has just suffered his first heart attack. Throughout marriage most women are forced by reality to revise their expectations to include the role of a widow with all that this entails. It may entail, for example, some revision of a total dependence upon a husband for companionship or decision-making, before widowhood becomes a reality. This, I believe, is a neglected aspect of marriage research and counseling.

2. *The most important goal for women in marriage is companionship: it is expected to be derived almost exclusively from marriage.* This statement can in general be supported for the middle class in the United States but with certain modifications. We might define companionship as the maintenance of a close personal relationship with a particular person or persons. We say that women, as well as men in contemporary society, marry for love, the one and only valid basis of marriage. If we examine this more closely, however, it becomes apparent that love is the criterion for selecting a marriage partner, but women marry in order to maintain a close relationship, to be with, to live with, the one they love. This is born out by the studies of Blood and Wolfe who discovered that companionship was deemed the most important aspect of marriage by the women they interviewed in the Detroit metropolitan area (Blood & Wolfe, 1960). In modern impersonal society where the need for companionship is great, marriage is one of the few sources for it. The geographic mobility of couples often creates a situation where their spouse is the only "close friend" they have.

It should also be noted, however, that while the marrige relationship takes precedence over all other possible relationships in the middle class, this is not as frequently the case in the working and lower classes. In the working class, where there is typically less geographic mobility, the woman does not expect to give up ties of companionship with her relatives, particularly her mother and her friends. Her husband also is more likely than the middle-class husband to maintain a separate group of friends. The "night out with the boys" is more typical of the working class where the wife does not expect that her husband will be her primary companion; if he is a good provider and doesn't get drunk or into trouble she may feel that no more should be expected of him. It is thus among the working and lower classes that wives often find their closest confidant in their mothers or sisters, not their husbands; and husbands communicate more closely with their friends than they do with their wives (Cohen & Hodges, 1963). Apparently more education brings about the development of more shared interests and activities which increases both the expectations for companionship as well as the attainment of it. It would be incorrect to label as a failure a stable, lower-class family in which the woman finds her companionship with others rather than her husband. It may well be part of her expectations. A serious problem does arise, however, when a woman whose husband is not a companion to her has no other adequate sources of companionship. The uneducated woman who has moved away from her family or friends has a serious problem of loneliness since her husband is not expected to be the primary source of companionship as is expected in the middle class.

It is also fairly clear that companionship is less expected and less fully attained as the marriage becomes older. In both middle and working classes it has been found that companionship decreases with years married from the highpoint of the honeymoon period. While companionship has been discovered to diminish when the wife is involved with caring for a number of children, the need for it on the part of the wife becomes greater when her children have grown up (Blood & Wolfe, 1960). In these post-parental years the husband is for a number of years still heavily involved in his occupation from which he retires perhaps at 65, whereas his wife has retired about 15 years earlier from her role as a mother. This period gives rise to loneliness due to a failure to fill the increased need for companionship.

3. *Women do not expect a high degree of differentiation between the role of wife-mother and that of husband-father.* This statement opens up a number of rather complex issues concerning the role expectations of women in today's world. Our starting point may well be the traditional roles of women and men which have on the whole been rather distinct roles. Not only was it the expectation that men and women would do different things both inside and outside the home, but also that their dispositions and interests would be quite distinct from

one another. Thus there existed a definite female culture or way of life, and a male culture. Such statements as "woman's place is in the home" or "the father is the head of the family and the mother is the heart" describe such expectations as to marriage.

Several changes in society have brought about a considerable alteration in this view of marriage. In the first place, women have received much more education, which has often served to allow them to break out of a female culture. In addition, the opportunity seized by many to work outside the home has changed their orientation from one directed only to home and children. The majority of brides have worked outside the home before marriage and thus have participated in part in the occupational world which was formerly male (National Manpower Council, 1958). On the part of the husband, with increased education, with fewer jobs being manual jobs and with shorter work weeks, there is more time, interest, and energy to be directed to the family and other non-occupational interests. These factors have brought about a greater similarity in the interests and roles of the two sexes. The process has been further stimulated by the emphasis in society on the marriage relationship—with the couple having a family life rather independent of relatives and in-laws. Thrown thus upon themselves, the maintenance of separate, distinct roles becomes more inappropriate.

These changes in the roles of men and women which have brought them closer together have been reflected in the expectations which women have about marriage. It is true that there are still some sex-typed tasks around the home, e.g., mending clothes vs. shoveling snow, but the expectations have adjusted to allow either the husband or the wife to handle most tasks in the home. One could describe this new expectation as one in which a household or child-care task is allocated to whichever one, husband or wife, has the ability or the time to handle the job. Thus if the wife works, the husband does more around the house; if the husband is heavily involved in a successful career, the wife does more (Blood & Wolfe, 1960). It is characteristic of this change that ads for interior house paint usually show a woman doing the painting and husbands can be much more frequently found helping with shopping in the supermarket or taking care of the children. While American culture permits either the traditional or the new roles, situational factors in families have apparently led more couples to adopt the new patterns in which the roles of men and women are not sharply differentiated. The expectations of women before marriage have not always caught up with the new patterns. One study found, for example, that among engaged couples husbands expected to be involved with household tasks to a greater extent than their wives expected them to be (Dyer & Urban, 1958). We also frequently find among the clergy the traditional expectations which are not in accordance with the realities of the family life of parishioners. The separate Sunday morning Communion breakfasts for men and for women, for example, do not reflect current family-life expectations. Some parishioners also question why there must be separate fathers' and mothers' clubs when parents have rather similar interests with respect to their children.

The changes I have been describing, however, are much more true of the middle class and the more educated segments of the population than of the working class. Recent studies have made clear that the traditional, differentiated roles of men and women are more common in the working class (Komarovsky, 1964). Situational factors help account for this difference. Without education, couples often do not have the common interests necessary for the merging of roles. The working-class job of the husband is normally a manual, often monotonous job in which neither the husband nor the wife has a great interest. These husbands report that they just do not have anything to talk about to their wives, since the wives are not interested in baseball or cars, and they themselves are certainly not interested in women's talk. When he comes home he just wants peace; he has done his part and it is the wife's part to take care of the house and children. Work and home are quite separate areas of interest. These expectations of the working-class woman with respect to her role begin in childhood where sharper distinctions are made between boys and girls than in the middle class. Her expectations are often, then, not frustrated by the marriage experience. Problems do arise, however, when a working-class wife must work outside the home and also handle the household tasks and children entirely by herself. They also arise when the husband or wife, but more frequently the wife, for one reason or another has middle-class expectations for the marriage. As a result of more education or from reading popular magazines, a woman in the working class may expect that she and her husband should be doing more things together, that they should have common interests; but he does not respond. Particularly in this area we must be careful about applying middle-class norms to the expectations and marriage patterns of the working class.

4. *Women expect to have an equal voice in family decision-making.* Much has been said and written about equalitarian expectations for American marriage. It is certainly true that the traditional patriarchal pattern receives little support in the society and rarely forms part of

the expectations of women. This is not to say that there are no patriarchal families in the society, but rather that the culture does not
prescribe them. In this respect American culture is quite permissive,
allowing either patriarchal patterns or equalitarian patterns. Only
marriages in which the wife is dominant do not receive societal approval. It is significant that marriages in which the wife is dominant
have been found to be associated with low levels of marital satisfaction
(Blood & Wolfe, 1960). It appears that within the range from patriarchal to equalitarian marriage, expectations are developed in accordance with the particular strengths of the two individuals. A woman
who marries a man who is far more educated or intelligent than she,
expects him to have a more dominant voice, whereas a woman who
works outside the home and contributes substantially to the family
income, expects more of a voice for herself. This is a good example
of the way in which marrige expectations are formed as a result of
experience in the marriage. Experience in marriage decision-making
may indicate who should make the decisions and the society gives
approval to either a husband-dominant or equalitarian pattern. Decision-
making which reflects the relative power or authority of the husband
or wife may be equalitarian in two senses. Either the decisions are
made collectively with the couple talking it over and coming to some
agreement, or the husband and wife each has a separate area which
he or she dominates. The expectations as well as the practice in the
middle class appears to be equalitarian in the sense of collective
decision-making in most areas of family life (Blood & Wolfe, 1960).
This is certainly consistent with the companionship orientation of
middle-class marriages. In other words, the middle-class woman expects
neither a sharp division of areas of dominance between husband and
wife, nor a power struggle against patriarchal patterns. For her the
struggle for equality is long since over; equalitarianism is well-institu-
tionalized and expected by both husband and wife.

In the working class and in the lower class the situation is somewhat different. In the lower class, where the husband has little power
to be derived from his economic contribution to the family, matriarchy
often prevails. This has been noted for both Negro families and for the
families of the unemployed. In part it is wife-dominance by default,
but the permanence of the situation leads to an incorporation of wife-
dominance in the marriage expectations of the lower class. It is often
the case that the husband lays claim to ultimate authority and feels
that "women ought to keep in their own place." He has little ability
to exert this authority, however, and his wife continues to make the

important decisions concerning the home and children (Komarovsky, 1964).

It is also clear that with higher status and more stable family life in the working class, the husband does exert more authority in the home and a form of patriarchy arises. It is only with more education and common interests that equalitarian patterns begin to emerge and the upper segments of the working class begin to adopt what we have described as middle-class patterns.

Dominance in decision-making is also related to the length of the marriage. Studies indicate that the mother with young children has less power and is more dependent upon her husband, but that as the children grow up, and especially after they leave the home, the woman can expect a much stronger role in decision-making. Other things being equal, a woman can expect a more dominant voice in decision-making at middle age than at any other period of her married life (Blood and Wolfe, 1960).

In general, we can conclude that the dominant expectation among American women is for an equalitarian pattern in marriage, but that the particular strengths which either she or her husband brings or does not bring to the marriage will pattern their roles. The greatest problem in this area is in the consistency between the wife's and husband's expectations.

5. *Women expect their sexual relationship to be an important source of satisfaction to them.* The expectations of women for satisfaction from the sexual relationship in marriage have risen within recent decades for most segments of the population. Our culture has certainly moved away from the view that sexual satisfaction is something for men but that sexual relationships are a duty for women, though one still hears in certain circles that sexual relationships are a "wifely duty" and should be engaged in for "the quieting of concupiscence." At the present time women expect that they and their husbands will have a mutual interest in sexual relationships, that they should expect to receive satisfaction from them, and that their husbands will also have the expectation of mutual satisfaction. The popular culture and literature on marriage has, however, led to extremely high expectations on the part of young women as to the satisfactions to be gained from sexual relationships, often equating the intensity of physical response with sexual satisfaction. It is quite clear that these expectations cause many couples unnecessary frustration. It is also clear that these expectations are based upon an exclusively physical view of the nature of sexual

relationships with little recognition that sexual satisfaction is determined as much by the psychological as by the physical response
(Landis, 1965).

In the working class we find more frequently the older expectations
as to sexual relationships (Rainwater, 1964). There is even suspicion
of sexual desire in women as being somehow impure or wrong. Mutuality or reciprocity in sexual relationships has not developed in the working class as it has in the middle class and the working-class wife is
not led by experience, as she is by the popular culture, to expect
considerable satisfaction in her sexual relationship. Here again the
imposition of middle-class norms on the wife when her husband maintains the lower-class norms is likely to bring frustration. There is also
an erroneous common expectation that sexual satisfaction is something
for the earlier years of marriage, not an expectation for the later years.
As the length of marriage increases many women learn to expect satisfaction from sexual relationships beyond menopause into the post-
parental years (Kinsey, 1953).

6. *Women expect to be mothers of moderate-size families, i.e., two-
four children.* Motherhood is a well-established expectation for virtually
all women. Considerable research has been conducted on the expected
and ideal number of children as viewed by women of all ages. About
90 percent of the women in a nationwide sample saw two to four
children as the ideal number of children with the expected number of
children being about three. Less than one percent wanted none (Freedman *et al.*, 1959). Recent decades have seen the diminishing desirability
of the no-child or one-child family, and at the same time the continuing
decline of the desirability of the very large family. Motherhood is seen
as second only to companionship as a goal of marriage for American
women (Blood & Wolfe, 1960).

The expectations as to the number of children, of course, have to be
revised for many women as they are or are not able to fulfill these
expectations. It is interesting to note, however, that in a nationwide
sample of married women, 15 percent stated that the number of children
expected was larger than the number wanted, but 23 percent stated that
the number was smaller than the number wanted. The degree of fulfillment of expectations here is revealed by the finding that 59 percent
expected a number of children within the range wanted (Freedman,
1959). However, here is an instance where expectations are frequently
changed to conform to reality. There appears to be little difference by
socioeconomic class in the original motherhood ideals of women,

although lower-class women are less likely to actually expect the two to four child ideal, since they have less ability to control their fertility (Jaffe, 1964).

7. *Women expect that their mariage alone will be sufficient for personal fulfillment: careers, jobs and community activities are unimportant.* We can recognize in this statement a current hot issue with one position being represented by Betty Friedan (1963) in *The feminine mystique* and the opposing position being championed by Phyllis McGinley (1964). It is the type of issue which we can place in context but certainly not solve, since the discussion revolves primarily around what ought to be the case rather than what is the case.

First of all, it ought to be clear that the issue is not the one of marriage *vs.* a career but rather marriage *and* a career, job or other activity outside the home. The possibilty of the latter has arisen because of the greater education of women, the opportunity in careers and jobs open to them, and the ability to control fertility. A woman may choose a domestic role with low or moderate fertility combined with a career, but the possibility of high fertility and a career is available only to "superwomen." While a career may later turn out to be a possibility because of low fertility, whether planned or not, the expectation that a career will be followed, when held by women before or at marriage, normally includes a plan for fertility control.

A recent study of a fairly representative sample of young women revealed that when the very few who did not plan on marriage were eliminated, about half the remainder opted for the domestic role alone and the other half for marriage *and* a career (Turner, 1964). We thus have a situation of a lack of homogeneity as to woman's role, a divergence of expectations, among women in the country. It is such divergence of attitudes which spawns the current controversy. However, while about half of the women expect to follow a career with marriage, another study—this time of college women—revealed that 87 percent felt that the most important source of their satisfactions in life would be their marriage; less than 10 percent believed that their career would provide these satisfactions (Goldsen *et al.*, 1960). Thus it is clear that we are not speaking about an alternative to marriage for personal fulfillment or satisfaction, but rather a supplement to marriage and motherhood. Most women want marriage and expect it to be the most important source of satisfaction. The question is: Is it enough?

The nature of the ambition which women have with respect to marriage and career was demonstrated in a study which indicated that

women sought extrinsic rewards, i.e., material gain or status, through
their ambitions for their husband's success, but that they also sought
intrinsic rewards, i.e. achievement or accomplishment for its own sake,
through a career (Turner, 1964). Left unanswered is the issue as to
whether marriage can provide by itself the intrinsic reward. Apparently
a large number of American women do not feel that it will. At this time
34 percent of all married women living with their husbands are working—40 percent of the mothers without pre-school-age children and 20
percent of those with school-age children (U.S. Department of Labor,
1965). These statistics on the percentage of married women and of
mothers who are in the labor force bear only indirectly on our problem
since they include both women who are working out of financial need,
real or perceived as real, and women who are working for "intrinsic
reward."

Here there are definite class and educational differences to consider.
In the working class a women more commonly does not have a "career"
but a "job" which is held for its financial value. There does not appear
to be a marital problem here since it has been shown that the increased
income which the wife provides more than compensates in marital
satisfaction for the difficulties occasioned by her being out of the home
(Blood & Wolfe, 1960). The jobs which these women have are also
very frequently not so attractive in themselves as to be in competition
with the home for the woman's interest. The problem is in the middle
class with the college-educated woman in particular, whose relative
financial contribution will not compensate for difficulties created by
her being out of the home. But, of course, it is precisely these women
who feel the greater need to follow a career for their own satisfactions
and who have the necessary education to embark on such a career.

The length of marriage should also be introduced into this discussion because the expectation has emerged on the part of many women
that they will work for a few years before their first child is born, withdraw from their job or career while they are bearing and raising to
school age about three children fairly close in age, and then return to
their job or career after the children have entered school or at least
after they have grown up. The expectation of some additional activity
is particularly strong in the post-parental years. This type of pattern
has opened up the possibility of a career or interrupted career for many
women and is a definite part of their marriage expectations.

We should also consider carefully the domestic role which is itself
a composite of many roles. This composite includes the housekeeping
roles and the roles of wife and mother. The woman who devotes her-

self to the joys of cooking, cleaning, knitting, sewing and decorating may have just as much minimized the role of wife and mother as the woman who is devoted to an outside career. For some the alternative becomes that of combining the role of mother and wife with an outside career or with a career in housekeeping.

We can conclude that American culture at this time allows either the expectation of marriage only or marriage with a career and that in the choice which many women must make on this point, half choose marriage alone and half marriage plus a career. The problems which arise are mostly due to conflicts between a wife's expectations for a career and her husband's disapproval of it, or the conflict between her desire of marriage only and a feeling that society expects something more of her.

Marital satisfaction may be achieved with the fulfillment of any of a variety of expectations. Since the culture allows a variety of roles and combinations of roles for women, we have a situation which can accommodate itself to individaul differences among women—all must not conform to one set of expectations. However, this has the consequence of not giving a woman a clear-cut role to follow. Rather she must choose among alternatives which may often appear confusing and even conflicting. It is a price we pay for individual freedom and a provision for individual differences among women.

8. *The expectations of women for marriage are unrealistic.* If we mean that women before marriage have expectations that do not accurately reflect the actual situations they will experience, then we can not but agree that women's expectations for marriage are unrealistic. But given the nature of marriage coupled with the emphasis on romantic love and the American value of optimism, marriage expectations are bound to be unrealistic. First of all, very realistic expectations are impossible as they would require prophetic abilities concerning future marital situations, which few in a changing complex society can possess, plus a knowledge of one's spouse which is virtually impossible to acquire prior to marriage. Since American marriage patterns are based, as we have mentioned, not on definite cultural prescriptions but upon the experience of the couple with each other in marriage, to have an accurate notion of what that experience will produce is difficult indeed. This includes not being able to perceive some of the good qualities of the spouse or some of the added satisfactions in marriage, as well as the unfavorable experiences.

In addition to these natural difficulties with developing realistic expectations, the American pattern of marriage, based as it is upon romantic love, heightens the unrealistic quality of marriage expectations. Romantic love includes a primacy of an emotional attachment and as such is not easily reality-tested. Thus the phrase, "love is blind." When the American tendency to be optimistic, to view the future as likely to be an improvement over the present, is added to romantic love, the unrealistic quality of marriage expectations is further enhanced. These unrealistic, optimistic expectations are more often found in the middle class than in the lower class where the harshness of the real situation hinders the development of an aura of "sweetness and light." In companionship, equality, sexual relations, and ability to control fertility, high expectations for marriage in the lower class do not realistically develop (Cohen & Hodges, 1963). Women do not perceive the attainment of these objectives in their own family and in those of relatives and friends. The lower-class women also do not typically spend a number of years away from home either in college or at a job. It is during these years that the middle-class women can prescind from the realities of marriage and family life they have known and construct their own unrealistic expectations. Of course, to the extent that the lower-class wife has derived a set of expectations from the popular literature aimed at the middle class, her expectations may be even more unrealistic than those of the middle class.

Marriage expectations, as we have pointed out, are revised as a result of marriage experience. This is marriage adjustment. As a consequence of a better knowledge of her husband and of the life situations they are experiencing, a woman's marriage expectations are likely to become more realistic as the length of the marriage increases. However, there is no end to this adjustment since marriage situations are always changing throughout marriage.

At the beginning of this paper we mentioned that marriage expectations serve both as a determinant of behavior and as standards by which marriage experience is judged as satisfactory or not. As a determinant of behavior, marriage expectations can be a stimulus to strive for higher quality in the marriage relationship or to greater attainments in personal life. As such, high expectations, even though they be to some extent unrealistic, serve a good function. High ideals, though never fully attained, can bring about efforts to improve married life. Marriage expectations also serve as standards, however, and as such may result in frustrations when they are not fulfilled. This may occur with respect to companionship, decision-making, or sex relationships, for example, where the woman's high ideals are so far from being attained that the whole marriage looks to her like a trap into which her high expectations led her.

Thus there is to some extent a dilemma in that high, unrealistic expectations may produce greater efforts in marriage but may also lead to greater frustrations. The answer to this problem is not, I feel, the one often attempted, i.e., to make marriage expectations realistic—which is, in part, to lower ideals. While in certain areas, such as with expectations concerning sexual satisfactions, expectations may with counseling be made more accurate without being to any extent lowered, nevertheless, high expectations, though somewhat unrealistic, should be allowed to continue in order to stimulate better marriages. However, there must be a recognition that considerable effort is required for women to achieve their goals in marriage: it just does not happen naturally, and often the competency of women to attain their goals can and should be improved. At the same time it should be remembered that the marriage expectations of American middle-class women are not the only intrinsically correct ones; allowance needs to be made for the important cultural and class differences, some of which we have mentioned. In general it appears to be better, through counseling and education, to increase the competency of women of various class and cultural backgrounds for fulfilling their expectations than to change the expectations.

REFERENCES

Blood, R. O. & Wolfe, D.M. *Husbands and wives.* New York: Free Press, 1960.

Cohen, A. & Hodges, H. Characteristics of the lower blue-collar class. *Social Problems,* 1963, *10,* 303-334.

Dyer, G. D. & Urban, S. The institutionalization of equalitarian family norms. *Marriage fam. Living,* 1958, *20,* 53-58.

Empey, L. T. Role expectations of young women regarding marriage and a career. *Marriage fam. Living,* 1958, *20,* 152-155.

Farber, S. & Wilson, R. (Eds.) *The potential of women.* New York: McGraw-Hill, 1963.

Freedman, R., Whelpton, P. K. & Campbell, A. A. *Family planning, sterility and population growth.* New York: McGraw-Hill, 1959.

Friedan, Betty, *The feminine mystique.* New York: Norton, 1963.

Jaffe, F. Family planning and poverty. *Marriage Fam.,* 1964, *26,* 467-470.

Goldsen, Rose, Rosenberg, M., Williams, R. & Suchman, E. *What college students think.* Princeton: Van Nostrand, 1960.

Goode, R. *After divorce.* New York: Free Press, 1956.

Jacobsen, P. H. *American marriage and divorce.* New York: Holt, Rinehart & Winston, 1959.

Kinsey, A. C., Pomeroy, W. B., Martin, C. E. & Gebhard, P. H. *Sexual behavior in the human female*. Philadelphia: Saunders, 1953.
Komarovsky, Mira. *Blue-collar marriage*. New York: Random House, 1964.
Landis, P. H. *Making the most of marriage*. New York: Appleton-Century-Crofts, 1965.
McGinley, Phyllis. *Sixpence in her shoe*. New York: McGraw-Hill, 1964.
National Manpower Council. *Work in the lives of married women*. New York: Columbia University Press, 1958.
Nye, F. I. & Hoffman, Lois W. *The employed mother in America*. Chicago: Rand McNally, 1963.
Rainwater, L. Marital sexuality in four cultures of poverty. *Marriage Fam.*, 1964, *26*, 457-466.
Turner, R. Some aspects of women's ambition. *Amer. J. Sociol.*, 1964, *70*, 271-285.
United States Department of Labor. Marital and family characteristics of workers in March, 1964. *Mon. Labor Rev.*, 1965, *58*, 260-265.

DISCUSSION

Eleanor M. Shattuck
Sociologist, wife and mother

The following discussion of Dr. Reiss' paper is subject to the qualification of being mostly applicable to middle-class married women, since this is the group with which I am most familiar and which has been the object of my study. Let me comment on his eight propositions, one by one.

1. "Virtually all young women expect to get married—and stay married for life." A recent study of college students corroborates this, but reveals a most interesting attitude on the part of the young women who have this expection.

Though most college women unhesitatingly choose marriage and the family, this wish to find a sense of worth in professional work rather than simply in family life stays with many. . . . For professional work among women in this country is viewed as an interlude, at best a part-time excursion away from full-time family life—the family life which the coeds yearn for, impatiently look forward to . . . and define as largely monotony, tedium and routine.

It is this basic contradiction which makes it difficult for college women to come to terms with themselves. They measure family life by standards that leave no doubt about its important—indeed its primary—value to them. At the same time, however, they apply to it other standards which determine value in our culture: self-expression, self-esteem, prestige, status, income, power, recognition and respect from others. In our culture these values are imbedded in the institutional complex of occupation, not of family [Goldsen *et al.,* 1960, pp. 57-58].

This suggests that perhaps the stereotype of the dewy-eyed, romantic bride may need overhauling.

2. "The most important expectation for women in marriage is companionship; it is expected to be derived almost exclusively from marriage." In our mobile society it is increasingly difficult for both men and women to form lasting friendships, particuarly among their neighbors, since both they and their neighbors are likely to be transients. This often places the middle-class married woman in the position of being dependent on her husband for adult companionship. At the same time, the woman who is a full-time housewife is seldom a very stimulating intellectual companion for a man whose mental development did not cease on the day of his college graduation or on the day he said "I do." Husbands who are executives or professional men have careers which demand a great deal of time and commitment on their part. This frequently means, particularly for those who commute from our ever-expanding suburbs, a 12- or 13-hour work day, six days a week. This leaves little time for togetherness. So I suggest that loneliness is one of the most prevalent problems of middle-class married women, not only, as Dr. Reiss suggests, for the woman whose children have grown up, but for the young mother as well.

3. "Women do not expect a high degree of differentiation between their role of wife-mother and that of husband-father." In any family where the husband-father works at a job which is located in a place other than his home, this simply cannot be the case.

The pressures are strong in the suburban setting for parenthood to be highly differentiated and skewed to an ascendant position of the mother. Women dominate the family, men the job world. . . . This is the pattern which prompted Margaret Mead to characterize the American middle-class father as the "children's mother's husband" and partly why mother looms so oversized in the lives of suburban children [Rossi, 1964, p. 635].

It is true that many men do spend much of their free time working around their homes, taking care of their children, etc., but they and society view this as "helping mother out" rather than as something proper to the husband-father role as such.

4. "Women expect to have an equal vote in family decision-making."
In the middle-class family many important things are automatically
determined by the husband's occupation—the geographic location of the
family, the frequency of changing location, the type or class of neighborhood and consequently of schools, the size and relative luxury of the
home, the social life of the family, e.g., country clubs, business-required
entertainment, the possibility of employing domestic help, the necessity
of the wife working, the quality of nutrition and medical care available.
In short, the life-style, the social and economic status of the middle-
class married woman, is determined not by anything she is or does,
but predominately by the prestige, wealth, power and authority which
her husband achieves. Thus, although she may have a voice in such
matters as what color the new family car will be or where the family
may spend its vacation, the truly basic facts of whether there will be
a new car or a vacation are the husband's responsibility.

5. "Women expect their sexual relationship to be an important
source of satisfaction to them," and

6. "Women expect to be mothers of moderate-size families." I am
purposely combining these two propositions because for the Catholic
married woman these two ideas have to be considered together. For
many women, the degree of satisfaction in the sex relationship varies
inversely with the number of children. Fear of conceiving another child
which she feels unable to care for physically, emotionally, or economically exerts a powerful inhibiting influence on a woman's physical
and psychological response to her sexual relationship with her husband.

With specific regard to the number of children—"the ideal three"—
it was not long ago that Catholics were encouraged to believe that
sanctity in marriage was directly related to the quantity of children a
couple produced. The good Catholic family had at least six children.
The Church now seems to recognize that the responsibility of rearing
children implicitly places limitations on the function of bearing children
—that responsible parenthood is an acceptable alternative to "a childlike faith that God will take care of everything." In other words, the
Church now agrees with the rest of society that population control is
a serious problem both for individual families and for society as a
whole.

7. "Women expect that their marriage alone will be sufficient for
personal fulfillment: careers, jobs and community activities are unim-

portant." This is becoming less and less true, particularly for educated women. Two of the principal functions which our society assigns to the married woman are those of childcare and homemaking. Implicit in this arrangement is the premise of homogeneous womanhood—i.e., since all women are biologically capable of giving birth to children, they must all, therefore, be qualified temperamentally, intellectually, physically, morally, and economically to rear said children. "Well, it ain't necessarily so." There are many women who simply do not find childcare and housework fulfilling for the simple, but overlooked, reason that women are no more homogeneous in their abilities or their interests than are men. We wouldn't entertain for a moment the ridiculous notion that all men should perform the tasks of bus drivers, or bank tellers, or sociologists.

Then, to add insult to injury, society does a hard-sell job to try to convince women that motherhood and homemaking are noble and glorious pursuits. However, the true value which our society places on these functions is most apparent in the fact that childcare and housekeeping are the lowest paid of all occupations. Those who are hired to perform them are frequently the least educated, least talented—often mentally retarded or those too old or too young to obtain other employment—marginal people. In contrast to this, we see other cultures like those of Israel, Russia, and Sweden placing a high value on childcare and consequently training and paying competent professionals to do this work well. Of course, those cultures also place a high value on the contributions that women can make to their societies, on the basis of their talents and interests, not just their biological capacities.

With regard to the work of homemaking or, more specifically, housekeeping, not much can be said for it. Most of it can be accomplished by turning on a piece of equipment which turns itself off when it is finished. It has to be done—continuously and repeatedly—but it requires very little time and effort and no intellect or imagination (although, as Betty Friedan [1963] says, in accordance with Parkinson's Law "housewifery expands to fill the time available"). This is at least partly attributable to what home has become in our society. In traditional society the home was the place where the work—the productive work—of society was carried on. The education of children and the life of the family were centered in the home. Today, work is done outside the home; children are educated outside the home; the sick are cared for outside the home; weddings, wakes and most other important events take place outside the home. The home has become a museum in which to exhibit the family status symbols, and the wife is the curator.

Despite the general favor with which male characteristics are viewed in our society, there is little evidence that most women want to reverse the normal pattern and abandon the traditional feminine role altogether. They *like* being women for the most part, but they wish it didn't seem to mean that they had to be so "unsuccessful." They don't want to feel —quite rightly—that being a woman dooms them to a kind of second-class existence—with lesser potentialities. . . . What is debilitating and anxiety-producing is lack of self-respect, a feeling of unimportance [McClelland, 1965, p. 186].

The second half of this proposition—that careers, jobs, and community activities are unimportant—must be measured against the facts that, as Dr. Reiss mentions, 34 percent of married women are working outside the home and that books like Betty Friedan's (1963) *Feminine mystique* and Phyllis McGinley's (1964) *Sixpence in her shoe* have stirred up the interest and controversy which they have. However, unless and until we institutionalize childcare in some satisfactory way, I believe that many gifted women will not consider the possibility of combining a career with marriage because they cannot accept the unsatisfactory childcare arrangements which are currently available.

In addition, for most women, the successful pursuit of a career will necessitate some family planning—both as to spacing and number of children. The so-called emancipation of women will certainly not be complete until women have the freedom to decide the questions of whether, when, and how many, with regard to the bearing of children and the manner in which they will be cared for.

In passing, I might add that the community activities in which women sometimes involve themselves have also been accorded a very low value by society and are increasingly being relegated to busy-work, e.g., the hospital volunteer who peddles candy bars and toothpaste while the nurses care for the sick.

There is yet another role, not yet mentioned, which is played by the married woman in our society—the role of consumer. Women spend 75 percent of the consumer dollar in this country. Would you not think this would entitle them to a little respect and affection from the economic institutions—from the purveyors of goods? Not on your life! These ungrateful wretches, the hucksters and image-makers, whose livelihood depends on the buying habits of women, spend their days devising new and clever ways to defraud, deceive, mislead and trick the helpless consumer. What possible defense has a poor housewife against some invisible thing that counts the number of times her eyes blink as she looks at the frozen squash? A recent survey by the Consumers Union found 49 brands and sizes of laundry detergents on a local (Westchester

County) supermarket shelf. These were in no way comparable with regard to size, price or cleaning ability. It is common supermarket practice to manipulate the size and price of merchandise in order to confuse the customer. There is a bill currently before the United States Congress to correct some of the prevalent abuses, but the industries are lobbying vigorously against its passage and, unfortunately, consumers have no effective lobbying group to promote or protect their interests at this time.

8. "The expectations of women for marriage are unrealistic." Society views the married woman as a set of roles. Unfortunately, the various institutions of our society impose on women a welter of confused, poorly defined and often conflicting role definitions. Therefore, I believe that it is more accurate to characterize women's expectations for marriage as confused than as unrealistic. This state of confusion is what social psychologists call anomy; in this case caused not by an absence of norms but by a surfeit of conflicting norms. So, those who are in the position of counseling married women (or girls who will someday be married) would do well to keep in mind that many of their problems arise from social conditions and not from individual constitutional weaknesses—they are not all neurotic.

The solution to these problems is not in counseling the woman to "adjust", but in helping the society to change, and here is where the Church must exercise its great institutional and moral force—to help bring about creative solutions to these problems. For example, on the parish level, can we conceive of spending some of the time, money, and personnel currently devoted to duplication of existing public school facilities to the creation of day-care centers for children; homemaker services for help in emergency situations; effective integration programs for new families in the parish, and other facilities designed to strengthen the family? On the educational level, much can be done to facilitate the further education of married women—things like scheduling classes more conveniently, giving credit for correspondence courses, simplifying transfer procedures to accomodate those who must move frequently, helping to provide childcare facilities, etc. In the field of employment there should be many possibilities for utilizing the skills of married women on a part-time basis during the years when family demands make full-time work impossible. These are but a few ideas of ways in which the Church as an institution could become relevant to the lives, not only of women, but of families in modern life.

REFERENCES

Goldsen, Rose K., Rosenberg, K., Williams, R., Suchman, E. *What college students think.* Princeton: van Nostrand, 1960.

Friedan, Betty. *The feminine mystique.* New York: Norton, 1963.

McClelland, D. C. Wanted: a new self-image for women. In R. J. Lifton (Ed.) *The woman in America.* Boston: Houghton Mifflin, 1965. Pp. 173-192.

McGinley, Phyllis. *Sixpence in her shoe.* New York: Macmillan, 1964.

Rossi, Alice S. Equality between the sexes. *Daedalus,* 1964, *93,* 607-652.

The Career Wife

ROSEMARY HIGGINS CASS

Rosemary Higgins Cass received her A.B. degree from the College of St. Elizabeth, Convent, N.J., in 1950; her L.B. degree from Columbia Law School in 1953, and her Ph.D. in Sociology from Fordham University in 1964. She is a member of the Essex County, New Jersey State, and American Bar Associations; a member of the Sections of Family Law and International Comparative Law of the American Bar Association, and was chairman for 1964-65 of the New Jersey State Bar Committee on International and Comparative Law. She is likewise a member of the American Sociological Association and the American Catholic Sociological Society. Dr. Cass is a practicing attorney in Bloomfield, N.J., and in New York City, and a frequent lecturer before women's groups on the subjects of women in international affairs, problems in family life, and similar topics.

Social action is prompted by human need. Man, for the fulfillment of his human needs, enters into systems of regulated interpersonal contacts with other men, which are known alternately as "groups," "social arrangements," "social organizations," "social structures," or "social systems." Recognition by any group of the human needs which caused

123

its establishment results in a set of values which the group must maintain if it is to survive.

Sociologists and psychologists may quarrel over what are basic human—that is, psychological—needs, though I believe that their differences are primarily semantic. Currently acceptable as the central human need is all that is implied by the term "status" (Parsons, 1954, pp. 89-103; Schneiders, 1956, pp. 338-348), including recognition of a person's intrinsic worth, acceptance of him as he is, and his meaningful relationship to persons and things around him. Closely allied to this need are the needs for affection and security, which, it could be argued, are subsumed under status.

Within a slightly different frame of reference we might call these basic human needs the needs for love and for work—love here defined in its broadest sense to include the whole spectrum of different types of affection toward which one can respond, and work—not thought of solely in terms of employment, but in the dictionary sense of conscious activity directed to some meaningful purpose or end.

Now, if we look for a moment at the family we see that it partakes of the characteristics of a group since it is a system of regulated interpersonal contacts prompted by human needs which are valued as essential to the maintenance of this group. These values are, broadly, the regulation of love and the provision for work; in other words, values corresponding to the basic needs of men for meaningful love and meaningful work in their lives. Investigating a little further one would find that the family is both historically the first known group, and, down through the centuries, in different cultures and in different patterned ways, the most lasting institution still seeking to fulfill the same basic needs.

Yet society is vastly more complex in the 1960s than it was in the year 2000 B.C. The meaning of love, the meaning of work, though essentially the same in definition, have connoted a variety of different implications to the hunter on the Asiatic plains, the cultivated Athenian gentleman, the medieval monk, the eighteenth-century adventurer, and the twentieth-century scholar. The highly sophisticated, deeply personal relationship a man is expected to maintain with his wife in western society is a far cry from the kind of dominion he exercised over her in nomadic and agricultural societies. The type of work engaging the mind and creative efforts of the president of a business corporation in the midwest United States today does not begin to compare with the leisurely involvement of a Roman senator in Caesar's day.

A further qualification which presents itself is that while in very simple societies man was enabled to fulfill the totality of his basic needs within the framework of the group known as the family, the changing structure of the family accommodating itself to the needs of an increasingly complex society has made it well-nigh impossible for most men to satisfy either their affectional or their productive needs solely within its confines.

This kind of analysis becomes relevant to a consideration of the roles of the married woman within the context of the family and outside of it. The woman, no less than the man, has these same basic human needs which she anticipates fulfilling, and again, like him, she expects to fulfill them within the framework of the family; but here, unlike him and indeed perhaps because of him, she has been socialized to the expectation that all of her love and work needs will be fulfilled within the family and only incidentally, if at all, outside of it. Whether this is a valid expectation depends on the extent to which the family group is capable of fulfilling her need dispositions, and, conversely, on the extent to which she is able to carry out within it those tasks which are essential to the maintenance of the family. Here it must be pointed out that what is essential to the family's survival as a social group may or may not be a task for the family itself. Contrast, for example, the rudimentary government of the ancient clan with the intricate patterns of the federal system, or the nursing care of ancient Egypt with that of the modern hospital. Yet both have maintained the family.

At this juncture a new element has been introduced, for not only can we look at the family from the viewpoint of the individual and his basic needs, from the viewpoint of the family itself and what is essential to its maintenance as a group, but we ought as well to view the function of the family within the wider perspective of the society in which it is located. Society expects certain things of the family, viz., that it will perpetuate the species, serve as an approved mode of control for the sexual drive, and provide for the transmission of the culture to the succeeding generation. Since these are recognized needs of society, to the extent that the family cannot or will not carry them out, society will seek other channels. So, e.g., the transmission of the culture is a simple matter in the primitive native villages of the Highland New Guineans, and both parents have their role to play. The transmission of the American culture, on the other hand, needs all the resources of family, school, church and other community agencies to pass on even a part thereof. Perpetuating the species—which would include material, mental, moral and spiritual provision for the person—was on the one hand a most difficult process in the days when disease, ignorance and poverty were rampant in every society, and, on the other hand, essentially a relatively simple process as one struggled merely to survive. Today, when the means for the elimination of poverty, disease and ignorance are close at hand for those who will utilize them, the process is nevertheless a complex one requiring all the skills that family, hospitals, social-welfare agencies, schools and community government can bring to bear on them.

THE WORK OF MODERN WOMAN

Where then does the role of the modern woman lie? Is it, as some maintain, within the home itself, and does she betray her role as woman by seeking outside commitments (Lundberg & Farnham, 1947)? Or is it, as others would maintain, by seeking only her own fulfillment without regard for, and even in disregard of, this basic group of which she is a member and to which she has duties (de Beauvoir, 1953, pp. xiii-xxix)? Could the answer lie somewhere between? This question necessitates a second look at roles within the family structure, and more specifically within the Judaeo-Christian tradition.

When a man and woman marry they form a new "family," a family that has four basic tasks to perform: reproduction, socialization of its young, affectional control among the members of the family, and the economic maintenance of the family group. All these tasks are carried on by the husband-father and the wife-mother. (We are not here dealing with the specific roles of the child in the family though evidently the interaction of parents and children is integral.) In other words, we could, indeed we should, call both "homemakers." Except for the actual capacity for childbearing, specifically the woman's, and in those activities demanding physical prowess, more common to men, none of the four basic tasks is inherently the prerogative of either man or woman (Callahan, 1965). Traditionally, they have been performed by those free to carry them out (Blood & Wolfe, 1960, pp. 73-74).

So in an agricultural society, the reproductive function—which normally occupied a woman for most of her adult life—kept her close to the house, and it seemed quite a sensible division of labor that she therefore cooked and cleaned and did the multitude of other economic tasks required about the house in a pre-industrialized society, while her husband tilled the fields, roamed the forests, hunted game, and fought the enemy. There were many other tasks common to both, including the socialization of the children and affectional interaction. Yet in terms of so-called economic maintenance, the work of each was indispensable to the family.

What has been lost sight of in much of the analysis of the modern urban family is the importance of the economic activity of the wife-mother in the economic maintenance of the family—the importance to herself in terms of her basic needs for meaningful love and work, to the family in terms of its survival, and to society in terms of the tasks it demands of the family. A simpler age could recognize these relative exigencies and provide for all of them within a single group—the family.

What appears to have happened today is that those intent on maintaining the family system have neither examined what forces are at work within the system to enable it to restore an equilibrium which was badly shaken by the Industrial Revolution, nor, in their zeal to preserve fundamental family values, have they re-examined the reasons for the existence of the family vis-à-vis the individual and vis-à-vis society, and how the values can be preserved in a family structure with differently patterned ways of action.

We have seen the tasks of socialization and affectional control increasingly assumed by the woman in the absence of the man who had formerly shared these activities with her but whose working hours no longer permit this. At the same time we have been faced with the specter of an occupational structure and a money economy which has placed more and more of the burden of economic maintenance on the man, where formerly it was a burden more evenly shared, except perhaps in those times when the woman was physically incapacitated in the throes of childbirth.

To illustrate the last point one has only to think of the tasks performed by the mother of a large family of moderate circumstances a scant hundred years ago. She not only baked the bread and made the clothes for her family, she spent long hours cooking, laundry was a two-day task and even a bath a major operation. But additionally, she was the dispenser of largesse, of advice and comfort to the less fortunate; she was the one who cared for the sick and the elderly of the community and gathered the children for schooling. Many of these tasks are either no longer necessary or have increasingly been taken on by other agencies within the community, agencies which are, however, supportive of the family and which require the work of family members outside of the home.

Is it a wonder then that when a great majority of the average women are asked why they are working they claim that their basic reason is economic (Nye & Hoffman, 1963, pp. 18-63; Cass, 1964)? Indeed, it is the reason. And in the struggle of men during this last century for shorter working hours and better wages has not one motivation been their desire for more time with their families and in their homes? What we see here is an apparent effort in working-class families to restore equilibrium within the family structure, an effort which is still being challenged in the professional class.

THE CAREER WIFE AND THE CAREER HUSBAND

Perhaps all of the foregoing has seemed like nothing more than a too-lengthy introduction to the subject of this paper, but it does not seem that any understanding of the role of the professional (career) wife will ensue in the absence of an understanding of family functions and of those changes in society which have affected the family generally and the roles of the family members specifically.

Though the family is committed to the continuation of certain tasks, which are related to the fundamental needs of the persons making up the family and thus represent values for it and for society, we must be careful to distinguish the values themselves from the implementing patterns of behavior for maintaining them. Reproduction operates both as a basic task of the family and as a value for the family. Yet no one says that a mother is not fulfilling her task and maintaining the value because today she has her babies in the hospital and no longer breast-feeds them. Socialization of the young remains a basic activity of the family and hence has a value attached to it; yet much of the socialization to become a mature member of society takes place in school, church or other community agency. Affectional control is achieved both through family and through peer groups, social groups, work groups, church groups, etc. None of these activities is any longer questioned as basic to the family, the *sine qua non* of its existence, but at the same time to be contributed to and supported by outside groups and other institutions within society. In fact there is even today a grudging acceptance that a woman can and should work in paid employment when her family has need of her economic assistance (Nye & Hoffman, 1963; Cotton, 1965, pp. 11-13).

But that a married woman, worse a married woman with children, should actually seek partial fulfillment of her basic need for meaningful work in a serious commitment to the profession for which she has been trained is seen as the very negation of her role as wife and mother. On the other hand, even though the man's professional commitment may be all-absorbing to the point where he fails in his socializing and affectional roles as husband and father, we are prone not to see the significance of his failure, since in this society we have ascribed to him the primary role of "breadwinner" (Parson, 1954).

One might question the use of the word "commitment," but within the framework of one's "commitment" to a particular vocation is there not place for a variety of other commitments to subsidiary goals, provided they are conducive to the attainment of the major commitments? We have recognized this for the professional man but not for the woman. Conversely, how seldom do we recognize when a man does not abide by his commitment to the vocation of marriage in an excessive zeal to become a business success?

What is actually involved here is a dual failure precipitated by the occupational structure. Educated woman cannot share the meaningful economic activity which once was hers within the framework of the family, and educated man can no longer share the affectional and socializing roles which he once could. Man's failure has been obscured by the woman's awareness of the unmet needs of their children for affection and socialization which she has attempted to fulfill, and woman's inability to exercise her economic function has been obscured by the man's increased preoccupation with his professional role. The result has been that we see among the educated class a generation of ineffectual fathers, dissatisfied mothers, and problem children.

More serious, however, has been the denial implicit in the present social structure of the invaluable role of woman in contributing to society's needs, not alone in terms of bearing children but also in nurturing and socializing them, a many-sided and complex task which can no longer be performed completely within the home. Woman herself has not risen to the challenge of society's need for her work (Sanders, 1960). Indeed, fearful of society's condemnation and what it might do to her marriage, she has shunned it. Hunt has said:

> The very forces that make women fearful of using their intellectual abilities, for instance, have also prevented them from serving their society well and relieving some of its problems. . . . The paradox of American women . . . can be restated thus: out of her very satisfactions (as wife and mother) she makes her dissatisfactions, and out of her disregard of society's needs there sooner or later comes her failure to meet her own needs [Hunt, 1962, pp. 6-7].

It is a simplistic answer to say that because women are made for marriage and children they should be content with the role which has been theirs throughout the ages, when this role has been robbed of a major part of its meaningful content in the very era when the life span of both men and women has been appreciably increased by more than 20 years since the turn of the century; when modern progress and technology have eased the burdens which impeded woman's full participation in public life, and education and enlightenment have permitted their penetration into all fields. Other societies in other times made possible meaningful work for women at every level. But since the Industrial Revolution, which eliminated the family as the basic producing unit of society and removed so much work from the home, to suggest that the married woman with intellectual capacities and training will find sustained meaningful work throughout a lifetime solely within the confines of her home is, I submit, unrealistic.

There are very real contradictions present in the situation of the professionally trained married woman. On the one side there is the prevalent attitude that she is somehow less of a woman, less the good wife and mother, and a selfish person because she yearns for or lives a professional commitment. On the other hand, she knows what her capacity and training are and how they may be utilized. She hears too the call of society for the fulfillment of many tasks, some of which in elemental form were the very tasks carried out by women in and through the family of another age—teaching, nursing the sick, giving counsel to the afflicted—and other tasks which have been necessitated by the greater interdependence of the various units and groupings in society and the progressive rise of new social, cultural, and political institutions.

For some women the reconciliation of this conflict is achieved through volunteer service and, while I would be the last to deprecate the outstanding contribution that is being made and hopefully will always continue to be made by these women, I do not think this should be the answer to those who prefer serious professional commitment. And all of us are familiar with the volunteer who is never satisfied with what she's doing! Other women hide their real motivations for working behind the false one of gaining supplemental income or through a lessened sense of obligation to their profession—e.g., the married woman teacher who is always first out the door of the school on the pretext of home obligations when they may not exist! And finally there are those women who remain at home, some from a sense of duty to husband and children, some because their lives are indeed rich, full and busy with the care of many children, sick relatives, and other obligations that allow no time for outside commitment, and some through sheer laziness.

I respect the woman who chooses to remain at home when duty impels her to it but I have little patience with women who simply run the bridge and cocktail circuit. With Edith Stein (1956) I believe that whenever the circle of a woman's home becomes too small for her time and talents then she has not only the right, but indeed the obligation to use her time and talents in the service of the wider society, whether this be in paid professional commitment or in serious volunteer service. There are all too many women who use their marriages and their families as an excuse for not fulfilling society's need for their services. Why else the shortage of teachers, nurses, doctors, social workers and other professionals? There are not sufficient men or sufficient single women to fill all these positions. In the total employment picture, if every married woman had left paid employment in the year 1960 and every unemployed but employable man or single woman had been employed in that same year, there would have been a surplus of over nine million jobs (President's Commission on the Status of Women, 1963).

ADDITIONAL PROBLEMS OF THE PROFESSIONAL MOTHER

There are, however, other problems which the professional mother must face, and in terms of interpersonal relationships often the most difficult of these are the differences in expectation of her role as she sees it and as her husband views it.

A husband is apt to see his wife's professional commitment as threatening in any of several ways: 1. as a threat to his comfort— unfortunately he is still socialized to the expectation that his wife shall be more or less at his beck and call; 2. as a threat to his status—both in terms of the income he can provide and in terms of the prestige which he enjoys. In this competitive society man inclines to look at his woman colleague as just one more competitor and he does not want this in his wife. Moreover, her presence in a professional field conflicts with the still prevalent conception of man as the "breadwinner" of the family. 3. Finally, there is the deeper inner threat to his sense of security as a man, for he still maintains the idea of his own superiority over woman and finds here in the professionally competent woman the last seeming vestiges of it overthrown.

These are serious difficulties and I would not gloss over them, but time does not permit more than a word concerning their resolution. Succeeding generations of men, it is to be hoped, will be socialized to rather different expectations of their own and their wives' roles: 1. that the wife shall be no more at her husband's beck and call than he at hers; 2. that rather than a competitor, woman truly is meant to stand beside man so that they both can "subdue the earth"; income and status will be matters of joint endeavor, and woman's status will be that which she has of herself and not merely as an appendage of her husband; 3. that man and woman are equals whose love, paraphrasing Saint Exupéry, will not consist in gazing at each other but in looking outward in the same direction.

Meanwhile there will be conflict and it will take love, patience and understanding, but perseverance as well, to reconcile the problem of the married professional woman's working with the perceived expectations which her husband still maintains about her.

There is still left unmentioned the problem which might appear central to any discussion of career or professional wives and mothers, and that is the care of the children. Yet I have deliberately left this emotion-laden question almost to the end so that we could view the roles of the woman in the family within the total perspective of her lifetime, which is now averaging almost seventy-five years.

Though left unstated, the implications of my previous remarks, I think, were clear in that there should be a much greater sharing of the socializing and affectional roles—child-rearing and homemaking, if you will—between husband and wife. It is to be foreseen that woman's outside professional endeavor will eventually permit to the professional man lesser hours of work and hence the resumption of these roles in the same way that the working-class woman's employment, coupled with shortened hours for the man, has seemingly permitted a restoration of the equilibrium for that type of family.

But meanwhile, the woman still bears the major responsibility for the care of the children, and here, for at least the span of years in which she bears children and has small children at home, there is the essential of actual physical care, and during all the years there are children at home who have not yet reached maturity, there is always the question of care adequate to meet the needs of their particular stage of development. How the mother copes with this situation is dependent on a variety of factors including her own health, the type of profession she has and whether it lends itself to part-time work in periods when she is much needed at home, the attitude of her husband, and the kind of help she can get with her household duties and with the children. There are no hard and fast rules and the decision is one to be made by husband and wife giving careful consideration to the needs of their own children and their individual circumstances.

What has been said raises some interesting questions for those engaged in the counseling of young people. I shall not reiterate those points dealing with expectations and perceptions of male and female roles. Rather, I would deal with one last point concerning motivation of the young woman to pursue a serious career where she has the ability for it.

Girls today are encouraged to go to college and to prepare themselves for a career, but only in case they do not marry, or in the event their husband dies, or if they should want a job to fall back on at some later date in their lives. This is hardly strong enough motivation for the pursuit of a medical, law, or other graduate degree, and the lack of real motivation implicit in such an approach can be seen in the fact that 60 percent of the girls starting college today drop out, while there has been a decline within the last 30 years in the percentage of women obtaining graduate degrees. This is perhaps the rather absurd but logical conclusion to be reached in a society which permits the education of women at every level, but would then deny them the full exercise of it because they marry. Apparently these young women are reasoning: why, then, become educated at a higher level?

Shall we not instead motivate and train the new generation of young women to see that their roles, like those of men, will be many and complex, that they have duties to themselves, to the husbands and children of the families they will create, and to the larger society of which they are a part, and that in the fullest development and use of their capacities they will serve their families and their societies best, and themselves be blest with the reward of the "valiant woman" of the Scriptures?

REFERENCES

Bettelheim, B. Growing up female. *Harpers*, 1962, *225*, 120-128.

Blood, R. O. & Wolfe, D. M. *Husbands and wives: the dynamics of family living*. New York: Free Press, 1960.

Callahan, Sidney. *The illusion of Eve*. New York: Sheed & Ward, 1965.

Cass, Rosemary Higgins. Maternal employment as a positive reaction of the modern urban middle-class married woman to the situation of anomie. Unpublished doctoral dissertation, Fordham Univer., 1964.

Cotton, Dorothy Whyte. *The case for the working mother*. New York: Stein & Day, 1965.

de Beauvoir, Simone. *The second sex* (trans. and edited by H. M. Parshley). New York: Knopf, 1953.

De Lauwe, P. C. Images of women in society. *Int. soc. Sci. J.*, 1962, *14*, 1-25.

Dohen, Dorothy. The working wife. In W. C. Bier (S.J.) (Ed.) *Marriage: a psychological and moral approach*. New York: Fordham University Press, 1965. Pp. 159-169.

Friedan, Betty. *The feminine mystique*. New York: Norton, 1963.

Hunt, M. *Her infinite variety: the American woman as lover, mate and rival*. New York: Harper & Row, 1962.

Lundberg F. & Farnham, Marynia F. *Modern woman, the lost sex*. New York: Harper, 1947.

Mannes, Marya. Female intelligence: who wants it? *New York Times Magazine*, January 17, 1960.

Mead, Margaret. Job of the children's mother's husband. *New York Times Magazine*, May 10, 1959.

Myrdal, Alva & Klein, Viola. *Woman's two roles, home and work*. London: Routledge & Kegan Paul, 1956.

Nye, F. I. & Hoffman, Lois W. *The employed mother in America*. Chicago: Rand McNally, 1963.

Parsons, T. *Essays in sociological theory* (rev. ed.). New York: Free Press, 1954.

President's Commission on the Status of Women. *Report of the Committee on Education*. Washington, D.C.: U.S. Government Printing Office, 1963.

Sanders, Marian K. A proposition for women. *Harpers*, 1960, *221*, 41-48.

Schneiders, A. A. *Introductory psychology*. New York: Holt, Rinehart & Winston, 1956.

Smuts, R. W. *Women and work in America*. New York: Columbia Univer. Press, 1959.

Stein, Edith. *Writings of Edith Stein* (selected, translated and introduced by Hilda Graef). Westminster, Md.: Newman, 1956.

The Childless Married Woman

AILEEN B. OSTAZESKI

Mrs. Aileen B. Ostazeski attended Alfred University, Alfred, N.Y., from which she received her A.B. degree in 1942. She received her professional training at the New York School of Social Work (now the School of Social Work of Columbia University) during 1944 and 1945. Currently Mrs. Ostazeski is Supervisor of Case Work in the Adoption Unit, Westchester County Department of Public Welfare. Previously she had been Assistant Case Supervisor, Westchester County Department of Public Welfare, Division of Family and Child Welfare.

The family is the foundation of our American culture. Its image depicted today in popular magazines portrays an inviting picture of the young married couple with their children living in their modern comfortable homes, participating actively in community projects and seemingly enjoying the roles of husband-wife-parent. It is the "good" life, it is comfortable with its wealth of satisfactions in the depth of love each one feels for the other. It is the hoped-for life which each couple reasonably expects for themselves when they enter the state of marriage. Although the woman who is happy in her marriage may hope for a few years of married life without children to give herself and her husband time together to adjust to their new life, she does want children eventually and when her first child does arrive her satisfaction and joys are abundant. As time goes on and her family is increasing she shows evidence of many gratifying experiences and some disappointments; she grows and matures, comfortable and secure in her role as a woman, a wife, and a mother.

Yet there are many women much less fortunate who also have the right to express hope for and to plan for children in their marriage, but who must, because of circumstances beyond their control, face their years ahead frustrated by the knowledge that they may never reach the fulfillment of their marriage through the birth of a child. Regardless of financial status or educational achievements these feelings are common to each woman in varying degrees.

THE STERILE MARRIAGE

In the early years of her marriage when a woman begins to realize that she is having difficulty in conceiving she becomes anxious, unsettled, and concerned. She knows that she may consult a specialist in the field of gynecology and that the result will be one of three possibilities. First, she may discover that she never will be able physically to conceive a child; secondly, she may be told that there is no medical reason that can be established to account for the fact that she does not conceive; thirdly, she may find that the doctor will be able to help her conceive naturally. I will consider first the woman who finds that she may never be able physically to conceive a child. The knowledge of this fact is an enormous shock to many women. Their feelings of inadequacy, failure, and bitter disappointment are intense.

For the most part married women are knowledgeable about the advances of medical science and the availability of help for them through medicine. The worry and strain a woman experiences prior to making the decision to consult her doctor threatens every emotion within her. In most instances she is reasonably sure that she can endure the physical pain and discomfort involved in the examination, but she questions her ability to face the results. If the total responsibility for childlessness rests with her, she naturally worries about how this fact will affect her marriage. Initially she may be conflicted and question whether she really wants to submit to the long medical exploration involved. If she does not seek medical help about her inability to bear a child, she can save herself from knowing and facing the facts. Yet she also knows that by not exploring her situation she must face herself and her husband, and live with the feelings of guilt that will be most difficult and frustrating. She

will have to face the fact that, by resisting this medical help, it can
mean she really may not wish to bear a child, and these feelings are not
acceptable. Generally her desire for parenthood is very strong, and this
helps her make the decision to consult her doctor. Her anxiety mounts
through the long months of testing and treatment. As the time goes by
this woman is forced to ask consciously and unconsciously over and over
again: "Will I ever conceive a child?" Although her frustration is increasing she does submit herself to repeated tests, new discoveries and
continued treatment, and finally may learn that her marriage is sterile.
Although during this time she has had suspicions of negative results,
her hope for successful results has sustained her.

It is an understandable phenomenon how in our work with prospective adoptive parents, when it has been medically established that a
woman cannot conceive a child she will speak about the possibility that
a "miracle" might happen. These can be particularly difficult situations
where professional counseling and help may be needed to afford the
individual the opportunity to work through her feelings and to accept
the reality of her marital situation. The woman who constantly hopes
for the impossible places an enormous obstacle on her ability to free
herself to accept her fate maturely and with sustained equilibrium.

When these findings in her individual situation are confirmed her
sense of failure as a woman—as a marriage partner—are further intensified. She will need strength to develop the capacity to face her disappointment bravely, not only in the present but also in future years.

The sterile adoptive mother must endure privations, she must forego
all the emotional experience involved in the birth process and the dreams
of what her child may be like. She is denied the joyful experience of de-
livery and the elation of seeing her own child (Deutsch 1945). Yet she
is allowed some opportunities for gratification. She is spared the fears
of expectation of what her child may be, she will not endure the bodily
pains, the fears and conflicts of the birth process.

> But deep in the unconscious there remains the unsatisfied longing for
> the masochistic experience she must miss and the reproach directed
> against the ego for having avoided this function. Both the woman and
> the man are deprived of the realization of the narcissistic wish for physi-
> cal immortality [Deutsch, 1945, p. 424].

A woman must first share the medical findings with her husband and she
must draw on all her inner strength to do so. Her feelings about her
own completeness as a woman are being threatened, and she is concerned about how her husband may respond to the medical findings.
It is a serious crisis in her married life. She looks at other women

pregnant and some mothers whom she considers so much more fortunate than herself, and asks herself quietly over and over again, "Why couldn't this happen to me?"

Many prospective adoptive mothers are most articulate in expressing their feelings of resentment and bitterness when they see a pregnant woman or a mother with her children. One young woman cried bitterly in an office interview when she told of her reactions to her situation. She rebelled at the thought of other women who were able to have children. Her deprivation was so acute that she could not accept her situation or find any solace in the fact that others too were deprived. Yet she must live with her feelings, struggle in her frustrations and continue to try to fill her life.

She may be blessed in the strength of her love for her husband and secure in her knowledge of his love for her. She knows this must sustain her if her marriage is to survive. With her husband's mature love, patience and understanding, and often with professional counseling, she can emerge a person most adequate and ready to seek satisfactions of motherhood through adoption.

Some women through natural means (use of rhythm method) or through artificial means (use of contraceptives) may elect to put off having children for several years until such time as she and her husband can achieve financial security and material wealth, only to discover at some future date that she cannot bear a child. Such discovery may come as such a shock that she will experience feelings similar to those previously stated but with a much greater degree of intensity. Her deep feelings of guilt and frustration can be multiplied.

We must comment also about the woman who physically is able to bear a child but whose husband is sterile. It may well be that the feelings of frustration can be much greater for her in this situation. She is called upon not only to handle her own disappointment that she can never bear her husband's child, but also to extend herself in every possible way to help him to fortify his self-worth and self-confidence.

This knowledge may be a greater psychological blow than when it is the wife—not that the latter is not a painful discovery—since infertility in a man is often equated with weakness though without real basis. It makes some men feel that they are not truly men [Gordon, 1956, p. 292].

Therefore a woman's burden is indeed great to help her husband in this crisis through her sympathetic and warm and sincere understanding, and at the same time to handle her own disappointment and frustration.

FUNCTIONAL STERILITY

There are reasons other than physical why a woman cannot conceive a child. Dorothy Hutchinson points out that

> it is not possible to separate arbitrarily functional sterility from organic sterility; nor does finding some basis for organic sterility always rule out unconscious conflict as a contributing factor [Hutchinson, 1943, p. 17].

After extensive medical exploration and treatment a doctor may find no physical basis for childlessness in either partner. The hope that a pregnancy will occur is ever present and often expressed consciously. Yet no pregnancy does occur.

In support of Hutchinson's point many provocative questions are raised by Dr. Deutsch, an eminent psychiatrist, about the

> psychologic motives for sterility and by the woman's reaction to her renunciation. Has her fear of the reproductive function proved stronger than her wish to be a mother? Is she still so much a child that she cannot emotionally and unconsciously decide to assume the responsible role of mother? Is she so much absorbed emotionally in other life tasks that she fears motherhood? Is her relationship with her husband so gratifying and fulfilling that she fears a change in the status quo? Does she think that her husband should not be burdened with the tasks of real fatherhood? Does she think that her body has been injured by forbidden actions? Does she hold her husband responsible for her childlessness? Does a deeply unconscious curse of heredity burden all her motherly wish fantasies? [Deutsch, 1945, p. 397]

Whatever the reason or reasons may be why psychologically a woman cannot allow herself to become pregnant, it is intensely bewildering and confusing to her. Her feelings may be so deep-rooted that only psychiatric help will give her a better understanding of herself and an ability to free herself sufficiently to allow a pregnancy to occur. To illustrate this point I present the following case history.

> Recently Mr. and Mrs. Dean, a young couple in their late 20s, applied to adopt a child. They had been married ten years and she had never conceived a child. Extensive medical exploration revealed no conclusive evidence for sterility. As the couple shared their disappointment they revealed a great deal about themselves. The young man, a high-school graduate, had been brought up in foster-home care and expressed overt feelings of satisfaction in this experience. He spoke freely of the reasons why foster care was necessary. His mother was a deaf mute and she was never married. He considered her a burden to her family, and showed

little compassion for her. He claimed to feel sorry for her, and mentioned her occasional visits to his foster home. The last time he saw her was to secure her signature to permit him to marry. His total identification was with his foster family. Although he knew where his mother was he had never suggested his wife meet her and completely divorced himself from any contact with his natural family. He had been told that his natural father was a neighbor who had "taken advantage" of his mother and later married another woman by whom he had two children. He revealed that his father had since died and he expressed little curiosity about him or his family.

Mrs. Dean, a somewhat obese, immature young woman, a high-school graduate too, claimed a lifetime of satisfactions, an exceptionally happy childhood, her father's favorite child, now enjoying a fine marriage with her only expressed disappointment being her inability to conceive a child. She told us that her relationship to her mother was an exceptionally fine one. She spoke most admirably and affectionately, with no evidence of envy, of her sister who was a college graduate, accomplished in the mastery of foreign languages, married to a professional man and the mother of a young son. Mrs. Dean's life experiences seemed almost "too good to be true."

As we engaged in a study of this couple it seemed clear in this marriage that the fear each partner had of conceiving a child naturally was deep-rooted. Mr. Dean, whose background contained many unknowns and certainly an obvious known, in the person of his mother, may have feared that their child too would inherit her defect. He evidenced much discomfort in discussing the fact that he had seen his mother only once in many years. He had little or no recall of her physical appearance and he admitted feeling ashamed of her. Mrs. Dean showed almost no interest in her husband's natural family, not even curiosity, and she related her own total life experiences in a manner that was consciously or unconsciously intended to present herself as almost "perfect." Both these young people spoke of their good marriage together and expressed disappointment in their inability to have a child.

If indeed this couple's fear of heredity prevented them from conceiving their own child because of the many unknowns, it seemed logical to expect that these fears and worries would justifiably lead to fears in adopting a child whose heritage carries many unknowns. Certainly there are many risks in having your own child, as there are many risks in adoption, and the capacity to face these risks maturely and consider them soberly is indispensable in adoptive parents (Bowlby, 1952). We encouraged this young couple to seek psychiatric help for a better understanding of themselves. We believe that they might, once freed of their concerns, be able to have their own child, or be more ready to adopt.

Beside the fear of heredity certainly it was clear that this young man needed too to work through his feelings of having been a foster child and to prove his self-worth by taking care of a child through adoption.

THE DEATH OF AN ONLY CHILD

The woman who has suffered the loss of an only child through death may experience such deep-seated guilt that she dare not have another child lest that child die too. She may find herself unable to turn her interest to anyone and feels she is unworthy to be given the privilege of having another child. She may feel herself the object of pity by her friends and relatives and tend to withdraw from their well-meaning overtures to her. Her period of mourning probably will depend upon the extent of her need to punish herself for the loss of her child. She may find the presence of other children a cruel reminder of her child and resent them fiercely. The frustration created by her desire to have her child back, her knowledge that this can never be, might well be insurmountable. Her childless world may be unbearable and her suffering intolerable. She feels so different, so hurt, that she terminates her former associations with other mothers. No woman needs more comfort and help than the woman who becomes childless because of the death of a dearly loved child.

ADOPTION OF CHILDREN

It is not possible for an adoption agency to consider favorably each woman who seeks motherhood through the process of adoption. Not every childless married woman can accept wholeheartedly a child not her very own. She may feel too that unless she secures a child somewhere, her marriage may end. These women must, for their own sakes, be rejected by an adoption service. To them this constitutes a double failure. Where previously a woman had to accept the fact that she was denied the right to motherhood naturally, she believes now that she has been found "unfit" to adopt a child. The sense of desperation, of complete and total failure which she realizes, could well cause a mental break. Her need for help is very real and her inability to accept herself as a worthwhile person is intensified. There is no childless married woman who needs more sympathetic sensitive handling than this one.

Married women, prospective adoptive mothers who are childless, express their frustrations in many ways. They verbalize their wish to make up in some way to their husbands for their failure to bear a child. They not only appear over-affectionate and more solicitous of their husbands but also quite the reverse. They may withdraw from their husbands and also be reluctant to fulfill their marital sexual obligations, since they believe the only purpose of their marriage was to beget a family.

They express feelings of being different from their friends and relatives. When they are with friends or relatives who talk about their children they often feel left out. Their tendency is to withdraw from the couples who have children, and they may seek their social satisfaction in different areas, where children will not be the subject of interest and conversations. Since they cannot be parents, they feel that they have no place in this group because they have no children to talk about, no experiences with children to share.

Their feelings may change from earlier interest in their friends' children to feelings of discomfort when children are around. They may find it difficult to talk with the children where previously they found it enjoyable because once they had anticipated having a child of their own.

Relatives can be particularly difficult for childless couples. They will chide them good-naturedly about the fact that there are no children. Culturally it may be extremely important to have children and couples may be regarded as peculiar, different, or even inferior when they have no family. Thoughtless and cruel remarks are made which can give a couple good reason to withdraw. Jealousy and resentment can be natural reactions toward those couples who do have children.

It is not unusual for the childless married woman to express strong feelings of hostility toward the unmarried mother or toward married parents who neglect their children or who "give them away." They ask such questions as "how could anyone bear a child and give that child to someone else?" It is an understandable remark when they are so eager for parenthood themselves. There are some women who question even their right to enjoy motherhood through adopting another woman's child. They may experience strong feelings of guilt in having taken another woman's child to be their own.

The well-adjusted married woman has less difficulty. Once she has lived with and accepted her disappointments she can continue to enjoy her friends, sensing some normal feelings of envy of those who have a family, but at the same time continuing with her husband in her secure relationship which is founded on love and mutual respect.

CONCLUSION

I have attempted to present in this paper the major areas of concern, together with the feelings and frustrations which the childless married woman has experienced and will continue to experience. It is reasonable to expect that even the woman who is successful in adopting a child may often wish that child might have been born to her.

Every married woman, with some exceptions, wants a family. Some of the exceptions want what they cannot achieve and yet they are unable to understand or accept why they cannot achieve it. The woman who has accepted the fact that she may never have a child biologically may indeed enjoy all the satisfactions of motherhood through adoption.

For the most part, adoption agencies, in approving a home for adoption, request and respect the comments of the couples' pastor in completing their evaluation of the home. It is indeed most comforting to an agency to suggest to a woman that she seek the counsel of her pastor when this is indicated.

Parenthood as it is related to sexual relationship is so intimate that it is difficult to discuss. And it is certainly true that for many the sociocultural milieu in which we live does not often permit comfortable discussion of sex. So at such time of crises in a woman's life she will need and welcome the spiritual comfort and the sympathetic response of her priest. I believe most sincerely that the clergy has a significant role to fulfill in helping the childless married woman to accept her on-going responsibility to herself as a woman and as a wife.

Every woman has the right to expect a happy fruitful marriage with healthy, happy children. We can only hope that those who are denied this privilege can continue to find satisfactions in their lives through spiritual guidance and sympathetic understanding and respect from those who cherish them.

REFERENCES

Bowlby, J. *Maternal care and mental health* (2nd ed.). Geneva: World Health Organization, 1952.

Deutsch, Helene. *Psychology of Women*, Vol. II *Motherhood*. New York: Grune & Stratton, 1945.

Gordon, Henrietta L. *Casework services for Children, principles and practices.* Boston: Houghton Mifflin, 1956.

Hutchinson, Dorothy C. *In quest of foster parents.* New York: Columbia University Press, 1943.

The Divorcée

THOMAS E. TOBIN, C.Ss.R.

Father Thomas E. Tobin, C.Ss.R., came to his present position as rector of the Liguori Mission House, Liguori, Missouri, and associate editor of Liguorian, *after some years as professor of psychology at the Redemptorist Seminary at Oconomowoc, Wisconsin. This background enabled him to cultivate the psychological-religious field to which he has contributed pamphlets and magazine articles on such topics as anxiety, self-confidence, scrupulosity and marriage problems. He is the founder and editor of* Scrupulous Anonymous, *a monthly publication begun in 1964 as a means of self-help for persons troubled with scrupulosity. Father Tobin is a priest genuinely interested in helping people, and it is in this context that he has become concerned about the plight of the Catholic divorcée.*

The Catholic divorcée finds little understanding and acceptance in many circles. She is desperately trying to remain faithful to her marriage vows and yet she hears from friends and relatives who should know better such advice as the following: "You need a husband and your children need a father." "A good God cannot expect you to live alone for the rest of your life." "The Church is too strict, but God will understand." "You can still be a good Catholic and raise your children as Catholics even though you cannot receive the sacraments."

144

On the other hand, the Catholic divorcée who wants and needs to be treated well by her fellow Catholics often encounters just the opposite treatment. Most ignore her, others avoid her, and some are openly hostile to her. The following extreme views were expressed in a letter received by the author after an article (Fleming, 1964) about the Stella Maris group, an organization for divorced Catholic women, appeared in *This Week* magazine:

> I thought that the Catholic Church was unconditionally opposed to divorce as one of the greatest of all evils. A divorced woman is a disgrace and deserves to feel like an outcast. Just tell her that she is a married woman, that she freely chose marriage as a vocation and was given sufficient grace to fulfill her obligation, and that is that! Above all, no priest should ever lose an opportunity to tell her that she is not free to marry. Beyond this she is not worth bothering about, because she just feels sorry for herself.

As Catholics, we should try to understand the Catholic divorcée and make her feel at home in the Catholic Church. To help further this understanding and acceptance is the purpose of this paper. It will not examine the reasons for the failure of the marriages, nor study the Catholic divorcée who has not been able to hold out and has entered into an invalid marriage, but the divorced woman who is trying to live a good Catholic life. The material is derived from work with the Stella Maris organization in St. Louis, retreats to divorced women, many hours of counseling, and especially 51 questionnaires answered by divorced women from different sections of the country.

Three points will be discussed: 1. The Catholic woman at the time of her divorce; 2. Her life as a Catholic divorcée; 3. The Stella Maris group as a means of helping the divorced Catholic woman help herself.

THE MARRIAGE

Before considering the divorced woman it will be worthwhile to take a quick glance at the married woman whose marriage ended in divorce. Of the 51 divorcées answering the above-mentioned questionnaire, 60 percent were between 21 and 24 years of age when they were married. The marriages lasted for an average of ten years—longer than usual— an indication that these women who were trying to save their marriages tried much longer than the average divorcée. Eight had no children, eighteen had one child, and fourteen had two children. Fifty-nine percent of the women were in the one-to-two-child bracket.

Forty-seven percent foresaw possible problems in their marriages but thought that love would conquer all. Their answers indicate their attitudes: "Of course not, although I was warned." "I was advised not to marry him by both his mother and my mother but I was young and very much in love." "Who thinks! Certainly not I." It is interesting that many of these women chose a type of husband which doomed the marriage from the very beginning. Often there was a personality problem antecedent to marriage which led them to select such a mate. Thus a woman with no confidence in herself could be attracted to a man who, she felt, had even less to offer. She could hope that this man would never look down on her, but would respect and love her for what she would give him as wife and mother. In this way she would build up confidence in herself and assure the success of her marriage. Incidentally, if a divorced woman becomes interested in another man frequently she is shocked to discover that he is the same type as her husband!

THE DIVORCE

Most of the women did not want a divorce. In at least ten cases the husband was the plaintiff and the wife countersued. In most other instances the wife sued for divorce either because the husband repeatedly insisted upon it or because the wife reluctantly decided that there was no longer any hope, and a divorce was needed to secure legal protection for the children and herself. In many divorces another woman was involved but it is difficult to say whether this was the cause or the effect of the failure of the marriage. Perhaps the attitude of many women can be summed up in the words of one: "I tried everything possible and finally reached the end of my rope."

The women become very descriptive in reporting their mixed emotions at the time of the divorce: "State of shock, a sense of guilt and shame, felt a failure and did not care if I lived or died." "Felt guilty that I had not been mature enough to make the marriage last, felt like an animated puppet." "I lived in a vacuum experiencing little or no emotion. Gave time to the children but in a rather mechanical way." "I was drained of any real feelings and wanted to get it over with." "Completely rejected." "I lost every speck of self-confidence and pride." "A numb nothingness and then fear and relief and finally the dominant one—the determination to turn the divorce into a good thing by giving the children security and a homelife without the traumatic experiences they have been exposed to."

Despite their feelings of rejection, failure and anxiety at the time of their divorce, nineteen of the women responding to the questionnaire said they still loved their husbands, twenty-seven said they did not, and five were undecided. Twenty-one of the fifty-one hoped for a reconciliation.

AFTER THE DIVORCE

The Catholic divorcée is alone and life is difficult! She has failed at the marriage that she wanted so much and worked so hard to save. She has lost a husband and has no right to obtain another. She faces the problem of raising her children by herself. Her family and her friends do not fully understand her. Her sense of failure, rejection, fear of being hurt, and lack of self-confidence tend to drive her into the narrow world of her own personality. All too easily can she build a wall around herself that no one can break down. She does not want to be hurt again.

Loneliness is the common problem of the Catholic divorcée. "Loneliness is my biggest problem so that most of the time I live in my own private hell." Many were so ashamed of themselves that they found it difficult to admit to others that they were divorced. Some hated the word divorce so much that they would not even use it. "Away from home I don't tell anyone that I am divorced unless I am asked and I usually am not. At home I say it bluntly and change the subject as it makes me feel unclean." "I never tell anyone if I can help it." "I have learned to express it in this way: 'To teachers, I am all the children have; to others, I am separated or a widow of sorts; to friends, I am married to a man, but he is not my husband. Please do not say the word out loud as we both will be embarrassed.' " In the course of time the divorcée finds that the best way to handle this situation is a frank and unapologetic statement of the fact, which explains all the person needs to know and puts a stop to further questioning.

THE CHILDREN

It is a truism to state that the children are the ones really hurt by the divorce. Both girls and boys need and want the love, discipline, and example of a father to supplement the loving care of the mother. "My greatest difficulty in raising my child was to convince my son that he cannot have another daddy so that he no longer looks at any man whether a gas station attendant or a friend as a potential daddy. For a time he also refused to visit homes where there was a daddy." Often children of divorce feel strange when with other children who have fathers. "The children find it difficult to explain their status to their friends and are envious of the children who have fathers. Often they seek out the companionship of children whose parents are divorced or have some marriage difficulty."

The use of visitation rights varies greatly. In our sample of respondents, sixteen fathers see their children regularly, eleven do so on rare occasions, and fifteen never see them. In sixteen cases these visits are upsetting, and in eleven they are not. Sometimes the children do not wish to go with their fathers, especially when forced to be with the second wife. The father who sees the children for only a few hours and can act as a Santa Claus has a great advantage over the mother who must discipline the children and say "no" to them at times. Yet even the children react against only an occasional appearance of Santa Claus. "The children are delighted to see their father and spend weeks afterward living and hoping to see him again, watching for the mail and running for the phone. But when he does not contact them bitterness sets in." Despite all the difficulties, the children do have a right to as much of a father as he cares to be, and the mother should not destroy the image of the father. If he is not well and cannot face responsibilities, this should be explained in such a way that the children will still love and pray for him. The children have a right to a father even if their mother does not have a husband!

WIFE AND EX-HUSBAND

The attitude of the divorced wife to her ex-husband depends on whether she is emotionally as well as legally divorced. It is an established fact that sometimes the legal divorce precedes the emotional one. The wife who still loves her husband and hopes against hope for a reconciliation suffers very much. Seven women among those responding to our questionnaire said that they still love their husbands, and nine were not certain. In most cases the husband's visits to see or pick up the children disturbs the divorced woman with painful memories and present angers and frustrations. The well-adjusted divorcée is able gradually to think about or even see her husband without allowing her emotions of either love or hate to overpower her. But she does pray for him.

THE DIVORCÉE AND HER FAMILY

Most of the families were very understanding and helpful at the time of the divorce. Some were embarrassed by the presence of their divorced daughter but most gave all possible aid and assistance. Only one woman wrote this sad statement: "They never accepted me before or after the divorce."

Many divorcées have to move back to their parents' homes for financial reasons. The usual difficulty is that the parents are over-protective and try to do too much for the daughter and her children. "My mother felt that the tragic mistake on my part gave me no right to make any decisions for myself. She tried to override me in every-thing." The divorced woman at home has to be a daughter to her family and a mother to her children, and usually is caught in the middle. Independence is a great necessity for the divorcée. In most cases it is better to live apart from the family so that the daughter feels mature and independent. In this way, too, interference with the raising of the children is lessened.

THE DIVORCÉE AND FRIENDS

It is not always easy for the divorcée to keep her old friends or to make new ones. Only nine of the thirty who did maintain contact with the friends of their marriage years saw them with any degree of frequency. Twenty-one had lost all contact with them.

New friends have been made through work, religious and political activities, and the Stella Maris group. Work with the children in the Brownies, the Cubs, the school, the parish cafeteria, and the P.T.A. has led to some fine friendships. Still, social contacts are very difficult for divorcées in our couple-structured society. They do not like to associate with others who either feel sorry for them or seek to find a new husband for them.

Often a divorcée lacks confidence and is afraid to open herself to others. "I am a devout coward and I feel if I don't get too close to people I will not get hurt. I am overly sensitive and lack confidence even though it does not always show." But new friends have been made by the friendliness of the divorced woman. "I have made friends by being interested in people and by being friendly and appearing to be happy." "It seems as though I am drawn more to the young work-

ing mothers who are closer to my state of life than the single girl or the
older career girl."

DIVORCÉES AND DATING

The divorcée has to make a difficult decision about dating. Her own
feminine nature prompts her to seek and enjoy the friendship and companionship of men. Twenty-eight of the fifty-one women in our sample
say they have dated since becoming divorced. If a woman has had a
happy marriage she misses this kind of companionship and wishes it
to continue; if she has had an unhappy marriage she wants to prove
to herself that she is capable of a happy marriage. In both instances,
she is attracted to men and marriage. Even though she may be bitter
and distrustful of all men after the divorce, she may gradually begin to
think that all men are not too bad. Then she may start to have an
occasional date with different men with no intention of getting serious
and falling in love. She feels that she must have fun and recreation
and needs the companionship of a man to have this. There is always
the danger that she will meet the "one and only" who really would
make the perfect husband and father except that she is not free to
marry him. Dating is dangerous and every Catholic divorcée who
entered an invalid marriage did so because she dated. Most of the
women in our sample have found dating "too heady a wine" for them.
The desire that many women have to date is not helped a bit by the
encouragement given by well-meaning friends.

Here are some of their reactions to dating: "I feel lonesome and
do miss dating, but I never allow myself to dwell on these thoughts
because I realize they are dangerous." "Usually dating only brings more
frustration as most of the men are looking for more than companionship." "Yes, I did date, and to my regret. When I came to my senses
it was hard for me to stop. It seems as though there was always a
man there blocking the view of everything I held dear—my children,
my family, my faith. Knowing that this was wrong did not seem to
help me. I was not wearing my wedding ring, so I decided to buy a
friendship ring and wear it as though it were a wedding ring, to remind
myself and to warn all others off." "Yes, I did date, but I have found
this impossible if I wish to receive the sacraments."

Many of the divorcées have definite thoughts about remarriage. Only
sixteen have seriously considered remarriage but many of them wish
they were free to marry again. "This problem has caused me the most
doubts, kept me from my religion for a time, and has caused me the

most concern. To be married and yet not to be married, to be a woman and yet not allowed to be a woman in the physical sense is part of what we must accept. Forced celibacy is rough and without my spiritual advisor I shudder to think of what may have happened. Then came along the Stella Maris group and now I have hope." "I was all set to remarry and I was ready to fight my Church, my family, my children, convention, my ex-husband without the slightest thought as to the results for me and the children. But the prayers of my family to the Blessed Mother caused me to come to my senses. I was able to gain my strength back and have since lost the deep bitterness that I felt."

This desire for remarriage is seen in the attitude of the divorcées toward an annulment. Twenty-five considered an annulment, twenty-one did not, and five did not answer this question. One woman consulted fifteen priests. Some of those who knew they had no grounds for an annulment wished that they did.

RELATION WITH THE CHURCH

The relation of the divorcée with the Catholic clergy, religious, and laity is a very sensitive one. The Church has preached so strongly on the sanctity of marriage and the evils of divorce that the term Catholic divorcée seems to be a contradiction. One is either Catholic or divorced. She cannot be both. Twenty-one of our respondents said that the Church was really interested in them, nineteen thought that the Church was not, five gave a "yes-and-no" answer, and six stated that they gave the Church little or no chance to help them. Those who did receive help from individual priests usually contented themselves with giving a simple "yes" answer to the question. But those who did not obtain assistance and thought that the Church was not interested in them were often quite bitter in their responses.

"I went to see three different priests and never at any time did I feel that I was anything but a burden and an imposition. Never was I made to feel that the Church cared." "My help came only in the form of the sacraments which continued to sustain me." "I felt that no one was really interested. After being referred to the Chancery I felt that no one in the parish cared if I remained a Catholic or not. But in fairness," the same woman continues, "I did not make much effort to know any of the parish priests, so some of this must be my fault. But I think there is improvement now in the way marriage cases are handled in the parish and in the Chancery." "Not the Church *per se*, but I was extraordinarily fortunate in meeting compassionate and wise priests and nuns. The Church as a body of men seems impatient with us, eager to sweep us under the carpet as unsightly mistakes. However, as long as the Church provides me with an avenue to God I don't really care. Through the Church, I receive Communion, the source of my life, and for that I am eternally grateful. I do distinguish between the Church and the sacraments as divine and the clergy as human. The clergy are men who do their best but, after all, they are just men faced with a difficult problem." "I thought the priest was too busy." "I thought the priest was trying to finish our discussion as quickly as possible. He offered no suggestions or encouragement and merely said that I could never remarry, which I knew before visiting him."

In many cases the divorcée has not fared any better at the hands of the religious and laity. School children are taught without any qualification that it is a sin to get a divorce and come running home to tell mother that she is living in sin. A divorced woman finds it hard to find her place in the Church. "I still don't think that the Church is interested in a divorced woman. I don't fit into school organizations or Church groups because I am single. I don't fit into single groups because I am married. Mostly we are tolerated and sometimes not too graciously." Another woman complains of "the ostracism and assumption by other Catholics that divorcées are immoral." Another expresses this wish: "Why can't married Catholics be made more aware of us so they will not shy away from us?"

A very touchy point is the position of the invalidly married woman in the Church. The woman who is openly not keeping the law of God is made more at home in the Church than the divorced woman who is heroically trying to be faithful to her marriage vows. She is more accepted in the married Ladies Sodality, at social functions such as dances, and the P.T.A. than the woman who is a living witness to the sanctity of sacramental marriage. At times the invalidly married woman holds elective or appointive office in Church organizations. This situation is very difficult to understand and to swallow.

FINANCES

Almost all divorcées have financial problems. Not many of them have money in their own names, or are well cared for by their ex-husbands. Only fifteen of the divorced women in our sample receive regular child-support, fifteen receive it irregularly, and thirteen do not receive any support. Even the fathers who are listed as being regular supporters often fall behind in their payments. One woman who indicated that she receives regular child-support is $180 short for the last year. The child-support money that the court awards is not sufficient to support a child, and the mother must in some way supplement this money. Often the only solution is to move back home and receive some financial help from the family. Sometimes the divorced woman is able to stay at home, swallow her pride for the sake of the children, and seek help from Aid to Dependent Children. But in most cases she has to become a working mother who is forced to make some provision for her children with relatives, a day nursery, foster home, or orphanage while she earns enough to support them. The divorced woman knows that the children need her love and care but above all else they need food and clothing and shelter. Hence she reluctantly leaves home to work, shares the responsibility for their care with others, and misses the joy of being with them when they are young. The fortunate ones are able to stay at home until the children start school.

HELP FOR THE DIVORCÉE

There are many personal suggestions of a psychological and spiritual nature that could be made to help the divorced woman find emotional adjustment and Christian fulfillment. But here we will content ourselves with looking at three groups that offer assistance to her.

The publicity for Parents Without Partners awakens her interest: "Whether you have children full time or 'on visitation'—wouldn't you like to know others in the same position—to talk over common problems, to hold group discussions with psychologists, lawyers, and so forth?" The Catholic divorcée attends a meeting and finds a representative group of widows and widowers, divorced men and divorced women. She enjoys their company very much but soon she realizes that many in the group approve of dating and of a second marriage. She knows that this can be a dangerous atmosphere for one who is lonely, misses the companionship of men, and is tired of supporting and raising the children alone. Unwillingly she stays away from the meetings and socials.

Divorcées Anonymous is dedicated "to preventing the breaking up of homes and the forwarding of all types of activities which will keep the family together." Divorced women serve as counselors to women with marital problems. But the Catholic divorcée can discover that talking about marriage and its problems can open up old wounds that are still not healed. Besides, she may not consider her own failure in marriage as a good qualification for the role of marriage counselor. Also she misses the Catholic atmosphere to which she is accustomed.

STELLA MARIS

The Stella Maris movement was founded in 1958 in St. Louis, Missouri. Its name was suggested by a Poor Clare nun. "Your marriages have been shipwrecked on the stormy sea of life. Therefore you should call upon Mary, the Star of the Sea, to guide you and your children to the eternal shores."

Its primary purpose is explained in a brochure: [1]

> To help the divorced woman find herself and to live a full and positive life in the fulfillment of her responsibilities to God, the Church, her children and community.
>
> The divorced Catholic woman who, by her religious belief, is not free to remarry feels alone in the Catholic as well as in the secular world. Hence, she feels security in the solidarity of a group of women who do live as she must. She is able to accept the fact of her divorce and to go forward to a positive and happy life. The group helps not so much by direct group therapy as by the mutual encouragement, individual aid and the example of other divorced women who are living happy lives. It is not a group whose concern is a backward look to the past, but the forward look to the future.

The secondary purpose is:

> The apostolic purpose of Stella Maris is to assist other legally separated or divorced women to adjust to their new status and to find fulfillment as women and Catholics within the framework of their status as divorced women. It reminds them that the graces of the sacrament of matrimony are still present to help them live without their husbands and to raise their children as children of God.

The founder of the group, the late Father Edward Dowling, S.J., often told the women that their lives were still lived under the influence of the sacrament of matrimony. When they married God promised them all the actual graces needed to act as Christian wives and mothers. And God does not go back on His promise even though the wife does not live with her husband and is raising the children alone. The realization that God gives light for the mind and courage for the will so that she can fulfill all the duties and overcome all the difficulties of her life is a powerful thrust to confidence and action.

[1] Information about the Stella Maris movement can be obtained from Stella Maris, Box 123, Liguori, Missouri 63057.

Since the women realize that they cannot live their lives as witnesses to the sacramental sanctity and Christian permanence of marriage without the grace of God, they have instituted a prayer program for themselves. The biweekly meetings open and close with prayer. Included in the opening prayers is this beautiful one composed by one of the women: "O my God, who didst raise the state of matrimony to a sacrament, grant to us who are endeavoring to uphold its sanctity the ever-continuing grace which comes from this sacrament so that, though we are living without our partners, we may lead chaste lives and raise our children secure in their faith. Grant us the serenity which comes only with the knowledge that we are doing Thy will." The meetings close with the *Memorare* and the blessing of the spiritual director.

The Stella Maris groups in St. Louis, Miami, Florida, and Austin, Minnesota, have sponsored closed retreats for divorced women. The women felt that they really belonged to the group making the retreat and that the retreat master was speaking to all of them and not just to a few of them. The retreats have been so favorably received that they have become annual events in these cities. The members are encouraged to receive Holy Communion each Sunday and on one extra day during the week, if possible. The *Memorare* is recited privately each day for the spiritual and temporal welfare of all the members.

The Stella Maris groups are not organizations but movements, and like all living things they live and grow by adaptation. Prospective members are first invited to a social gathering where they can meet members of the Stella Maris. Both the woman and the Stella Maris members can decide whether the Stella Maris can offer something to the woman and whether the woman wants to become a member. Sometimes a specialized group such as Alcoholics Anonymous or Recovery, Inc. would more meet the needs of the divorced woman. In the experience of the St. Louis group, ventilation of a woman's emotions about her marriage and divorce is best done privately with the spiritual director, a psychiatrist, or a mature member. When some of the meetings were devoted to detailed descriptions of marriage and divorce problems many of the members were greatly disturbed because painful memories were brought back. Interest in the group and attendance at meetings dropped off when this public-ventilation method was followed. It has been found absolutely necessary to devote the principal part of each meeting to a study and discussion of some point of Catholic doctrine or practice. The St. Louis group has studied the Gospel of St. Matthew, the Book of Genesis, and is now engaged in a course in psychology. Discussion is not held rigidly to the topic and many points of interest are brought up and discussed during the meetings. There is also a small lending library which the members are encouraged to use.

SOCIAL LIFE

The members of this group are not staid and solemn women who sit around and feel sorry for themselves. They are happy and well-adjusted women who enjoy many good times together. Each month a member prepares some social event which she feels the members will enjoy. Dinners at restaurants, Dutch treat and spaghetti dinners at homes, a tour of the zoo with the youngsters (fifty attended this, the largest crowd at any event), outdoor picnics and swims, hayride parties, trips to the theater and shows, and ice skating parties were happy occasions that left memories. Besides the group activities many friendships developed that lead to many pleasant hours spent together.

The Stella Maris movement has received publicity in the secular and religious press and has begun to grow. There are active chapters in Miami; Austin; Appleton, Wisconsin; St. Louis; Detroit, Michigan and Garden Grove, California. Priests and divorced women from many sections of the country have written for informaton about forming a group.

The aim is not to keep the divorced women in a ghetto but to help them find themselves so that they can take their rightful place in the community and in the Church. These women who are so lacking in self-confidence regain this confidence by the example and encouragement of others. With this newly found confidence they are better mothers because they are better persons. These are some typical comments from members: "I was glad to know that the Catholic Church was still interested in me and welcomed me at the altar rail." "I no longer feel like an outcast. Now I have a sense of belonging. I have a place in society." "The Stella Maris group helped me stay away from an invalid marriage by showing me that I did not have to date or remarry to be happy." "The example and encouragement of the group has helped me follow God's laws, when my own weakness and the encouragement of others made it seem so easy and even so necessary to go against the law of God and of the Church against remarriage after divorce." "Through guidance, friendship, and the example of the Stella Maris group, I have found a way toward spiritual development and emotional security."

Catholic divorcées need much help and understanding. Priests can take the initiative in this great apostolate for these women who feel so neglected and abandoned. Every priest knows divorced women who would benefit by knowing other women in the same situation. He can introduce them, encourage them to form a group and serve as an active spiritual director. These women will finally believe that the Church is really interested in them and will grow into fine Christian women of whom the Church can justly be proud.

REFERENCES

Champagne, Marian. *Facing life alone.* Indianapolis: Bobbs-Merrill, 1964.
Despert, J. Louise. *Children of divorce.* Garden City, N.Y.: Doubleday, 1962.
Faherty, W. B. (S.J.) *Living life alone.* New York: Sheed & Ward, 1964.
Fleming, T. J. The divorced ones. *This Week* Magazine, January 26, 1964.
Goode, W. J. *Women in divorce.* New York: Free Press, 1965.
Jones, Eve. *Raising your child in a fatherless home.* New York: Free Press, 1963.
Kling, S. G. *A complete guide to divorce.* New York: Random House, 1963.

The Widow

MADELINE H. ENGEL

Madeline Helena Engel received her A.B. degree from Barnard College in 1961. She then came to Fordham University for graduate work in sociology, receiving her M.A. degree in 1963 and her Ph.D. in 1966. During her graduate work she was variously a research assistant in the Sociology Department at Barnard College, and a teaching assistant, a research fellow and an instructor in the Sociology Department at Fordham. At the time of the Institute in 1965, she was a lecturer, and is currently an instructor in the Department of Sociology of Hunter College of the City University of New York. Dr. Engel is a member of the American Sociological Association, the American Catholic Sociological Society, and the American Academy of Political and Social Science.

Bereavement is an ubiquitous phenomenon, as is the home broken by death. In many primitive societies, this sudden rupture of the family was almost automatically mended by some socially institutionalized mechanism. Despite the fact that a woman generally died at an early age, she knew exactly what to expect and what would be expected of her in the event of her husband's death. She was socialized to be cognizant of the possibility of widowhood and she was prepared to meet the situation. Her cultural setting absorbed for her the experience which in the modern Western world causes shock and strain for the widow and her fatherless children. A recent study noted, ". . . strangely, it is [in] our highly civilized part of the world where women live longer and men are known to die earlier, that there is no preparation or pattern for life as a widow" (Langer, 1957, p. 26).

The adjustment made by a widow varies sharply from society to society, and decade to decade, in relation to her personality and the definition of the situation provided for her by the cultural system in which she is a participant. Some groups define and expect a particular status, role and function for the bereaved woman. Others, however, notably those in the United States, lack consensus on such definitions and leave the widow to her own resources, frustrated in a situation for which she has had no anticipatory socialization, no preparation. Furthermore, American society actively deters adjustment to widowhood. In the absence of clear, explicit expectations and socialization for meeting death, it not only acts in ways less functional than primitive societies, but at times acts in ways *dysfunctional* for widows. For example, our society sets no standards as to the period of time, form of dress, or sequence of social relations for those in mourning. Moreover, it places a high premium on independence and self-sufficiency, equating their absence with weakness in emotional and moral fiber (Langer, 1957, p. 93). Clearly, when a widow must question her own adequacy if she seeks help, comfort, or structure in her crisis and new life, society itself has precipitated part of that crisis. The American way of life seems to hinder, rather than facilitate, a woman's adjustment to the death of her husband.

WIDOWS IN THE PRIMITIVE WORLD

Prior to the advent of modern Western civilization, communities generally defined the behavior which they expected of widows. In the first place they had formal rituals of mourning, periods of isolation, and special dress marking the woman's own ceremonial death, followed by a ceremony marking her rebirth (Langer, 1957, pp. 26-28). In the second place, the communities systematically made practical arrangements for the widow, and gave to her a set of explicit rules governing her behavior, especially her remarriage.

For example, suttee was a practice, common among Hindus, whereby a woman could choose to be cremated on her husband's funeral pyre. The practice provided the woman with a voluntary means of acting honorably and virtuously according to cultural prescriptions. Where suttee gained religious approval, the widow gained not only social rewards from her action, but also religious ones—specifically, she was assured that her own and her husband's family would be cleansed of evil and that she herself would become a saint.

Levirate marriage is another practice illustrative of a culturally recommended action. Many ancient peoples, the Hebrews included, required or permitted a man to marry his brother's widow, especially if she was childless, so as to keep property within the clan or perpetuate the family name (Gen 38: 8-10; Ruth 4: 5). Although its major functions were familial, the practice also served to arrange for the care of the widow herself. The custom carried the weight of social, religious, and legal sanction. The Old Testament records specific comment regarding society's obligation to protect the weak, widows included, who are without human protector or physical force to defend their rights (Exod 22: 21). The civil law of Israel gave to the deceased husband's brother an obligation cast in terms of family loyalty. When he failed to live up to this duty, he fell under the curse of abject poverty, and the widow had the right to disgrace him publicly (Deut 25: 5-10).

Societies which did not practice levirate marriage, for example ancient Greece, often bequeathed the wife to a close male relative or friend who would be her protector (Langer, 1957, p. 28). Other primitive peoples explicitly forbade remarriage or disapproved of it, punishing such action with social, religious, and/or legal ostracism. Such was the practice in traditional Japan and Nepal (Bernard, 1956, pp. 26-30).

The preceding is meant not as an apologia for specific primitive actions but rather as an indication that the various patterns mentioned served economic, religious, biological, and quasi-political functions. They were primarily means by which group solidarity and allegiance were assured. But when combined with generally strong religious and kinship systems and respect for elders (widows were usually aged), primitive social patterns and cultural dictates also helped the widow to face her situation. American society, however, with its secular and individualized ethic is less helpful to her. As a group, we fail to define for the woman what she is to do; we fail to sustain her emotionally, especially if she happens to be aged. An American woman is ill-equipped to acknowledge the possibility—probability—that her family will be broken, in time, by the death of her husband. She has never consciously expected this. Her expectation, socially inculcated, was one of never-ending marital bliss, and so widowhood is an experience for which she is unprepared and in which she constantly feels frustrated.

THE AMERICAN WIDOW: AN OVERVIEW

Unlike ethnologists involved in a study of primitives, those who would study American widows are faced with a paucity of data regarding the family crisis which results in dismemberment and, all too often, demoralization (Eliot, 1942, p. 490). A few pertinent insights are to be found in American literature:

> In the more somber tradition of American literature, reaching from Hawthorne, Melville and Poe to Faulkner and Hemingway, one finds a tragic depth that belies the surface thinness of ordinary American death attitudes. By an effort of the imagination the great writers faced problems which the culture in action is reluctant to face—the fact of death, its mystery, and its place in the back-and-forth shuttling of eternal recurrence [Lerner, 1957, p. 618].

Scattered information is also available in narratives by widows, occasionally published in popular women's magazines, and in the files of religious counselors and doctors. The federal government and insurance companies provide a broad statistical view, which complements this case perspective. These agencies compile statistics on widows in order to facilitate the allocation of finances, especially during war years and immediately thereafter. According to the Metropolitan Life Insurance Company, the United States contained, by 1960, more than eight million widows, indicating a steady increase over more than three decades. One-half of these women are over the age of 65, with another two-fifths falling between the ages of 45 and 64, and the remainder being under 45. Most widows (73 percent) live in urban areas, and most maintain their own households which, especially in the case of young widows, are likely to include children (*Science News Letter,* 1954). Widows far outnumber widowers, a fact attributable to the higher death rate of men, their higher remarriage rate, and their greater age at marriage. Men are less isolated financially, have a greater need to remarry especially when they are left with small children, and fall victim to fewer subtle social conventions which restrict remarriage (Eliot, 1942, p. 495).

However, in all, there is little objective or empirical material pertinent to a study of American widows, and there is virtually no integrated conceptual analysis of that which does exist. Some of the reasons for this dearth of material lie deep within the American attitude toward death and the taboos which surround the phenomenon, making it a sacred area which provokes an anxious, recoiling response.

The typical American, we are told, living in our affluent society, is interested or concerned with death only when it can be used to bolster his pride, assuage his guilt and remorse, and symbolize his status (Mitford, 1963, p. 15). The elaborate funeral now customary in America is devoid of meaningful ritual or social function in the primitive sense, and is couched in pseudo-psychological terms and euphemisms (Mitford, 1963, pp. 17-18). It would seem that the sugar-coated is the only side of death for which we are prepared, or which we find tolerable. Relevant to this point, one study of American national character observed:

> Whether through fear of the emotional depths or because of a drying up of the sluices of religious intensity, the American avoids dwelling on death or even coming to terms with it: he finds it morbid and recoils from it, surrounding it with word avoidance (Americans never die, but "pass away") and various taboos of speech and practice. A "funeral parlor" is decorated to look like a bank; everything in the funeral ceremony is done in hushed tones, as if it were something furtive, to be concealed from the world; there is so much emphasis on being dignified that the ceremony often loses its quality of dignity [Lerner, 1957, p. 619].

America, the very society geared to mental hygiene and science, is the one least able to understand death or console those facing it. The paradox is tragic for the widow and society as a whole:

> In some of the primitive cultures there is difficulty in understanding the cause of death; it seems puzzling and even unintelligible. Living in a scientific culture, Americans have a ready enough explanation of how it comes, yet they show little capacity to come to terms with the fact of death itself and with the grief that accompanies it [Lerner, 1957, p. 619].

We never prepare the young or the old for death; we never help them to realize that death is as much a fact of life as is birth. We ignore the possibility of widowhood, and when it comes we try, at all possible costs, to rush the woman through the initial phases of the experience, by quickly burying her husband and forcing her to resume "normal" social relations and activity. The very speed with which the process is forced upon her retards adjustment, rather than facilitating it, but enables those around her to avoid dwelling on death or the values that transcend life. In the long run, such culturally induced practices are more detrimental than helpful to all concerned.

Given American attitudes towards death, the study of bereavement is seen as a pathological absorption in the gruesome and morbid. Almost every cultural group fears death, yet in most this carries with it a fascinated absorption not found in America.

> The recoil from death in itself betrays a lack of sensitivity toward its implication for the spirit. . . . American culture cuts away the sensitivity

to death and grief, suicide and immortality, emphasizing the here-and-now as it emphasizes youth and action [Lerner, 1957, p. 620].

It was not too long ago that the term "pathological behavior" was leveled at those who sought to study and discuss sexual practices or mental hygiene. These too were once areas hidden by shadows of fear and guilt, to which one could allude only in jokes, novels and plays (Eliot, 1930, p. 544). The topic of death is now cast in this position, surrounded with a culture complex of folkways, taboos, superstitions, and compulsions which make research all but impossible, and allow allusion to death only in black wit, or fictionalized contexts; never in candid, objective terms.

Another part of the research problem is internal to science, and quite divorced from the values with which its would-be subject is imbued. The collection of detailed case analyses is time-consuming; they must be awaited and meticulously recorded over the months, even years, of mourning, bereavement, and familial adjustment. Such research may provide interesting insights but rarely permits generalization. Furthermore, since widowhood does not involve a violation or contravention of mores, as does divorce or desertion, it arouses little interest (Komarovsky & Waller, 1945, p. 450). Lastly, grief or bereavement, adjustment, and many of the other relevant aspects of the widow's frustrated situation can not be quantified or even measured. This too deters scientific research, especially within American behavioral and social science, which is mathematically oriented.

Despite the problems inherent in research, the skills of the scientist must be brought to bear upon widowhood, if it is to be better understood and guided, and made more bearable. When a society fails to define expectations for a widow, and then militates against objective research into her chaotic situation, it does her a disservice. It leaves the frustrated, unprepared woman at the hands of well-meaning friends and "mortuary salesmen" (Eliot, 1942, p. 517). It leaves the public without the insight necessary to improve mental hygiene and family functioning (Hansen & Hill, 1964, p. 815). A few researchers have pioneered in the study of bereavement in general, and widowhood in specific. Their rudimentary studies have, over the last forty years, begun to supply us with relevant information. In order of development, these studies can be categorized as: economic, psychiatric, and sociological. Each provides us with a different set of findings and each makes a unique, and still unintegrated, contribution to our knowledge.

THE ECONOMIC VIEW

Early studies of the widow's situation were exclusively concerned with her economic status (Fritz, 1930, p. 553). The economic aspects of her situation are those which are most immediate and obvious, even to the untrained eye. They are, too, the needs least involved with death itself and those which an affluent society is relatively well-equipped to meet. Since the mid-1920s the widow has been afforded social security payments or a pension for herself and her children. Although reception of government funds no longer constitutes acceptance of charity in the public eye, many women have been socialized to refuse them or accept them only with reluctance. Widows prefer, and are encouraged by society, to be self-supporting.

However, the American wife is traditionally protected and kept in relative ignorance of her husband's financial affairs during his life. Once he is dead she is immediately called upon to assume the role of financial manager and expert. Often for the first time, she must now file tax returns, maintain the home or see to its maintenance, take care of insurance premiums and investments, the bank account and the will. Often, too, under the most awkward and stressful conditions, she must meet and work with a lawyer, broker, and banker (*Business Week,* 1955). These are problems faced only by the "fortunate," those widows left with financial resources of their own. Advice, guidance, and practical assistance from a male relative, friend of the family, or professional counselor is most welcome, if offered in such a way as to permit the widow to maintain her independence. Sudden, major changes such as selling the home or moving away from friends and relatives should generally be avoided, but prompt handling of financial matters is crucial (Rochford, 1953, pp. 135-138).

In most cases, the cost of medical care for the now-deceased husband and/or his funeral expenses, exhaust the financial resources of the widow. Fortunately, our society is increasingly oriented towards training women, educating them, and employing them. Resistance to, and resentment of, the working woman and working mother has sharply declined, especially in cases where she is employed out of necessity, as in the case of the average widow. Work can provide the widow with income, security, and new social contacts, but it is a poor substitute for the absorption into a kinship system which was characteristic of societies in the past. Furthermore, working is not without its problems, the least of which is finding a job to which the woman can return after years of absence, or finding a first job when she is middle-aged or older and equipped with only minimal skills. The widow's more severe conflicts and problems, however, may come when she tries to arrange for care of her children during working hours and when she must relearn ways of relating to men. The latter, whether remarriage is the goal or not, is particularly difficult for the already emotionally exhausted woman (Langer, 1957, Ch. 4 *passim*).

Familiarizing the woman with the family's total financial picture, from the time of her adolescence or, at least, from the earliest days of her marriage, would greatly ease her entry into the economic sphere as well as the familial. It would also alleviate much of the economic panic which comes with finding herself a widow. Extension of, and new attitudes towards, governmental subsidies, day-care centers for the children of working mothers, and vocational training for adults, are desirable if the widow is to make a successful, less frustrated adjustment in society. At the very least, counselors and the public should be equipped with knowledge of existing services, and they should be able to direct the widow to relevant agencies as soon as her needs arise.

THE PSYCHOLOGICAL VIEW

World War I and the years immediately thereafter produced an ever-increasing number of widows. The 1920s also produced a growing interest in Freudian psychology. The government had no sooner acted to establish financial support for widows, than the prime interest in the academic arena shifted from the socio-economic to the sociopsychological aspects and processes of life as a widow (Eliot, 1930, p. 549). Although hindered by attitudes and other research problems previously mentioned, several scientists began to study grief and the readjustments which follow it.

Psychosocial analysis of grief

Thomas D. Eliot and his students led the field, with a series of case studies, monographs, and articles on bereavement. Their works suggested that one of the most fruitful approaches to the social-psychological analysis of grief was that which viewed adjustment in terms of stages. When made applicable to a study of the widow, these range from the initial shock phase, through interim periods, to a stage of final readjustment, in which remarriage is but one type of response.

Bereavement is a family crisis, which occurs within a cultural system replete with its unique rituals, mores, and attitudes. But it is also an individual experience, which can severely and permanently affect the depths of the widow's personality. The immediate effects of bereavement, according to most researchers, are intense longing and grief, manifested in one or another forms of sorrow. The patterns typically observed are:

1). impulsive, unrestrained wailing and violence; or
2). tearless, mute self-control; or
3). paralyzed discouragement; or
4). active frenzy [Becker, 1933].

Each can be a relatively normal, temporary response to the same cause— the death of one's husband. But society defines which form is the *most* desirable expression of sorrow; Americans favor the self-controlled response, especially while the widow is in the public eye or with company (Eliot, 1929, p. 185; Eliot, 1932, p. 88).

The second phase of reaction is also socially conditioned, and judged in terms of social standards. In it, one or more psychological mechanisms are unconsciously called into play by the widow to insulate and protect her in the crisis (Langer, 1957, p. 16). The mechanisms observed during this stage of adjustment range from escape through drugs or suicide to repression, masochism, sublimation, identification with the deceased, and compensation through rationalization and ritual. Identification and compensation are the favored mechanisms in American society (Eliot, 1929, p. 186), and a widow may suffer psychic conflict and censure if her actions do not correspond to this preconceived, admired model. American society minimizes the standardization of grief, yet many women develop a concept of what they "should" do and "should" feel. When they do not act or feel in this way, they develop guilt and anxiety (Eliot, 1929, p. 187). If the society were to set no patterns whatsoever, or very clear patterns, much of this guilt would be eliminated.

The secondary reaction usually lasts until the end of the funeral activities (Eliot, 1932, pp. 88-92). Many widows fight against the reality of their situation. Finally, some acquiesce, and play an active role in arranging for their husband's funeral, without being overly dependent upon others. These women realistically comply with society's implicit behavioral code. Others act in an overly excited manner and attempt to manage the funeral single-handedly. They become so absorbed in detailed arrangements as to almost forget their meaning. Still others react with protest, levelling accusations against others: God, the devil, the doctor, friends, themselves. This type of response typically leads to a minimal role in the arrangement of funeral rites. A final group of widows may be characterized as detached and/or despondent. They are completely nonactive, and the period of mourning aggravates their psychological state. In the United States, the acquiescent response, facilitated by semi-formal mourning, is the most desirable response. Other patterns represent extreme responses which in our culture should be guarded against.

A transitional stage falls between this initial adjustment and the final adjustment. During this phase, the woman's response is that of trial-and-error, especially in interpersonal relations. She alternates between activity and depression, forced sociability and attention-seeking. A society which fails to set clear-cut standards and patterns of expectation leaves the widow without a storehouse of realistic notions to fall back on, and the notions she has internalized are frustrated by the very absence of her husband.

Lastly, most women repattern their lives and resume social relations in a normal schedule of activities. Some never reach this stage of adjustment, but seclude themselves, suffer, and resist consolation and help. However, most widows do reach the final stage, the last plateau, and find release for their tensions and frustrations in substitute relations including remarriage; increased activity on the job, in volunteer work, or in women's clubs; identification with the role of the deceased, and phantasy, which is a psychological safety-valve, when it does not completely exclude reality (Waller & Hill, 1951, p. 63).

The Widow's need for personal relationships

In almost every phase of readjustment, the woman intuitively seeks to share her chaotic despair with others, to evoke their sympathy. However, her behavior estranges others, alienates them, and makes them uneasy. She is apathetic, withdrawn, inconsistent, and is not a good companion (Marris, 1958, p. 125). She reacts in unexpected ways which confuse her friends, because the behavior does not meet their expectations. They, in turn, react with behavior which does not meet the widow's expectations, and further frustrates her. She is left alone, deserted; her friends appear to lack tact and sympathy. While undergoing the changes and upheavals in her life, the woman must believe she is acting as her husband would have wished. She must also feel that she is needed and that she can talk with friends, if she so chooses. The outpouring of emotion should take place under the "tourniquet principle," whereby alternately it is released and allowed to flow, and then shut off (Eliot, 1955, p. 344). Contact with others, in suitable amounts and contexts, can do much to ease grief and the practical help (e.g., housework, caring for children, funeral arrangements) is invaluable (Marris, 1958, p. 126).

From the psychological vantage point (Marris, 1958, p. 21), a widow is a woman whose grief aggravates or precipitates physical ailments, to which she gives voice in search of comfort and attention. She is apathetic and unable to understand what is going on around her. The widow often loses contact with reality, and feels her life is futile and without purpose; she feels she has no reason to live. She is a woman withdrawn from people, rejecting the consolation or interests which might provide her with an escape from sorrow. This last point is especially significant. The woman seeks personal relationships and needs them desperately; yet, at the same time, she acts in ways which fend them off. She is lonely, but she inadvertently pushes people away. Her paradoxical and inconsistent behavior is difficult to understand, especially if the person to whom she is relating is unprepared for it.

Perhaps the problem is largely that the American woman has been trained to be a wife and a mother, even a grandmother, but never a widow. She is unprepared for this stage of life and finds it completely frustrating (Langer, 1957, p. 12). Sorrow is a frustration of impulse, a cry for help and security, and not simply a sign of weakness or failure (Shand, 1920, pp. 311-314; Becker, 1933, p. 391). It consciously rebels against distraction, but unconsciously seeks and finds it. Much understanding of the widow's situation is to be found in the concept of "frustrated expectations," and the role of a society in creating them or alleviating them.

Even under the best social conditions, with which our widows are *not* blessed, acute grief is a definite syndrome. It has a psychological and somatic symptomatology, which usually occurs immediately after a crisis (Lindemann, 1944, p. 141). A morbid or abnormal response is one which is postponed or delayed, exaggerated or apparently entirely absent, or indicative of other distortions of the normal syndrome. These include: overactivity, illness—especially the one which claimed the life of the deceased—agitated depression with suicidal tendencies, lasting alteration and loss of social relations, and great hostility against specific persons (e.g., the doctor) (Lindemann, 1944, p. 142). Generally, even despite society's negative influence, these distortions do not occur, and the widow enters into successful "grief work," by which she is emancipated from the bondage of the deceased, and readjusts to her new environment by forming new relationships (Lindemann, 1944, p. 145). Religious and psychiatric counselors can be most helpful at this juncture, by providing the bereaved with spiritual support and insight into death and ritual.

The Widow's altered self-image

The social living of the widow changes. Her feelings about her husband, friends, relatives, and herself are altered. The husband's name or image evokes guilt, loyalty, and especially rose-colored memories (Marris, 1958, p. 75). Reactions towards friends and relatives run the gamut from anger, resentment, and envy (especially of those whose families are intact), to hostility and projected blame. The woman is absorbed in herself and her own problems. But the immediacy of daily living, particularly caring for children, leaves her exhausted, empty, restless, and unable to cope with the situation by herself (Langer, 1957, p. 18). So it is that she must turn to the very people towards whom she has ill feelings.

The widow needs to completely rebuild her self-image. She needs to reestablish an identity, as a person and especially as a woman. Her husband's death leaves her emotionally and sexually frustrated, and leads her to question her femininity. She loses esteem for herself as a woman, and is confused about the role and degree of dependence that is appropriate to her position. The widow becomes increasingly egocentric; she suddenly becomes aware that she too may die; she is afraid of being alone, of going out alone. The woman feels there is no one with whom she can share her anxieties and dreams, her worries and hopes. All too often she clamps down on her children, restricting their mobility, so that she will have company and they will be protected from a world she now sees as dangerous (Ilgenfritz, 1961, p. 38). The widow is hostile towards others, especially men, who, she thinks, view her as "fair game" (Ilgenfritz, 1961, p. 39). She is, at once, outwardly less dependent upon others and inwardly more dependent upon them (Waller & Hill, 1951, p. 487).

Presuming that the widow loved her husband, certain laws of sorrow can be stated which summarize and give insight into her behavior (Shand, 1920, pp. 320-370):

1. sorrow is attracted to its object (the husband) and seeks to maintain union with it—the widow idealizes the memory of her husband, is loyal and faithful to that memory, and resents those who would distract her from her grief;

2. sorrow restores the beloved object—the widow develops a rich phantasy life and storehouse of daydreams in which she recaptures idealized moments and events once shared with her husband;
3. when sorrow is impeded, it increases; when it is allowed controlled expression, it decreases—the widow must be allowed to verbalize and demonstrate her feelings, if she is to make a satisfactory readjustment to life;
4. sorrow decreases when feelings are or can be expressed openly and in a group, so that they evoke sympathy—the widow should not be left alone, even if she is not very good company;
5. sorrow tends to arouse feelings of anger, futility, and contempt—the widow's resentment and depression are normal responses which, in time, will pass, if she is helped by those around her.

Sorrow establishes and preserves love. It becomes dysfunctional for the widow's personality only when it is uncontrolled, relative to the form and degree of expression common in her society (Shand, 1920, pp. 366-370).

Clinical accounts and psychoanalytic case-records provide us with clues as to the range of normal responses to the crisis of widowhood. They, therefore, help us to determine a course of action for the widow which will effect better mental hygiene and family functioning. Eliot has suggested, for these reasons, that narratives or diaries be kept by those involved in crises. The case records would include detailed accounts of the deceased and the nature of his death; the social adjustment of the widow after bereavement (e.g., changes in her interpersonal relations, attitudes, religious practice); her experiences during the crisis (e.g., reception of the news, immediate response, telling others, later feelings, care for the body, neighborly services, funeral and burial arrangements); comments by the bereaved woman on the study of which she has allowed her experiences to become a part (Eliot, 1933). The emphasis in such a study is on normal stress, not abnormal distress (Eliot, 1930, p. 545), so as to make the widow more aware of what to expect and less frustrated. Without a modern, empirically based image, people react to the widow in terms of a fictionalized or archaic stereotype, and implicitly or explicitly criticize her when she does not conform to their preconceptions (Eliot, 1930, p. 546). Some women find consolation in group therapy, clubs for parents without partners, and recreational outings with other families with similar problems (Ilgenfritz, 1961, p. 41). However, more adequate solutions to the widow's varied problems might be forthcoming, if better and more complete psychiatric and psychological data were forthcoming. This necessitates a revision of society's attitudes, so as to permit scientific research to aid those in crisis situations.

THE SOCIOLOGICAL VIEW

The psychological approach added a new dimension to the study of widows. The sociological approach examines these women in a still broader context. Within this framework, two distinct types of studies can be discerned: (1) studies of interpersonal relations; and (2) structural functional analyses.

Studies of interpersonal relations

The widow, regardless of her economic position or personality, can not be understood completely unless she is also viewed in terms of the roles and statuses which she assumes in her community. The death of her husband leaves the woman without some of her former roles, notably that of wife, and creates for her new ones, perhaps that of employee. The more immediate role transformations occur within the family setting, leaving the widow with a new burden of responsibility for her children. For some, these changes mark a new solidarity in a family now unified by crisis; for others, it marks a decline in solidarity and aggravated intrafamilial conflict. In all changes, the woman has a tendency to take on roles played by her late husband. For example, she often tries to be both mother and father to her children.

If her roles change abruptly, the woman may face a conflict in them, especially if she is young, when her desire to work and rebuild a life for herself may conflict with her obligation to her small children. In other words, her role as employee or companion conflicts with that of being a mother. Once her roles take on a new configuration, she may become confused, especially in her relations with men. Her husband's very presence or existence had protected her, but now she is susceptible to advances and open to sexual exploitation. The combination of new roles, conflicts among them, and the widow's confusion over them, greatly affect her identity or self-image. In this regard, the psychological and sociological frameworks are particularly compatible and complementary.

An emphasis on interpersonal relations leads to the conclusion that the degree of bereavement and the length of time needed for the widow to adjust will depend in large part not only on the more objective characteristics of the deceased—e.g., his age—but more importantly on his role in her life. Where he was a (the) key figure, her loss will obviously be greater than where his role was merely one of several important ones. The woman who was fairly independent of her husband, by virtue of her personality and the roles which she played within the household and outside of it, will be better equipped to deal with her husband's death than one who was completely dependent upon him. The latter's roles cast her in a position of submission, in which she reflected in a minor way the socio-economic, political, religious, and other statuses of her husband.

Structural functional analyses

Since the 1940s, with the war and the special problems which it generated, the skills of structural functionalists have been brought to bear on a study of family disorganization, including widowhood. Researchers have found that bereavement and adjustment to widowhood vary, not only with the status-role set of the woman, but also with the structure of the groups to which she and her husband belong, and by which they have been socialized.

Structural functionalists have been interested in a number of aspects of widowhood, including the functions served by anticipatory grief and mourning. Anticipatory grief refers to a separation of the spouses by something other than death (e.g., the husband's hospitalization or departure with the armed forces), which slowly prepares the wife for total separation, and eases her adjustment to widowhood by reducing the intensity of the husband-wife relationship during a prolonged period before death, so that when it comes it is less of a shock (Lindemann, 1944, p. 147). However, if the husband survives and returns to the wife, the separation may have been dysfunctional, because it leaves the woman detached, independent, and virtually unable to relate to him. But this is an extreme case, which does not invalidate the notion that preparation for death is helpful to those left behind. Forewarning and partial shock serve as pre-bereavement rehearsals, and reduce the effects of the final shock of death (Eliot, 1955, p. 342). Previous bereavements will act in the same way, and will cushion other deaths for the survivor.

1. *Function served by mourning.* Mourning too has been subjected to analysis by various researchers. Psychologically oriented theorists discuss it in terms of "grief work," and the benefits to the psyche derived from openly expressed emotion in a controlled manner. Those more sociologically oriented discuss mourning in terms of its role in gradually restoring social functioning and group participation. Both psychologists and sociologists, however, seem to agree that a short period of mourning is usually functional, rather than dysfunctional, for the widow.

Our society may be underemphasizing the importance of mourning with its special dress and ritual (Waller & Hill, 1951, pp. 488-490).

The adjustment to widowhood by native-born, white, middle-class women is not as successful, in some ways, as that by foreign-born, Negro, or lower-class women. The latter groups, along with their emphasis on kin and religion, have a tendency to maintain the mourning ritual. Consider, for example, the Orthodox Jews' practice of sitting *shiveh,* seven days of intensive mourning after the death of a close relative. During these days, everything is done for the widow by distant relatives, in-laws and friends, gathered together to help, to socially recognize the bereavement, and to share in the grief. After the seven-day period, social relations are resumed by the widow, as is relatively normal functioning in society. Although shorter in time, and less formally structured, the wake characteristic of first-generation Irish-American families serves similar functions. In these situations, friends communicate their sentiments and protect the widow in ways far more effective than those which our larger society has devised (Langer, 1957, p. 103). The wake and the practice of sitting *shiveh* are, in terms of public functioning, the reverse of primitive initiation rites (Eliot, 1942, p. 522). The initiation heralded man's entry into the adult world; ethnic practices in America today mark a notice to the world of his withdrawal or exit from it.

2. *The Psycho-social adjustment of the widow.* Growing out of a concern with mourning and its function in reestablishing social relations, theorists have been led to a study of the widow's entire social life. Her contacts with relatives tend to increase, especially immediately after the death of her husband, but her social life is severely reduced and greatly impoverished (Marris, 1958, p. 127). This is particularly true for those widows who had travelled in a circle of married couples, as opposed to same-sex friends. Here again we see why middle-class women may have a harder time adjusting to widowhood than their counterparts in lower socio-economic positions who are accustomed to being with other women, and to being excluded from male activities or shared functions attended by couples (Komarovsky, 1964, esp. Chs. 9, 14).

The widow's status and age-identification change suddenly in the eyes of her friends. This results in a loss of single and dyadic relations and a loss of status, as well as in an image of her as an aging woman (Blau, 1956, p. 202). The most detrimental effects on friendships and social life occur when the widow is a "deviant," that is, when the ma-

jority of her peers are still married. Thus, widowhood is most restrictive
of the young. Class, however, is a contingency factor. The middle-class
woman may be able to reestablish activities which she used to share
with her friends. The lower-class woman lacks this reservoir of relations, and because of finances and social patterns she will not turn to
bridge, shopping, travel, or attending lectures with friends. Instead,
she falls back upon renewed and strengthened kinship ties (Blau, 1961,
pp. 432, 436).

Studies by structural functionalists suggest that the best adjustment
to widowhood is made by those women who, before the death of their
husbands, were relatively independent of them. Economically, the
woman who adjusts best is the one who can fall back upon her own
resources—education, knowledge and skills, and her ability to cope
with bureaucratic structures (Langer, 1957, pp. 236-255). The woman
who is able to find and make use of personal and vocational guidance,
childcare services, legal and social aid, and associations for leisure-time
pursuits, is equipped for a life alone. The woman untrained to operate
in secondary associations, and accustomed only to dealing with family
members and close friends, finds adjustment to widowhood a difficult task.

Repeated studies have shown that the socio-cultural milieu of the
middle class enables its members to cope with bureaucracies, whereas
the lower class does not socialize its members to this particular skill.
In fact, some evidence suggests that the lower class trains its members
to be unable to deal with bureaucracies, and to be alienated and confused by their procedures, red tape, and emphasis on high verbal ability.
Economic adjustment is hindered by poor education, and minority-
group or foreign backgrounds. Although it is true that women in these
groups are accustomed to being employed, they are particularly in need
of community-sponsored economic props and services administered in
a warm, personal way, perhaps through an individual counselor.

It is more difficult to analyze psychosocial adjustment, but it appears, in general, that the very groups which facilitate the economic adjustment of their widows indirectly hamper other aspects of their adjustment. The middle class is characterized by a family system which,
quite unlike that of lower-class and ethnic groups (e.g., the Italians,
Negroes, or Puerto Ricans), operates at a high level of emotional intensity, with little margin for "shock absorption" (Parsons & Fox, 1952).
In the middle class, mates are almost entirely dependent upon each
other and their shared activities for psychological satisfaction (Waller
& Hill, 1951, p. 473). When the husband-wife ties break, the surviving

partner is entirely frustrated and without satisfaction. Her mate is gone and their shared friends disappear. She is cast in the role of a fifth wheel when out with couples who used to be friends of hers and of her husband. In ethnic groups and in the lower class, spouses are relatively less dependent upon each other. A major source of their psychological satisfaction comes from the kinship structure and same-sex friends. The family (kin) absorb the shock of death, and the circle of friends endures. This family system is not unlike that which proved so functional in the primitive world.

Furthermore, death is a part of the everyday life of lower-class and ethnic groups, as witnessed by their high death rates compared to native-born whites of high socio-economic position. Death, therefore, comes as less of a shock to them; it frustrates them less, perhaps because they expect it. Moreover, the middle class, with its secular ethic, has less on which to fall back than the lower class, with its religio-magical value system. Judaic-Christian religious systems provide emotional supports for the survivor through her belief in the immortality of the soul, whereas to the secular, materialistic ethic, death represents merely a meaningless end or finality. The latter provides little comfort for the widow. But a religious woman, prepared for death, who has a position within a larger family unit, is equipped to meet crises and finds them less disrupting than does one reared in the native-born white sectors of our population.

Industrialization and urbanization invariably affect religion and kinship structures, weakening them all. This type of society, e.g., American society, brings to its inhabitants social advantages and goods—mass production, high standards of living, education; but it also brings unanticipated consequences, when in its development religion and kinship are curtailed and nothing is created to fulfill the functions previously met by them. The widow left alone, without guidance or standards, falls victim to her situation, and may resort to extreme behavior. Durkheim, for example, noted the higher relationship between suicide and widowhood as compared with suicide and married life. He explained this correlation in terms of the absence of social controls on the widowed, and their subsequent leanings towards individualism (Durkheim, 1951, pp. 179-180).

More recently, Kraus and Lilienfeld showed that even where death comes by natural causes, widows die younger than married women (*Science News Letter*, 1959, p. 197). The authors offer several possible explanations for this fact: (1) individuals with short survival potential choose like mates; (2) widows shared with the deceased unfavorable environmental conditions; (3) grief, worry, responsibility, and alterations in daily life routines take their toll. If the last hypothesis has any validity, and we believe it has, then society's negligence and responsibility for this death rate are indicated. Community programs are necessary to fulfill functions once served by the kinship system now destroyed under the pressures of civilization and modern living. In our society, it is up to the community to see to the care of widows and their adjustment.

A complete restructuring or rehauling of society, with a return to a rural, underdeveloped economy and strong kinship ties, seems unnecessary and unwarranted. It is, nevertheless, the community's function to intervene between those left without social constraints and negative forces in their environment, so as to facilitate their sound psychosocial adjustment. This suggests that the community must become involved in helping the widow establish or reestablish group ties. The group, for example, might consist of several widows, brought together under the guidance of a counselor, who would help them evolve standards of behavior mutually agreed upon and functional for all, yet inoffensive to society. The adjustment of the group would be accomplished by increasing each individual widow's functional independence, thereby bolstering her self-image and self-sufficiency.

A sample of mature American widows, aged 55-84, recently listed as their five basic needs (*Science News Letter,* 1955, p. 121): (1) physical health and comfort; (2) a need to feel useful; (3) a need to believe in something; (4) a need to love and be loved; (5) a need for emotional security and freedom from anxiety. In the absence of kinship systems, the community must play a role in developing medical facilities, job training centers, and counseling services for widows, which would work to improve mental hygiene and social organization. To date, the best efforts along these lines seem to be those by labor unions seeking to aid their retired members and the members' families. However, these services are in dire need of supplements from other sources, including religious bodies and governments at various levels.

3. *The Widow's children.* As we have seen, structural functionalists have studied mourning and the adjustment of widows. More recently, however, they have turned their attention to the widow's family, especially her children. In general, young children recover quickly from the shock of their father's death, because they have not been long habituated to a response to him and his role is minimal in their lives (Eliot, 1942,

p. 518). However, there are a number of problems faced by the widow in regard to her children and their subsequent development and adjustment. In the first place, there are numerous practical problems, including proper supervision of the children now that the father is dead and the mother, in all probability, must go out to work.

In the second place, there are other, far more pressing problems which revolve around explaining the finality of death to the children, a finality which the widow herself finds difficult to comprehend. The children should be told of their father's death in simple, factual terms. Grief should not be kept entirely from them, but rather shared with them, so as to ease their adjustment and that of their mother, and bring the family closer together. "Protecting the children" by keeping things from them may, in reality, merely protect the mother, who can temporarily postpone the inevitable ordeal of giving them an explanation and answering their questions. Controlled emotion and feeling are of value to children (Langer, 1957). Furthermore, they do not interpret things the way adults do, and if they are not told the truth, they may think their father willfully deserted them. If they are not told the truth, or are sent away "for their own good" during the funeral preparations and mourning, they may interpret these actions as desertion and rejection by their mother. The fact of death may be far easier to accept, and less damaging to the children's personalities, than the distortions conjured up in their minds when they are left alone in crises. In relation to this, several researchers have noted the need for literature concerned with education for death, similar to that which is now available to aid parents in explaining sex to their children (Eliot, 1955, p. 346). Pamphlets and books could be supplemented by the more personal guidance of a religious or psychiatric counselor, or by their candid, open discussions and public sermons.

Children usually forget death quickly, if their mother does not constantly relive the experience, thus complicating the shock (Eliot, 1955, p. 346). They need help, however, in adjusting to their loss and in keeping a realistic image of their father (Ilgenfritz, 1961). The widow's tendency to glorify the father is dysfunctional because it keeps their memory of him too vivid and makes it impossible for anyone (a would-be stepfather included) to take his place in the children's eyes. This not only complicates the initial shock, but also makes it difficult for the widow to bring men into their lives. The children develop the tendency to measure the men whom they meet against their dead, heroic father's image. Needless to say, the men do not fulfill the children's expectations (nor the widow's), but are necessary to their adjustment, especially when young boys are left without a male figure with whom they can identify.

In addition to glorifying the father, the mother tends to err in handling the children by granting them special privileges to compensate for their loss. Far too often, in showering them with material things, she acts in a way just as damaging to their proper psychological development (Ilgenfritz, 1961). In these cases, the mother's actions and not the father's death *per se* affect the children's development, usually in a negative way. The widow must recognize that she can not be both father and mother to the children, nor should she even try to be. She can not live their lives for them either, and overprotection, like too much love, is damaging to the young.

With each year that passes, new light is shed by economists, psychologists and sociologists on the widow's marital frustrations, her problems, and those of her children. However, research to date is still inadequate and precludes detailed, sound guidance for families undergoing crises. While we await further studies, the role of the community, especially its religious and psychiatric counselors, is to be noted and increased, in order to meet the needs already indicated and to help alter American attitudes towards death.

WIDOWHOOD COMPARED WITH DIVORCE

At the present time, academicians know so little about the widow that some suggest temporarily making use of materials relevant to people in a position comparable to hers. Those advocating this approach generally suggest a comparison of the widow with the divorcée, who has been long and well studied.

Mourning is similar to the post-divorce period (Eliot, 1942, pp. 525-526), in that both involve a slow adjustment to the loss of a love-object. Both leave the woman with a yearning, frustration, and emptiness which necessitate a reconditioning of her daily habits, her philosophy of life, and her life itself. Much of the reconditioning, or reintegration, is facilitated by momentary psychological escapes into the past, through daydreaming and phantasy. However, in time, reality cancels out the memories, and the woman reactivates roles which she had played before her marriage. Moreover, there is a shift in the family configuration, with the woman taking on, willingly or not so willingly, new roles in her relations with her children and others. The widow and the divorcée both become increasingly self-centered, but recover by involving themselves in a job, the household routine, or ceremony. The tendency to conceive of themselves in an unhappy role outlasts the actual tension of unhappiness, and gradually the women discover new interests or love-objects.

The differences between the status and problems of the widow and those of the divorcée, however, far outweigh these similarities (Eliot, 1942, pp. 524-525). Convention makes different demands on the widow than on the divorcée. In bereavement, the mind is free to idealize the deceased—in fact, society actively encourages this practice in its adage which warns us to speak well of the dead. We have a tendency, whether out of fear, guilt, or justification for our grief, to praise the dead and remember only their positive traits (Eliot, 1942, p. 525; Langer, 1957, p. 21). The divorced, if they are to maintain a good self-image, can not speak well of their husbands, for if they do, they admit that the dissolution of their marriage is entirely their own fault. The widowed, on the other hand, bask in the reflected glory of their dead husbands. Society's admiration for their husbands and the blissful state of their marital unions spills over onto the widows themselves. The widow identifies with her husband and wishes to be so identified; the divorcée does not.

Society creates no conventional period of protection or recovery for the divorced woman as it does, through mourning, for the widow. The situation of the divorcée is less final and less convincing to her and to those around her. It evokes little sympathy. Furthermore, the misery of the post-divorce period is accentuated by wounded pride, self-praise, aggression, and social stigma. The attitudes of friends, especially the males among them, towards a divorced woman are more complex than those faced by a widow. These too complicate her situation. The parallel between the widow and the divorcée is weak as far as their children are concerned. Those of the divorced woman may have the benefit of a living father figure, but the tendency of divorced parents to use their children as weapons against each other often leaves the children torn between the two mates. While the fatherless child undoubtedly suffers from his loss, and the widow feels she must be both mother and father to him, his position is clear and he is not trapped between two conflicting adults.

One of the chief reasons for a comparison between the divorcée and the widow is that both lend themselves to a study of remarriage. The widow and the divorcée have to get to know men again. They both often feel that they need someone to whom they can cling, and someone with whom their children can identify and relate. They resent pressures to remarry, but are afraid of being alone and independent. But the similarities between remarriage for the widow and the divorcée end here.

In many cases, our culture so pities and venerates the widow that it grants her the would-be privilege of living alone. The divorcée, however, is stereotyped in such a way as to evoke very different responses. She is not put up on a pedestal, and so is far more free to act however she wishes in regard to remarriage. Her problem is that she is often forced by society to become Bohemian or immoral, thus fulfilling its prophecy and substantiating its stereotype.

Our attitudes towards remarriage for the widow are as nebulous and contradictory, though pervasive and influential, as are those related to mourning. The society, in its laws and religions, neither prohibits nor prescribes remarriage, but is ambivalent towards this type of union. It will be accepted only after a "decent" interval—usually defined as one year—after the husband's death.

Even if society openly condoned and encouraged remarriage, certain other socially inculcated practices—specifically the idealization of the dead—work against it. The widow idealizes her late husband, and then compares the men that she meets with his image. They do not stack up well against her standards—no mortal could! (Langer, 1957, p. 212) Not only do living men fail to meet idealized images, but the widow's concept of an ideal husband and father is now obsolete. It is personified, perhaps, only in a valiant young knight, aged 25 or 30, who in reality is not well suited to the needs of the widow or her family. Nor is the young man anxious to make himself suited to their needs. The widow, typically over 45, previously married for a number of years, and left with children, is not in a good bargaining position (Waller & Hill, 1951, p. 497; Bernard, 1956, pp. 12-13).

Remarriage is least problematic, be the woman a widow or a divorcée, when she is young and it occurs three or more years after the first marriage ended. By this time, the woman's tendency to relive the past is lessened, she is more aware of changes within herself, and she is more realistic than she was immediately following the end of her first marriage (Langer, 1957, p. 226). Before this time, she usually retreats from relations with males, even when these do not include sexual advances. Second marriages are not less successful than first ones, although the former spouse exerts an intervening role in the new relationship. For the divorcée the role of her first husband is an active one; for the widow it is passive and, as we have already noted, idealized. The latter may be the more difficult for a new husband to overcome.

Second marriages do not have the support of the American romantic love ideology. Clearly the husband is a second choice, second to the first mate. This is complicated in the situation of the widow because the first marriage was not ended voluntarily, and both she and her new husband are constantly aware of this fact.

It would appear that the issue of remarriage is a crucial one in any study of widows or divorcées. However, this is not to say that the factors are precisely alike for the two types of women, or that a study of one necessarily provides insights into the other's situation. The phenomenon of widowhood is a unique entity, and must be studied as such. A comparison with the case of the divorcée is somewhat helpful, but should be undertaken only with extreme caution. Data concerning remarriage can be used, however, to further support our argument—namely, that society plays a dysfunctional role in the adjustment of the widow.

CONCLUSION

The paucity of reliable and objective materials relevant to a study of widows is attributable to methodological problems and American attitudes towards death. The few studies that are available indicate that widows today find their status unexpected and frustrating. Their problems are complicated by the fact that, in their frustration, they are left alone, without the psycho-social supports which women in other societies and other decades derived from kinship ties, religion, and consequent mourning rituals. Our findings are subject to modifications arising out of the widow's personality, her group affiliations, and the composition of her nuclear family. It is to be hoped that additional research and community programs will be forthcoming to help the American widow meet her problems.

REFERENCES

Becker, H. The sorrow of bereavement. *J. abnorm. soc. Psychol.*, 1933, *27*, 391-410.
Bernard, Jessie. *Remarriage.* New York: Dryden, 1956.
Blau, Zena S. Changes in status and age identification. *Amer. sociol. Rev.*, 1956, *21*, 198-203.
Blau, Zena S. Structural constraints on friendship in old age. *Amer. sociol. Rev.*, 1961, *26*, 429-438.
Business Week. August 20, 1955, 151-152.
Durkheim, E. *Suicide* (trans. by G. Simpson). New York: Free Press, 1951.
Eliot, T. D. The bereaved family. *Amer. acad. pol. & soc. sci., Ann.*, 1929, *160*, 184-190.

Eliot, T. D. The adjustive behavior of bereaved families: a new field for research. *Soc. Forces,* 1930, *8,* 543-549.

Eliot, T. D. —of the shadow of death. *Amer. acad. pol. & soc. sci., Ann.,* 1932, *229,* 87-99.

Eliot, T. D. A Step toward the social psychology of bereavement. *J. abnorm. soc. Psychol.,* 1933, *27,* 380-390.

Eliot, T. D. Family crises and ways of meeting them. In H. Becker and R. Hill (Eds.) *Marriage and the family.* Boston: Heath, 1942. Pp. 489-536.

Eliot, T. D. War bereavements and their recovery. In M. B. Sussman (Ed.) *Sourcebook in marriage and the family.* Boston: Houghton Mifflin, 1955. Pp. 339-346.

Fritz, Mary A. A study of widowhood. *Sociol. & soc. Res.,* 1930, *14,* 553-561.

Hansen, D. A. & Hill, R. Families under stress. In H. T. Christensen (Ed.) *Handbook of marriage and the family.* Chicago: Rand McNally, 1964. Pp. 782-819.

Ilgenfritz, Marjcrie P. Mothers on their own: widows and divorcees. *Marriage fam. Living,* 1961, *23,* 38-41.

Komarovsky, Mirra. *Blue collar marriage.* New York: Random House, 1964.

Komarovsky, Mirra & Waller, W. Studies of the family. *Amer. J. Sociol.,* 1945, *50,* 443-451.

Langer, Marion. *Learning to live as a widow.* New York: Messner, 1957.

Lerner, M. *America as a civilization.* New York: Simon & Schuster, 1957.

Lindemann, E. Symptomatology and management of acute grief. *Amer. J. Psychiatry,* 1944, *101,* 141-148.

Marris, P. *Widows and their families.* London: Routledge & Kegan Paul, 1958.

Mitford, Jessica. *The American way of death.* New York: Simon & Schuster, 1963.

Murdock, G. P. *Social structure.* New York: Macmillan, 1949.

Parsons, T. & Fox, Renée C. Illness, therapy and the modern American family. *J. soc. Issues,* 1952, *13,* 31-44.

Rochford, E. *Mothers on their own.* New York: Harper & Row, 1953.

Science News Letter. Predict more than eight million widows by 1960. March 6, 1954, *65,* 147.

Science News Letter. Five basic needs of widows determined. March 12, 1955, *66,* 121.

Science News Letter. Widowed die sooner. Sept. 26, 1959, *76,* 197.

Shand, A. F. *The foundations of character.* London: Macmillan, 1920.

Waller, W. & Hill, R. *The family: a dynamic interpretation* (rev. ed.) New York: Dryden, 1951.

IV

THE SINGLE WOMAN

Why Women Do Not Marry

ROBERT J. CAMPBELL

Robert Jean Campbell, III, M.D., is Chief of the Out-Patient Psychiatric Service of St. Vincent's Hospital, New York City; Instructor in Psychiatry, Columbia University, College of Physicians and Surgeons, and Adjunct-Associate Professor, Fordham University Graduate School. Prior to assuming his post at St. Vincent's Hospital, Dr. Campbell was Senior Clinical Psychiatrist at the New York State Psychiatric Institute. After graduating from the University of Wisconsin, Dr. Campbell received his M.D. from Columbia University. He is a diplomate in psychiatry of the American Board of Psychiatry and Neurology, a contributor to various medical journals, and is currently editor of Hinsie & Campbell's Psychiatric Dictionary (1960). The present Pastoral Psychology Institute is the fifth one to which Dr. Campbell has contributed as a faculty member.

Living across the street from Ignatius Loyola Church I am weekly provided with ample evidence that marriage remains an acceptable goal for many of today's youth. It is somewhat distressing, therefore, to find that I must look at the negative side of all this, and must direct your attention to the stranger to these nuptial rites—the perpetual bridesmaid, the spinster, or, whatever you call her, the woman who does not marry.

Perhaps, unconsciously, I volunteered for my present-day role as harbinger of gloom in the 1963 Institute (Campbell, 1964), when I gave some consideration to the none-too-reassuring prospects for the long-term outlook in marriage. The reported figures do not confirm the fiction of living happily ever after, once the marriage bond is tied; on the contrary, more than one marriage of every four ends in divorce, and it is estimated that one in every three of the remaining is an unhappy marriage.

Despite these rather sobering figures, most people do marry, and many of those who do not would like to. It seems quite clear, therefore, that any symposium devoted to woman in modern life would necessarily be concerned with the woman who does not marry; let us try to evaluate some of the factors that appear to be related to what I might call spinsterism.

THE OBLIGATORY SPINSTER

In a monogamous society such as ours, marriage involves a relatively permanent pairing off; such a dyadic partnership, if it is to be entered into by the entire population, requires that the two elements—male and female—be matched at least in number. And here is the first rub; as anyone knows who has followed census reports during the past years, males have been outdistanced—at least in this respect—for a long time. The ratio of males to females at the present time in the United States is approximately 97 to 100, so all else aside we know that at least a percentage of the eligible women in our country cannot be offered the chance to marry, even though there may be no other factor working against them. This group could be called obligatory spinsters—or, in the fashion of my youth, old maids—to distinguish them from maiden ladies, the unmarried women who at some time in their lives had been asked to marry, but had refused the offer. There seems little hope that the size of this group can be reduced, for the ratio of males to females has been declining steadily for five decades. This is related to several factors, among which might be mentioned the more rapid growth of the female population, the greater increase of life expectancy among women than among men, and the passing of a generation of immigrants, among whom males predominated.

THE VOLUNTARY SPINSTER

But what about the other women who do not marry—the facultative spinsters, if you will—for whom potential husbands exist, at least? We are not yet so automated or computerized that we can depend upon some giant machine in Midtown, U.S.A., to match up our 97 males with appropriate wives; we must, instead, depend upon the human element to do our selecting and our matching for us. What goes wrong in that selection process that leaves so many of the potentially married still single? Some women, of course, do not wish to marry, and we must consider the factors that determine such a position. Others sincerely believe they want to marry and appear to go through the expected maneuvers of mate selection; yet we detect a false note or two in their behavior which leads us to suspect that their unconscious motives may be the exact opposite of the goals they claim are theirs. Still others do want to marry but are held back by a number of very real obstacles—families, money, illness, and the like, to say nothing of all the anti-marriage factors in what appear to be eligible males.

But let us stick to our subject of woman in modern life and ignore the recalcitrant bachelor, in favor of the reluctant debutante. What are some of the reasons for choosing not to marry? The way I have posed the question would seem to indicate that I deem marriage the most appropriate goal for everyone in our society. Let me hasten to deny that such is my position; for I believe very strongly that marriage is not for everybody, and certainly it has never cured any emotional or psychological disorder. As we discuss some of the reasons for women not marrying, I think it will become clear that in many cases these reasons are quite legitimate, despite what the girl's family, or friends, or fellow-workers might think. To be sure, some of these legitimate reasons may be an outgrowth of conditions that might be modified or changed, and are not of the type that confer permanent ineligibility on the woman; and perhaps our discussion later will provide an exchange of ideas concerning those underlying conditions.

For the woman, as well as for the man, marriage is a dynamic state and not a static condition, an ever-changing and shifting relationship between two people whose personalities will certainly clash at some points yet must generally complement one another's; whose goals and aims in life in general must be very similar; whose preferences, and tastes, and interests, and dislikes must be shared to some extent or at least be tolerated; whose interdependence must be of sufficient intensity as to constitute a repetitive if not a continuous cementing of the relationship, and yet not so intense as to hamper the continuing growth and development of each of them. Even more, marriage is an occupation, and one that makes increasing demands without guaranteeing any proportionate increase in emotional or material returns. And still more, at least for many people, it is an irrevocable contract that once entered

into cannot be dissolved, and it requires a final decision on the part
of participants who by definition can have had no experience in how
the contract might operate. Indeed, looked at in this way, it is amazing
that any marriage turns out to be successful, and it seems but small
wonder that some will pale at the thought of the far-reaching consequences of accepting a proposal. That even some marriages are successful is a telling argument for the basic mercifulness of the Almighty.

THE RELIGIOUS WOMAN

Because marriage is an occupation, all by itself, it can be absolutely
or relatively incompatible with other occupations. A religious vocation
in the woman, for example, certainly removes her from the ranks of
the marriageable. I am sure it has occurred to many people that those
with a religious vocation might account for a sizable proportion of the
three women in every hundred for whom no males are available, and
that the group of obligatory spinsters might therefore be of minor significance. Let me, though, sound a word of warning here; we are all
agreed, I think, that whatever it might be that constitutes a religious
vocation, taking the veil as a second best when no marriage proposal
is forthcoming is hardly the optimal route to the convent. Rather, the
girl who goes into the religious life should enter because of a positive
choice, with awareness of alternative courses of action, and not as a
rebound phenomenon or an escape from frustrating reality.

THE CAREER WOMAN

The religious life is not the only one that leads women to decide
against marriage, however. In a society which overvalues competitiveness and achievement, and fosters activity and accomplishment, it is
not hard to understand that the girl who has been reared in almost
identical fashion as the boy should come to value an outside-the-home
profession in preference to housekeeping. If she has established herself
in an occupation or profession, and has tasted of success, it is asking
a great deal to relinquish all this for a job of housekeeper and nursemaid
that goes on 24 hours a day for 365 days a year. Particularly is this true
if the woman's success in her position has been greater than that achieved
by her suitor in his. The woman may well wonder, if she follows
the marital adventures and misadventures of some of the country's
more famous career women in the newspapers, whether a career and
marriage are not mutually exclusive, or whether the combination is not

a guarantee of unhappiness. A career and marriage can, of course, be combined felicitously, but the suspicion is strong that the woman who can achieve the combination, and the husband who can tolerate it, must be rather special sorts of people.

THE HOMOSEXUAL WOMAN

Another type of woman in whom the decision not to marry is more or less understandable is the overt homosexual. It has long been believed that homosexuality in the female is more common than in the male, but specific data on relative incidence do not support this belief. The investigations of Kinsey and his associates, even though they share with others the failure to solve completely the vexing methodologic problems inherent in estimates of homosexuality, might be considered as fairly representative of the recent work in this area. Defining a homosexual experience as overt genital contact to the point of orgasm, Kinsey found that 37 percent of his male sample had had homosexual experiences, but only 13 percent of his females. Moreover, in any age period the number of women who were primarily or exclusively homosexual was never more than half the percentage reached by the male.

Speaking as a psychiatrist, I am somewhat hard-pressed to explain this finding, for psychodynamically one would have predicted homosexuality to be more frequent in women. The original love-object in both sexes is, of course, a woman—the mother; and it is easy to see that should anything go wrong in one's love-object relationships there would be a tendency to return to a repetition of or substitute for that earliest relationship. In the case of the woman, such a return would constitute a repetition of her primary homosexual attachment to the mother. In clinical psychiatry, this is certainly what we see happening in our patients, but of course any conclusions based upon clinical experience are always subject to the criticism that psychiatrists generally see only disturbed people and cannot therefore talk about people in general.

Be that as it may, it seems likely that not only conscious, overt homosexuality will influence a woman to decide against marriage, but that unconscious or latent homosexuality might operate as an even more potent factor in keeping her unmarried. Such women will often have had a background of a rejecting, cruel, brutal, and/or alcoholic father, who was not able to extend love, gentleness, or affection to them in their formative years. Finding themselves frustrated by the male at every step, they turn to the mother and to mother-substitutes; these are the spinsters who are most comfortable in the company of older women and seem to enjoy a life of enslavement to an older person. Another outgrowth of the kind of background I have described is to become involved with younger people, who represent the self, and as a teacher or a social worker, for example, to act the benign, protective parental role that the woman missed in her own rearing. Another type, which depends upon even more complex frustrations throughout the childhood years, becomes vindictive and vengeful toward the father and all males; such women enter into more or less open and hostile competition with the male, and much of their lifetimes is spent in seething rages against their rivals.

The Case of Joyce

In this connection, I am reminded of a patient, whom I shall call Joyce. She is a 28-year-old, single, Irish-Catholic teacher, and was referred by a priest, who felt that her scruples about dating might be indicative of some underlying emotional disorder. When I saw her for the first time in my waiting room, I was at once struck by the way she had got herself turned out, I supposed for her meeting with me. Her rather plain, square, and freckled face was wreathed with teased ringlets of hair, reminiscent of Shirley Temple at age eight. Yet her cheekbones were etched in thick rouge, and it must have taken conscious physical effort to hold her eyelids open, piled as they were with bluish-green eyeshadow. Her clothes also had a curiously contradictory or inconsistent aspect. It was mid-winter and she wore a blouse and skirt; the blouse was décolleté to a degree that would have been more appropriate to midnight than midday, and of a thin fabric that clung revealingly to her body. Her skirt, in contrast, was a rough tweed sack, totally shapeless, much too large around and yet not quite reaching her knees as she stood up. Below all this could be seen large, muscular calves that disappeared into tiny, fur-edged booties of the kind worn by very mature, if not to say elderly, women. Her manner of dress hinted at an indecisiveness concerning her life role that was mirrored in her actions and her speech. While her heavily mascaraed lashes flapped away like hummingbirds' wings during our first sessions, the rest of her face was totally expressionless, and remained so no matter what she talked about.

She appeared to be very direct, at first, and began listing her complaints even before I had had a chance to tell her that she was sitting in my chair in the consulting room. In any event, she told me straightaway that she needed my help in fixing up her relationship with her father, who is an alcoholic, and in finding some workable compromise between sex and her religion. Until three years ago, she had felt certain that she had a religious vocation. She had always had many scruples about sex, and felt uncomfortable with boys, and was sure that her father did not want her to marry. But then, in one of his drunken rages, he asked her what was wrong with her that she couldn't find a man, and after a period of soul-searching she decided that she would marry after all. It is since then that she has had all her troubles.

She worries sometimes that she is losing her mind, she has developed all sorts of physical ailments, and she seems always to be run-down and exhausted. She has many doubts about her femininity which she tries to solve in a characteristically inept and aggressive fashion—by going to dances, asking the boys in the stag line to dance with her, and demonstrating how she can dance circles around them. She cannot understand, though, why they never ask her to dance, even after she has shown her willingness by making the first move. She has had several bona fide dates, but is conscious of something having gone wrong; closer questioning brought out the fact that she turns every date into a classroom lecture. Before going out with a boy, she learns what his interests are, bones up on the subjects, and spends most of the date showing him where his ignorance lies.

She is a professional Roman Catholic and spends many of her sessions denouncing the bigotry of other religious groups. She interviewed girls as possible roommates a few months ago and from each extracted a signed statement that such-and-such holy pictures would remain on such-and-such walls, and was enraged when one girl asked if she might hang a star of David over her bed instead of a crucifix. She can describe to you exactly what her husband will be like—a combination of Job's patience, Adonis' beauty, Augustine's wit, a pope's holiness, and an Irish heritage—but in her three years of searching she has failed to meet one Irish Catholic boy her own age—not even on Third Avenue on St. Patrick's Day! With the best possible response to therapy, I think we might get this girl married off by the time she is 48—and I hope you have some idea of all the hurdles that would have to be cleared by then; but the question would remain—should someone like this marry at all?

MARRIAGE IS NO CURE FOR NEUROSIS

Proceeding from the knowledge that the typical woman's adult identity is to a large extent dependent upon her marital partner, and her performance in her role of homemaker, wife, and mother, it might be argued that marriage in itself would foster maturation. And it is not unheard of that women, and men too for that matter, with glaring and blatant emotional disorders, are advised to marry as a way of getting better. But no one has ever married himself out of a neurosis; marriage can certainly be a maturing experience, but only for those in whom the potential for growth and development exists. Probably you are all familiar with the well-established findings that mental and emotional disorders are much more frequent in the single than in the married. It would be a gross error to interpret this as evidence that marriage cures psychosis, however; that would be putting the cart before the horse. What such findings reflect is the need for greater, rather than lesser, emotional stability on the part of those who marry. The ones with serious emotional disturbances often do not wish to marry, or are not able to marry in the first place.

But neither can it be said that there must be something wrong with the woman who does not marry. Like the male, the woman is limited by accidental factors in her choice of a mate, factors such as availability of men and proximity to them. It is fortunately less common nowadays, but women can still be found whose spinsterism was largely forced upon them by a family's demands that the youngest daughter, or the 'good' daughter, or the most intelligent daughter, or the like, devote her young womanhood to nursing a father through his extended terminal illness, and her middle age to acting as nurse-companion to her elderly, bereaved mother.

The Case of Anna C.

An instance of the above, in a family whose pathology certainly exaggerated and intensified the passive dependency of the patient, is Anna C. She is the sixth of eight children, but the only girl in an obsessively perfectionistic Roman Catholic family. She had been treated as something very special almost from the moment of her birth—her father's favorite, jealously guarded and overprotected from the evil world, and the mother's only hope to mold someone in her own image.

Lurking within the family's repetitive rituals and frenetic religiosity was a heavy taint of superstitiousness that approached the savage; for when the father died unexpectedly when Anna was nine, the mother and her first three sons gave serious consideration to sacrificing the girl to appease the Almighty. They reasoned that God must certainly have been displeased with their father to have taken him so suddenly and that perhaps the only way to ensure his salvation would be to sacrifice the child who had been his favorite.

Somehow, she was spared such an end, but each of her older brothers in turn took over as head of the household as their older brothers went into the world and married. And each, in turn, looked upon Anna as his special concern, and each to this day is proud of the fact that Anna was never introduced to a young man while he was head of the house. Soon they all had married, even the younger ones, and Anna was left behind with her mother. But by now, the mother was crippled with arthritis, and everyone agreed that it would be cruel and heartless to desert a fine Catholic mother who had borne so many children. The boys, of course, had their own families and young children to worry about; Anna's election to the office of constant companion was unanimous. She settled into her role without too much obvious discomfort; indeed, she was hardly aware of any change from the rest of her life.

By the time she was 21, she was even allowed to go out one evening a week, so long as she visited one of her brothers or went with some of the unmarried women in her parish. Life creaked along in this fashion until 7 years ago, when Anna was 27. Then one of her brothers was killed in a freak railroad accident, and his widow and four children moved in with Anna and her mother. Anna, of course, was expected to become handmaiden to the new arrivals, and she did in fact take on the new assignment with nary a murmur.

The duties included getting the children back and forth to school, and Anna's own punctiliousness, reinforced by that of her family, ensured her getting the same bus day after day. She soon became friendly with the driver, 27 years her senior, one thing led to another, and when she was 34 years old she received his proposal of marriage. From the moment he popped the question, her panics started. They last about two hours and come several times a day—her heart pounds, she breaks into a cold sweat, feels sick to her stomach, fears that she is physically coming apart, has to pace the floors, breaks into hysterical sobs, and on several occasions has had to be restrained from jumping out the window.

She wants to marry the busdriver, her family (in one of those characteristic about-faces that sick families will show) thinks she should marry, but no one can figure out how to get her to the altar in the midst of her panics. Training of the sort she has had will stick, whether wanted or not, and 30 years is too long a time to be overthrown in an instant. For Anna, marriage with the older busdriver was forbidden on many counts—he was too clearly the reincarnation of her father, she could not forget the training from her brothers that all men are beasts and want only one thing from a girl, she could not abandon the mother whose care had been placed in her hands almost by papal writ, and at the same time she is petrified of the physical dangers (as she sees them) of the marriage bed and of childbirth, and loathe to commit herself to the further responsibilities of children, and of perhaps having to nurse still another person through his senility.

Anna's was an extreme case, but one that illustrates the bizarre twist that can be given to moral precepts and rules of conduct—in this instance by her family, but in others by teachers or counselors.

Many more reasons for spinsterism could be adduced, but in the time remaining I should like to focus on a large group which probably accounts for the majority of women who believe they want to marry but somehow can never find a man who meets their criteria. These are women with disturbances in their ability to form enduring object relationships, women with various kinds and degrees of ego defects.

One could subsume under this rubric the woman with an intense fixation on the Oedipal object, the father; for her no man is satisfactory because he is not enough like her father. There is a variant of this, the woman who can be interested in a man only so long as he belongs to someone else and who therefore—fortunately—always finds some last-minute excuse for terminating her engagement. Then there is the woman who has been too free with her favors, and has not only made herself so available that the men in her neighborhood no longer find her desirable, but has discovered that she is incapable of loving any one person, and is doomed to a life of short-lived, unsatisfying attachments.

However, the most important member of this group is the autistic, schizoid woman with the kind of personality that has been termed "as if" or "false self." The woman generally impresses one as being completely normal, and yet a look at her style of life reveals a lack of genuineness in her relationship to reality, and an almost staged quality of experience. She may be intellectually gifted but cannot create; she can only repeat and copy what she has done before or what others are doing. Emotionally, she is cold and tensely formal; this is not an overcontrol of intense feelings lying just beneath the surface, but rather a betrayal of affectlessness and emptiness. Being without feelings of her own that she can recognize and accept, she is uncertain as to how to conduct herself through life; she adopts a formalized exterior to hide her lack, and with this combines an alert readiness to pick up the slightest cue from those around her as to what expression to adopt, and what role to play.

As a consequence, she is a willing, compliant, passive partner to anything suggested to her; having no convictions or feelings that are truly her own, she can harbor no resentment of yours. She makes an apt pupil, and often spends most of her life in a teacher-pupil relationship, where little independence will be expected by her professor, who will hardly object to her slavish reproduction of his contributions. The only catch is that once she loses contact with the teacher, all productivity goes;

she seems unable to absorb anything from a relationship, and can only operate on moment-to-moment mimicry.

The longer one knows such a woman, the more he is tempted to preface any description of her with the term "pseudo." She is enthusiastic, but hers is a pseudo-enthusiasm to cover her apathy. She can seem to be active, energetic, and even expansive, but such pseudo-energy is an attempt to hold people off, to push them away before they get too close, and make too many demands. Men generally find something very appealing about such a woman; she brings out the protective warrior in a man, and leans heavily on the optimism she engenders in him. But soon his best efforts are reduced to futility, and he feels defeated, useless, inept, and foolish.

This is the type of woman who will consult her parish priest for all sorts of headaches in living. The problems she faces are always very involved and complicated, and it is clear that she needs some level-headed, sober-minded older man with common sense to help her put her affairs in order. Her pastor spends days telephoning lawyers, accountants, relatives, and what-have-you, and after much effort schedules a meeting for all the principals involved. She telephones ten minutes after everyone else has gathered in his sitting room to say that she has decided what she really needs is to get away from it all; she's terribly sorry about that meeting this morning, but she is afraid she cannot get packed as it is and her plane leaves at noon. So the good father will understand, won't he, if she doesn't come over to the rectory. Perhaps she'll be in touch again when she gets back.

She deals with potential suitors in exactly the same way, and while one would have no difficulty in identifying her as a problem from her life story, it is amazing how in the living of it she can continue to enmesh more and more people in her tangled web of unrelatedness.

This last, large group of which I have spoken brings us to the question of borderline mental disturbance, such as the ambulatory or pseudo-neurotic schizophrenic, and that could be a whole chapter in itself. We can not do that now, but I would like to restate what I consider the core theme of my presentation: not all people are suitable for marriage, and the difficulty that many women have in finding a mate is often a reflection of their own deep-seated psychological and emotional disturbances.

REFERENCE

Campbell, R. J. Sexual adjustment in marriage. In W. C. Bier (S.J.) (Ed.) *Marriage: a psychological and moral approach.* New York: Fordham University Press, 1964. Pp. 102-113.

The Career Woman

ALBA I. ZIZZAMIA

Alba I. Zizzamia has an A.B. degree from Trinity College, Washington, D.C., and a doctor of literature degree from the University of Rome, Italy. Formerly, she was associate professor and head of the Italian Department at Trinity College, and she has also been a faculty member at St. Joseph's College in her native Hartford, and at the Catholic University in Washington. Currently, she is assistant to the director of the NCWC Office for United Nations Affairs and is the representative of the World Union of Catholic Women's Organizations at UNICEF. Dr. Zizzamia has translated a number of books from French and Italian into English, and writes and lectures on a variety of subjects. She was the recipient of the medal Pro Ecclesia et Pontifice *in 1953.*

For several years I have been participating in panel discussions, seminars, and conferences dealing with women in political life, family life, international life, in the Church, in societies in transition, and so on *ad infinitum*. And I have begun to feel a little like Omar Khayyam who

> . . . did eagerly frequent
> Doctor and Saint, and heard great argument
> About it and about: but evermore
> Came out by the same Door where in [he] went.

194

Current literature—both popular and scientific—seems to stress that men and women today are confused as to their respective roles in society. Women, whether married or single, are entering and making their way in the professions against a background of history in which their role and their "nature" have been defined for the most part by men. They live and work out their salvation in a preeminently male culture. The basic orientation of psychoanalysis, sociology, social anthropology, however "modern," also remains predominantly male-oriented. What emerges from many studies or from their subsequent popularization— due to both a certain conservative bias and the selective use of findings —is the "traditional image of woman . . . who finds complete self-fulfillment in her exclusive devotion to marriage and parenthood" or, failing that, in the "predominantly . . . nurturant" functions in the broader society (Rossi, 1964, pp. 611-613).

Yet both the definitions and the traditional image have always been accompanied by paradox, as a study of cultural attitudes towards women and the actual circumstances in which they have lived and worked will show. Even the highly sentimentalized "pedestal" concept attributed to the Christian attitude toward women has not saved them from conditions of social and legal inferiority.

In fact, for religiously motivated persons the influence of war and especially of economics in emancipating disadvantaged groups—whether slaves, Negroes, ethnic minorities or women—deserves some pondering. A report of the International Labor Organization for 1958 notes, for example, that the demand for women's services and cultural attitudes towards women's employment depend in large measure on whether or not the economy is healthy and expanding. "Where this element of growth is a feature of economic life," the report states, "women have been welcome additions to the labour force in most countries. Where economies are stagnant, women workers or would-be workers have far greater obstacles to surmount."

EMERGING STATUS OF WOMEN THROUGHOUT THE WORLD

A close study of the conclusions of various United Nations-sponsored regional seminars on the status of women makes it difficult not to agree with the Asian participant who observed that the role and status of woman are determined by the economic and social structures of the society into which she is born, and that religion then supplies the justification and the gloss. When economic and social structures change— under the impact of industrialization or other economic forces, or of sudden independence as in many of today's new nations—there is an inevitable time-lag before mental attitudes adjust to the new situation and discard or modify traditions that are no longer necessary or valid, or before the misidentification of certain prejudices with religious values is corrected.

The increasingly rapid changes produced by modern science and technology would seem to require not only more intensified research but also considerable flexibility in outlook and definition. Spiritual directors and counselors particularly must not be trapped by yesterday's stereotypes, some of which still persist in terms of "feminine occupations" and "womanly characteristics." The current concern over a separate "theology for women" is not particularly reassuring. Discussions of the concept of "complementarity," appearing in increasing number, often sound as if old ideas had been given a new label. In fact, the term runs the risk of becoming another shibboleth unless it is recognized that whatever the "problems" and "confusion," they will be solved only by men and women together in a developing community or social organization—a fact which some of the new nations seem to be more aware of than we. Even a fraction of the study and analysis expended on women, if it were devoted to the role of men in changing societies or to the "masculine mystique," might conceivably be helpful.

It is not irrelevant, I think, to mention here the considerable influence on cultural attitudes towards women and their work which has been exerted in recent years by various UN or UN-related agencies. These have emphasized the need for the "advancement of women," first to accord them their basic human rights and then to ensure their active involvement in the economic and social development of developing countries, if efforts to combat poverty and raise living standards are to meet with success. It is here that the relation of women's "advancement" to the improvement of the community as a whole is most clearly reflected; it is of special pertinence to missionary work and plans and the institutional framework in which they are carried out.

The principle of respect for fundamental human rights for all, "without distinction as to race, *sex*, language or religion"—confirmed as criteria for all societies in the much-quoted Universal Declaration of Human Rights, and recalled in a long succession of other declarations, conventions and resolutions—has had a direct influence on the legislation not only of the newly independent countries but of older nations as well. In this field, and that of the status of women particularly, there has been a genuine interaction between secular developments and their reflection in Catholic teaching, including papal statements. For example, in the preparation of studies and formulating recommendations, the UN Commission on the Status of Women relies heavily on the co-operation of international women's organizations, among which the World Union of Catholic Women's Organizations has been steadily active. It has benefited over the years from a succession of addresses by Pius XII, in which he acknowledged the changes taking place, with some reluctance evident in his phrasing, but with confidence in woman's competence and ability to ". . . be present everywhere where the soul of a nation is being forged" (Pius XII, 1947, p. 171). In *Pacem in terris* Pope John XXIII (1963), with his usual cheerfulness, lists the emergence of women and their demand to be respected as human persons as one of the three distinctive characteristics of our time. We may perhaps question whether we would have had these statements from either Pius XII or John XXIII if it had not been for the ferment created by these international discussions and activities and the participation therein of Catholic international organizations, which ensured the presence of Catholic teaching, defended certain positions despite some difficulties and, guided by the encyclicals, formed a kind of two-way channel between official Catholic thought and practical economic and legal levels on which the advancement of women was being considered. I have mentioned this because I feel it is an area which is perhaps less familiar, and also because it is in its way a fruitful example of dialogue between the "Church and the world" through the instrumentality of the laity—by no means a new phenomenon.

CAREER OPPORTUNITIES

Despite the increasing scope of professional opportunities for women —some of which are outlined elsewhere in this volume [1]—the rosy expectations are often belied by actual treatment, and women's access to various professions, their opportunities for advancement, and their rewards, are still limited by the persistence of old prejudices and other social factors, as well as certain attitudes on the part of women themselves.

In 1958 at the request of the UN Commission on the Status of Women (United Nations, 1958, 1959), a number of studies were prepared on professional opportunities for women in teaching, law, architecture and engineering. These were followed in 1963 by similar inquiries on the professions of accountant, statistician, draughtsman, and that of techni-

[1] The career wife, p. 123; The employed woman, p. 210.

cian in chemical, biological and bacteriological laboratories, fields in which the shortage of competent practitioners opened them quickly to women. A total of 78 countries were covered. These surveys reveal a certain universality in the prejudices affecting women's entrance into fields traditionally regarded as male preserves, and a basic similarity in the factors preventing or hindering women's advancement in the professions.

First among these have been religious or cultural taboos and social customs, which have been reflected in parental attitudes and in the personal bias of counselors, with differences in the vocational guidance given to boys and girls. The economic factor is also important, either when means for advanced training are lacking or when a choice is to be made between a son and a daughter. In the latter case, the son is invariably and universally given preference for reasons too well known to go into here. Boys or young men are accorded the same preferential treatment when scholarships or fellowships are being awarded or candidates are being chosen to fill the limited places available in graduate schools or other advanced training courses. This is still true even in the United States which enjoys the same reputation of unlimited opportunities for women it once had for immigrants—and with somewhat the same subtleties of discrimination.

Other obstacles are presented either by apprenticeship conditions or the field-work training required in some professions. For example, architecture and engineering require field work on construction jobs, and it is argued that men are reluctant to work with or be supervised by a woman. In some countries executive traineeship in certain industries is almost inaccessible to women, for somewhat the same reasons. Where on-the-job training is necessary, employers consider women a poor investment since they are expected to marry and leave.

Other employer reactions reflect a number of preconceptions, derived usually from folklore, as to woman's ability or character. It is claimed she is unambitious (one would think this might be balm to the competitive male), that she lacks self-possession and daring, that she has a greater tendency to emotional instability because of her monthly cycle (though the cause-effect relationship here is by no means inevitable), that she is absent more often than men and less productive in her work. Recent studies on absenteeism and productivity have disproved these last arguments (Peterson, 1964, p. 692). And when the Civil Service was asked to give reasons why certain job openings were designated for men or women the designation was dropped altogether. Finally, there is the attitude of women themselves—fundamentally the universal fear that if a woman is too bright, too intellectual, too competent, she won't get a husband. Ever since Annie Oakley let herself be outshot, women have played down their intelligence in the presence of a potential husband, for in all societies, including our own, marriage is promoted and idealized as the one ultimate means of fulfillment for a woman. Even today when young men for the most part believe in equality of education and opportunity for women, girls tend to choose a career by what some intended or hypothetical husband will tolerate (Reisman, 1964, p. 730).

In developing countries, however, women are moving ahead faster than their sisters have in the West, chiefly because of the great shortage of trained manpower. Many governments are taking specific measures to ensure the employment of women in fields into which Western women had to battle their way, and several international women's organizations conduct scholarship programs to enable them to receive the necessary training.

In practically every profession—unless she goes into private practice or free-lances—the ceiling for advancement is lower for a woman than for a man. The bright young man is promoted over a woman of comparable ability, and it is rare for her to become a partner in a firm unless she is married to a man of similar profession—such as architecture or law—and forms a partnership team with her husband. In some countries judgeships and certain other judicial posts are barred to women. Where they do become judges they usually sit in children's courts.

Even in teaching, that genteel ancestor of "suitable feminine" professions, women tend to find both employment and advancement easier at the elementary level. Promotion to executive and administrative posts becomes more difficult the higher the educational level. There are, of course, some notable exceptions in the United States, since the present shortage of teachers at the college level is a factor of tremendous proportions.

In the fields covered by the UN studies cited above, it was found to be easier for a woman to pursue a professional career in government service than in private enterprise or independent practice, but even here her ceiling is lower than that of a man. The United States government, for example, reported (U.S. Department of Labor, 1963) that women economists and statisticians hold high-level research and administrative positions, especially in the Federal Government, but continued: "there is evidence that their opportunities for advancement are better in specialized staff positions than in executive posts." According to Esther

Peterson, Director of the Women's Bureau in the U.S. Department of Labor, ". . . many employers still feel that men should play a dominant role in the economic world." She continues:

> The National Office Managers Association surveyed 1,900 firms and found that 65 percent of those replying questioned the advisability of putting a woman in a supervisory position. Some felt that men would resent working for a woman, and others claimed that men would feel restricted in their actions and language. Women are also denied advancement, particularly to executive positions, because employers feel that they are "too emotional." However, there is no evidence to show that a woman cries more often than a man "blows his stack" [Peterson, 1964, p. 693].

Public relations and advertising are often pointed out as fields of burgeoning opportunity for women. Yet quite recently one of my friends, who is a public relations expert and "ad-woman" of great talent, was passed over for promotion in a large corporation in favor of a man. The question of competence was not involved. She resigned and went into business for herself, and that same firm, ironically enough, is now one of her biggest clients and periodically holds out enticing offers for her to return to the corporate fold. Incidentally it would cost them less if she did.

Dr. Caroline F. Ware, in an unpublished memorandum prepared in 1962 for the President's Commission on the Status of Women, has this to say about the woman who chooses to devote herself to a career:

> At best, her path is a difficult one. Though virtually all fields are technically "open" to her, in reality she encounters all manner of rejections. She meets direct refusals to hire or promote women; she finds she must prove herself much superior to a male candidate in order to be hired or, especially, to be placed in a supervisory or administrative position; she must overcome the widespread assumption that she is not a serious candidate and the mere habit of not considering women which results in her simply being overlooked [Ware, 1962, p. 40].

I would add that, whatever the profession, a woman has to work twice as hard as a man to maintain or advance her position, and she usually earns a lower salary.

The subject of "equal pay for equal work" has been the concern of the International Labor Organization for some fifty years, and it is a continuing item on the agenda of the UN Status of Women Commission. The ILO defines the principle as "the establishment of wage or salary rates on the basis of characteristics and requirements of the job and irrespective of the sex of the worker." About forty-five countries have ratified its 1951 Convention on this subject, but there is still a wide divergence of opinion, interpretation and practice in different countries. The first "equal pay" bill was introduced in the United States Congress in 1945, but it took nineteen years to arrive at the Equal Pay Act of 1963. Arguments against it were much the same as those against women's access to the professions or their advancement to responsible positions. Only twenty of our fifty-one states have enacted "equal pay" legislation.

Trade unions and women's organizations (including the Catholic ones) advocated and are still engaged in promoting the adoption of this principle, which works to the advantage of men as well. It has also been recognized that many single women—and we might better say "women alone" to include widows and divorcées—have family obligations: ill or aging parents, growing children who must finish their education. Despite the fact that many mothers work, with today's spiraling tuition costs it is not unusual for unmarried women to help with the education of nieces or nephews, especially where they are children of large families, or to be called upon to help a brother or sister, or their families, in times of financial difficulty or misfortune, such as disabling illnesses or accidents. Since it is assumed that the single woman "has no one but herself to look after" there is often little hesitation in appealing to her.

COUNSELING STEREOTYPES

There are four stereotypes that still persist in much of the written and other advice to which women are subjected, and they seem to have persisted longer in Catholic circles than elsewhere, at least on the nonscientific level. One of these is the myth of "suitable feminine" occupations, despite the fact that concepts of what makes them "suitably feminine" tend to be mainly social or cultural. There is increasing recognition today that differences in so-called male and female characteristics are due quite as much to cultural conditions as to physiology, that they vary from one culture to another, and that a great deal more needs to be learned about them (Dohen, 1960).

The occupations most frequently mentioned are good examples of the quality of paradox that has always accompanied definitions of woman's role and nature. Teaching, despite its "gentility" and its much advertised scope for satisfying the womanly or maternal nature, did not prevent the caricature of the school teacher as someone of didactic or tyrannic manner that made her unfit for business and likely to be a "bossy" wife. This has changed as more and more married women have returned to teaching and as more men have entered the profession with the rise in prestige and salary scale. Even the teaching nun—however noble a vocation she had been assured was hers—has not been free from priestly deprecation in references to the "good sisters" and their limitations, with little thought that their formation derived in most part from the "good fathers."

It can hardly be said that nursing was quickly and easily accepted as a "suitable" occupation, or that Florence Nightingale had an easy time of it. Women had to overcome tremendous opposition to gain access to medical school, though if tending the sick is so congenial to the feminine nature it is hard to see why women should have been confined to its ancillary aspects and hindered from access to the fuller powers of healing. The secretarial career which has produced the indispensable Girl Friday—a "service" profession, ostensibly suited therefore to "womanly" inclinations—was once the exclusive province of men.

Or take social work. An administrator of my acquaintance recently had to fill the post of director in one of several voluntary community centers she supervises. She had been unable to find a suitable woman candidate and so had to hire a man and, she observed, "of course, at a much higher salary." There are two aspects to this story—the unequal pay for the same job, and the fact that once a specific type of work acquires professional status and a certain salary level it no longer remains a strictly feminine occupation. At a recent meeting of the UN Social Commission, a delegate from a North African country remarked that it had not been possible "for a number of reasons" to recruit women for social welfare training, and so his government had had to recruit men instead.

A second stereotype it would be well to bury is the admonition, addressed to single women especially (who are somehow expected to make some compensation for remaining unmarried), to bring a distinctively "feminine" or "womanly" contribution to the exercise of a profession. I have often heard and read this, and have as often been struck by its superficiality in the context in which it was used. When women got the vote it surprised observers that they did not vote "as women" but as individuals. Surely it is as individuals that they must be expected to work in whatever career they choose, with the competence and professionalism their education and capabilities provide.

If by "womanly" is meant a capacity for understanding, compassion, gentleness and courtesy, a spirit of charity, I have always been of the impression that these are suitable characteristics for Christian gentlemen to cultivate as well. If what is intended is the old 19th-century ideal of docile passivity and sweet accommodation, then the poor girl might just as well give up at the start—she'll never make it—unless, of course, she uses those other strictly "feminine" characteristics guaranteed to get her ahead in a number of professions, though I doubt these are the subject of the pastoral exhortations I have in mind.

In fact, as Alice Rossi (1964, p. 646) points out, the professional man in today's complex economy needs "understanding in human dealings, social poise, and persuasive skill in interpersonal relations"—qualities which in women are called "charm, tact, intuition." For both men and women, the Christian virtues—particularly of humility, resignation, and charity—the precept to do unto others as you would have them do unto you, are fundamental to happy personal relations and adjustments, especially to failure or disappointment. But they have rough going in the highly aggressive and doggedly competitive tribal warfare of the organized jungles of politics and business. In short, the conflict between religious and secular values is much the same for both men and women. The success with which they resolve it depends on their personal spiritual formation and stamina and the degree of drive in their individual ambitions.

Thirdly, in much advice given to women there is a strong emphasis on maternalism. If she is single, she is told that she does, or she must, exercise a "social" or "spiritual" motherhood, and the "feminine" occupations noted above are often neatly categorized under this heading. I suspect that this, too, is often intended as some sort of compensation for her unmarried state. With all due respect for motherhood and the maternal instinct, it should not be overdone and above all it should not be over-sentimentalized. I am reminded here of a friend who is credit-manager in a fairly large manufacturing firm and who is as traditionally "feminine" as anyone could wish, but if she were "maternal" in her particular job she would not last a week.

The single career woman is better advised to develop a certain degree of detachment. If she is carried away by "motherly instincts" she runs the risk of emotional involvements that may do neither herself nor the object of her maternal concern—whether male or female—much good, and they may lead to heartache on her part and to irritation or rejection on theirs. The temptation to mother one's male colleagues, especially the younger ones, is not uncommon and often not particularly intelligent. Its wisdom is doubtful even when its object wants to be mothered.

If woman's biological structure is considered to render her inescapably a mother, is it too ingenuous to ask why man's physiology does not make him inescapably a father, whether he likes it or not? Why do we not hear so much about the obligations of "social" and "spiritual" fatherhood, and the benefits to society and the professions of the traditional "manly" qualities?

Finally, there is the old bromide about "feminine" education, which presumably is to take into account woman's physiological and psychological uniqueness. How the gender of a mind is to be determined in the context of acquiring knowledge and learning to think for oneself is never explained. With all the anxiety expressed today over the predominance of maternal influence in the rearing of boys, woman can hardly be confined to some theoretically "feminine" education if she is not to pass on a "typically feminine" education to her family and thence to the nation.

From a Christian viewpoint, much more emphasis could be placed in the educational system and in counseling on the the need to integrate a chosen field of work with one's purpose in life, as an instrument through which one fulfills one's obligations and earns one's salvation. A profession and the preparation for it, therefore, cannot be determined by some preconceived or generalized traditional concept; it must be suited to the talents and inclinations of the individual human person and should provide the potential for one's full development. It would be helpful if more counseling included the concept of vocation in the choice of each career or profession, as well as the importance of competence in and responsibility to one's work.

STATUS AND PERSONAL ADJUSTMENT

It is commonplace today to liken the disadvantages encountered by women to those of minority groups. If this is a true analogy, then single women may be said to form a subgroup in a minority situation. The unmarried career woman today has—paradoxically again—far less status than her pioneering Victorian predecessor, and even in the Church she is still somewhat of a second-class citizen. Most of the literature on working or professional women is devoted to married women. The single woman tends to be viewed as something of an anomaly or a problem. Until fairly recently religion courses made it quite clear that a woman should either marry or enter the religious life. If she did neither she was a vocation "manquée"—vocationless—even if she had made a choice. Pius XII helped to remedy this concept, labeling the vocation of the single woman providential if somewhat mysterious. Opportunities for service, such as volunteer work in the missions, in PAVLA [2] and

[2] Papal Volunteers for Latin America, begun in 1960, is the lay-mission aspect of the assistance being rendered by the Church in the United States to the Church in Latin America. See also Opportunities for service to the Church and the world, p. 263.

similar movements or associations, have also helped to remove the curse from the unmarried state.

As for secular society, the pressures in favor of marrying begin with early teenage dating and never let up. Parents, movies, TV, advertising, from cosmetics to cigarettes and Coca Cola, remind every girl that her chief aim in life is to get a man and hold him. If she doesn't, she has somehow failed as a woman. A recent episode in a popular TV serial is typical. A beautiful and brilliant science teacher, anxious to have an exceptionally gifted girl student (the superlatives are in the script) go on for higher education in oceanography, loses the battle to the girl's marriage-bent mother and uncomprehending high school sweetheart. The girl does not even go to college, and the beautiful young science teacher, smarting under the mother's attack, is forced to seek reassurance from the bland, blond hero of the series that she is a "woman" despite her interest in science.

It is against this background that the young woman embarking on a career must make her choice. If she is planning or hoping for an early marriage, she is unlikely to take advantage of the numerous opportunities for advanced study now available to most gifted girl graduates. She may well settle for a secretarial job or some other short-term employment and concentrate on finding a husband. Still another factor militating against serious consideration of a career is a tendency among many of today's graduates to change jobs every year or so in the search for new and varied experiences. This, too, has advantages as well as disadvantages but is generally geared to eventual if not-so-early marriage.

If a girl's hopes of marriage do not materialize—for one of the many reasons mentioned by Dr. Campbell—then she is trapped in a routine and not particularly satisfying job. Some would advise her to seek other employment where marriage opportunities are greater (Dohen, 1960). But any move she takes with this in mind—short of going to Alaska or some other area known for its shortage of women—she must take with the knowledge that it is a gamble and she may lose. She must also realize that if she does, all is by no means lost. There is still time to seek or train for work more suited to her capabilities and temperament and to build a useful, happy life for herself.

Given the longer life span and the fact that women are increasingly returning to work when their children are grown, many girls are now being encouraged to choose a profession which they may either wish to continue through marriage or to which they may return later, and consequently go on for the necessary advanced training in preparation for it. This would seem the most practical course, especially if they are not the type to despair at the age of twenty-two or three.

Whether she remains unmarried from choice, necessity or circumstance, it is important for the single woman not to go through life "tentatively," always dreaming of the bridal veil until she is well past fifty, always not quite satisfied with her unmarried state or her work, sticking finally to a job because it would be too costly to lose the fringe benefits. At some point she must grow up, face her internal and external realities and go on from there.

While a married friend may occasionally envy her her freedom, the single woman will have to cope with moments of depression, when she will long for what seems the peace and security of family life and the relief of masculine care and protection. She will at times wonder if indeed she has let "life pass her by" as popular literature keeps reminding her and married friends frequently imply. The complacent question "Are you still in the same job?" does not permit her to reply, "Are you still married—to the same dunderhead?" for somehow, one cannot remind a married woman of her mistake, if she's made one. Nor is it very helpful when a benevolent pastor asks, "Why don't you do something about getting married?" Unless one has sound, practical advice to give it is better to give none at all, and better still not to raise the question in the first place. A disturbed single woman, obviously, would need expert counseling and not amateur helpfulness. For most unmarried women, the advice that it isn't the decision that counts so much as the will power not to regret it, is often quite sufficient.

The single woman's freedom, her greater mobility, her ability to devote extra time to her work when necessary, unfettered and unbeset by family considerations or worries, give her certain advantages over the career wife. On the other hand, she must develop an inner strength if there is no loving family at home capable, even in its thoughtlessness, of rubbing off the rough edges of the day and restoring her perspective. She must maintain this herself, and in doing so it is obvious that she finds support in her friendships, her voluntary activity and her involvement with other members of her family, for whom she often fills a unique and valued role that is deeply and affectionately appreciated.

In pursuing her career, the single woman at times may feel the lack of a partner unless she has one among her colleagues. And she must rely on herself to build the "background" against which advancement in many professions and business organizations is measured. To the question why women often do not seem to reach the degree of achievement attained by men in the same field, one prominent career woman replied, "because they haven't any wives."

When all this has been said, however, the fact remains that if the single woman enjoys her chosen field, if it has meaning for her so that she pursues it with a sense of purpose and vocation, and if she develops a reasonable and satisfying range of outside activities, she will have little time left for the passing moments of depression or loneliness.

One aspect of American society may constitute a special difficulty for the single woman educated in the Catholic ethic, and this is the pre-eminence of sex in American mores and the fact that sexual relations are the test of maleness or womanliness. I am not speaking here of the neurotic who fears or sees "danger" where none exists; nor does one have to be more than ordinarily attractive to encounter the problem. In our society virtue no longer has its own armor, absolute chastity is a coin of archaic mintage and the line formerly drawn between the "good" girl and the "bad" girl is completely blurred.

When a problem arises with male colleagues or other contacts in her profession, especially those important to her work, it requires tact and self-possession and a flair for human relations to fend off their "advances" (they used to be called "improper") and still retain their friendship and a relationship of easy camaraderie. This is, of course, entirely possible, and a sense of humor is an invaluable aid. It also helps if she has not been bemused by that hoary but quite unrealistic teaching—prevalent at least in the past in most Catholic schools— that men are almost helplessly susceptible to sexual stimulation while women are the guardians of control.

This same problem will bedevil her social life, which is not the subject of this paper. I would merely like to call your attention to the fact that whether it is a business contact or a social engagement, refusal to comply on the basis of religious conviction will not necessarily help her with a Catholic. She may, in fact, find a readier acceptance of her reserve on religious grounds from men who are not Catholic. In defense of chastity she stands alone. It not only brings her no tribute, it often subjects her—if she makes the mistake of taking them seriously —to a number of humiliations: she is told she is not a "complete woman," that she is frustrated, or frigid, or "doesn't know what she is missing," or she is perhaps homosexual. The ease with which the latter charge attaches, at least in New York, to two persons of the same sex who share an apartment if only to cope with astronomical rents, is a commentary in itself.

Eva Firkel (1963) has a perceptive discussion on the loss of true friendship in modern society, due among other reasons to overemphasis on the erotic element in human relationships. Yet it is possible, she concludes, for persons of emotional maturity to form warm lasting friendships with persons of either sex, without hidden sexual motives, based on common intellectual or professional aims or interest.

"The single woman is not a defective type," Miss Firkel asserts toward the end of her discussion, "but fully woman in the unmarried state" (Firkel, 1963, p. 212). One might wish that her translator had found a more felicitous phrase, or better still, that the assertion did not need to be made at all.

In the plethora of discussions on "woman" today I am invariably reminded of two lines of a dialect poem written years ago by the famous Negro poet Countee Cullen:

> Ise not a problem, Ise a pusson
> And I craves to be so regarded.

I am afraid that, given the context in which this discussion is taking place, I, too, have fallen into the pattern of stressing the problem aspects in the life of the single career woman. It would be a disservice not to mention the great majority of unmarried women who have achieved success and satisfaction in their work and are not only well-adjusted but happy in their personal lives. If there is a conclusion to be drawn it is simply this: that the woman who remains unmarried for whatever reason has a right to her place in society, to recognition that she has a work to perform, a contribution to make, a personal vocation to fulfill. She is quite capable of being happy and of taking care of herself. In other words, she is not a problem but a person, and she craves to be so regarded.

REFERENCES

Degler, C. L. The changing place of women in America. *Daedalus,* 1964, *93,* 653-670.

Dohen, Dorothy. *Women in wonderland.* New York: Sheed & Ward, 1960.

Firkel, Eva. *Woman in the modern world.* Notre Dame, Ind.: Fides, 1963.

John XXIII. Pacem in terris. Encyclical letter of April 11, 1963. *Acta Apostolicae Sedis,* 1963, *55,* 257-304. English translation: Peace on earth. *Cath. Mind,* 1963, *61,* No. 1175, September, 1963, 47-62, and No. 1176, October, 1963, 45-63.

Peterson, Esther. Working women. *Daedalus,* 1964, *93,* 671-699.

Pius XII. Allocution to the delegates of the International Union of Catholic Women's Organization, September 11, 1947. *Acta Apostolicae Sedis,* 1947, *39,* 480-488. English translation: *Papal teachings: the woman in the modern world.* (Selected and arranged by the Monks of Solesmes.) Boston: St. Paul Editions, 1959. Pp. 163-174.

Reisman, D. Two generations. *Daedalus,* 1964, *93,* 711-735.

Rossi, Alice S. Equality between the sexes. *Daedalus,* 1964, *93,* 607-652.

Ware, Caroline F. Women today: trends and issues. Unpublished background memorandum prepared for the President's Commission on the Status of Women. Washington, D.C., 1962.

United Nations. *Documents of the Commission on the Status of Women.* E/CN.6/341 (1958); E/CN.6/343 and Add. L, 2, and 3 (1959); E/CN.6/345 (1959); E/CN.6/411 and 412 (1963).

United States Department of Labor. *Women in the world today: international report.* Washington: U.S. Government Printing Office, 1963.

The Employed Woman

LOUIS F. BUCKLEY

Louis F. Buckley, who received two degrees from the University of Notre Dame, an A.B. degree in 1928 and an M.A. in 1930, was, at the time of the Institute, the Regional Administrator, Bureau of Employment Security, of the U.S. Department of Labor. He had a long and distinguished career with the Federal Government from which he retired on January 1, 1967. In 1962 he was the recipient of the Meritorious Service Award of the U.S. Department of Labor. Mr. Buckley is a member of many professional organizations, and served as the president of the Catholic Conference on Industrial Problems from 1948 to 1958, and as president of the Catholic Economic Association from 1947 to 1948. He is the author of an impressive number of articles in professional and occasionally in popular journals, most of them bearing on labor and economic problems. Currently, Mr. Buckley is an associate professor of industrial relations in Loyola (Chicago) University's Institute of Industrial Relations.

To say that the working woman is not new to the American scene is, of course, to say something familiar to all of you. Nevertheless, a brief sketch of background conditions and trends will serve as a frame of reference for our discussion of the more recent changes and developments in this area.

HISTORICAL BACKGROUND

According to Elizabeth Baker, women probably never worked harder than they did in their own homes under the domestic system of production prevalent during colonial times and during the early days of our American nation (Baker, 1964). The very inventions which resulted in the shift to the factory system of production, however, were responsible for the early employment of women outside the home. By 1832, for example, most employees of textile factories were young women.

By 1900, 18 out of every 100 wage earners were women. The largest group, representing 40 percent of all employed women, was in the service industries, including domestic service. The second largest group, consisting of 25 percent of the working women, was employed in the manufacturing industries, in some manner of manual operation. The third largest group, comprising 18 percent of the employed women, worked on farms.

Although one in every three professional jobs in 1900 was held by a woman, the women were mainly concentrated in education, where 73 percent of the teachers were female. Significant concentrations of women also occurred in such clerical and sales occupations as telephone operator, bookkeeper, stenographer, typist and saleswoman. Two industries notably employing a high concentration of women in 1900 were trade and transportation.

The typical employed woman at the turn of the century was young, single, and had little education. She was usually the daughter of immigrant parents and was spending the years between school and marriage in one of the many unskilled jobs available in a city. The main types of variants from this pattern were widows, wives whose husbands did not support them, wives of immigrants in the cotton mills of the north, and Negro women in farm or domestic service jobs in the south (Smuts, 1959).

Nearly half of all American women lived on farms in 1900. The work of these women usually included the care of the kitchen garden and much of the work of caring for cattle, pigs, and poultry. The women of the family also produced most of the housekeeping needs such as brooms, soap, and mattresses, and made almost all of the clothing. The family's food supply was largely dependent on the work of the women in the home. They grew and preserved vegetables and fruits and even churned butter.

Many women living in cities often produced part of their food supplies. Parts of New York City, as well as parts of most other cities, were semirural in 1900. In New York City, this was particularly true of Queens, Brooklyn, and Staten Island. Thus, it is not surprising that many families were as dependent on the women's small-scale agriculture as on the man's industrial or commercial employment. The women in these homes were responsible for preserving, canning, and baking, and for making most of the clothing for themselves and their children. City women also supplemented their husbands' earnings by sewing at home, or taking in boarders.

The overall picture of the changes which have taken place in the employment of women outside the home is reflected in the shift in the numerically important categories of employment since 1900. The prominent position occupied by agricultural work declined markedly along with the shift to an urban-industrial culture. Substituted was a marked rise in the importance of clerical and sales occupations. In 1964, 39 percent of the employed women were in clerical jobs, by far the leading occupation. Domestic servant, teacher, and nurse stand as numerically important occupations for women both in 1900 and today.

EMPLOYMENT AND THE SINGLE WOMAN TODAY

The proportion of single women employed declined from 67 percent of all women working in 1900 to 23 percent in 1961. Over the same period, the proportion of married women rose from 15 percent to 55 percent; while the remainder, consisting of widows, divorcées, and married women with the husband absent, remained at a constant 19 percent.

In spite of the sharp increase in the number of women working since 1900, the rate at which single women participate in the labor force has risen but slightly during normal periods. From a level of 41 percent in 1900, the proportion of single women working rose to 44 percent in 1961. Only during the production emergency of World War II was there a significant rise in the proportion of single women working. At that time, 59 percent of this group were in the labor force.

The lack of a growth trend in the rate of labor-force participation among single women probably resulted from the counteraction of several factors. The movement toward the increasing gainful employment of women was counterbalanced by the emphasis on longer schooling. Because of this, a more meaningful statistic for our purpose relates the labor-force participation rate of the single woman to her age grouping. Thus, while only 26 percent of the single women in the 14-to-19-year age group were employed in 1961, 79 percent of the 25-to-29-year-olds and 82 percent of the 45-to-54-year-olds were employed.

As mentioned previously, the single woman represents approximately one in four of all employed women. However, the single woman in the labor force may be divided into two groups. Sixty percent are young women under 30, the great majority of whom will marry in a short time. The remainder, about 40 percent, consists of unmarried women over 30, most of whom will remain single.

The work pattern for women who remain single bears a strong resemblance to that for men. Those who enter the labor force before age 20 and remain unmarried will probably continue working for about 40 years, not quite as long as the 43 years averaged by men. They then live an average of 13 years after retirement.

As can be expected, the two groups of single women occupy quite different positions in the labor force. Of the group under 25 years of age, approximately half are in clerical or sales jobs and one-third are operatives or service workers. Only one in ten is in a job requiring considerable training and responsibility, most being teachers or nurses. On the other hand, almost four in ten single women in the age-45-to-54 group are employed in the upper levels of the occupational structure, as professional workers, managers, supervisors, owners of a business, or as skilled workers. Only a slightly larger number of males in this age category, 45 percent, are employed in these occupations (National Manpower Council, 1957).

CLERICAL OCCUPATIONS

Clerical work represents a particularly important source of employment for women. Forty-six percent more women were employed in this field in 1960 than in 1950. Two-thirds of all clerical workers are women, and almost one-third of all working women have clerical jobs. This concentration is even more striking among single women workers. Forty percent of all employed single women are clerical workers. Perhaps one reason for the heavier concentration of single women in the clerical field is that a large number of jobs require relatively little specialized training or experience. These are entry jobs having a relatively low pay scale. In addition, more single women are able to accept the full-time, year-round conditions required by most clerical jobs.

Over 1,400,000 women were employed as secretaries in 1960, the largest single occupation for women. An additional 258,600 women were employed as stenographers, and 496,700 as typists. Virtually all the workers in these occupations are women. A large number of women are also employed in such occupations as bookkeeper, office machine operator, mail clerk and carrier, and telephone operator.

For all but the most routine clerical position, the minimum educational requirement is normally high school graduation. Many people in clerical occupations also have additional education in a college or business school.

Many hundreds of thousands of clerical vacancies occur yearly because of employee turnover. In addition, a relatively large increase is expected in the number of clerical workers employed in the next ten or fifteen years because of the ever-mounting volume of communications, record-keeping, and paperwork generally, far beyond the labor-saving features of electronic computers and other new office equipment. By 1975, we expect an estimated volume of clerical workers 45 percent above the level of 1960. One significant reason for the rise is the expected rapid expansion of the finance and insurance industries. The secretarial and stenographic occupations expected to be most seriously effected by the expansion are already marked by serious shortages of workers.

The employment opportunities for typists will also increase, but somewhat less rapidly. The increased use of duplicating and other office machines is expected to eliminate most of the need for routine typing.

The trend toward specialization which characterizes so many occupations is also evident in some of the clerical occupations. Many business and professional employers prefer secretaries who are familiar with a special field, either through study or experience. There is a growing demand for law secretary, medical secretary, engineering secretary, and secretaries familiar with the needs of the education field or with government contract negotiations. Bilingual secretaries are becoming increasingly important to export-import offices, banks, travel agencies, manufacturing companies with overseas operations, embassies, and international organizations. Certain other specialties, such as court reporter, can bring greatly increased salaries.

The need for office machine operators is expected to rise rapidly. This still relatively small group, which includes operators of electronic and other kinds of data-processing equipment, is expected to expand faster than any other group of clerical worker. On the other hand, the impact of automation in the next ten years will be greatest on the office worker handling a large volume of relatively routine and standardized procedures. Bookkeeping, now employing the services of 764,000 women, will probably decline in importance as a result of increased use of mechanical equipment. On the other hand, the number of female cashiers, which almost doubled between 1950 and 1960 when it stood at 368,000, will still continue to grow although at a slower rate than in the previous decade. Many of these openings will be for part-time employment, thus attracting married rather than single women.

A recent study by the U.S. Department of Labor summed up the outlook for clerical employment as continued change all along the line: in equipment, duties, requirements, training, and personnel, and continued expansion. Employment probably will mount at a slower rate, however, than in earlier periods.

The ratio of the number of women workers to the number of men in clerical occupations is constantly changing; for example, men outnumbered women as bank tellers in 1950. Over the following decade, however, an average increase of 211 percent in the number of women tellers contrasted with an average increase of 12 percent for men tellers. As a result, the ratio of women to men in 1960 was nine women to four men. Men also outnumbered women as payroll and timekeeping clerks in 1950, but the 1960 ratio was three women to two men. Other clerical occupations in which the number of women has been increasing at a more rapid rate than the number of men include insurance adjuster, examiner, and investigator, stock clerk and storekeeper, and ticket, station, and express agent. On the other hand, although the number of women office machine operators increased 95 percent between 1950 and 1960, the increase in men's employment in this occupation was almost 217 percent.

WOMEN IN PROFESSIONAL POSITIONS

The 2,941,000 women performing professional and technical work in 1962 represented a 58 percent increase over the number in 1950 and 84 percent more than in 1940. Seventeen percent of single employed women are professional and technical workers compared to 13 percent of employed married women. As the occupational group with the second largest number of single women, the number of single professional workers is exceeded only by the number of single clerical workers.

With the demand for teachers to staff the nation's expanding school system continuing to rise, teaching remains the most popular profession among women. The 1,258,000 women teachers in the elementary and secondary schools at work in April 1962 comprised 43 percent of all professional women. About one in five of the women teaching below the college level is single. Enrollment in elementary schools will continue to rise, but at a slower rate than in the past, and will level off towards the end of this decade. By 1975, an increase of 20 percent is estimated for elementary schools and 26 percent for high schools. The greatest increases will be in the junior colleges, the colleges and the universities. Although women constitute only 20 percent of the college teachers, half of the women teaching in college are single women.

As the second largest occupation of professional women in this country, now providing jobs for more than a half-million women, nursing resembles teaching in many respects. In both occupations a constant shortage has existed and will probably continue. A somewhat larger proportion of women in nursing—one in four—are single than in teaching below the college level, where the ratio is one in five. The outlook is especially favorable for teachers and nurses with a bachelor's or master's degree for administrative and supervisory positions. In addition to teachers and nurses, the 1960 census recorded over 20,000 single women in each of the following occupational groups: librarian, medical and dental technician, social and welfare worker, religious worker, accountant, musician and music teacher.

About 26 percent of all women in professional positions are in medicine and other health fields. In addition to professional nurse, this group includes a significant number of women as doctors, medical technologists, x-ray technicians, physical therapists, dieticians, pharmacists, occupational therapists, and medical record librarians. Population growth, increased awareness of the need for proper medical care, greater coverage under health insurance plans, and the availability of more funds for medical research and facilities are among the leading factors which have created a strong demand for health services.

During the 1950s, the professions in which women made their most significant employment gains, either in terms of percentage increases or number of workers, were those related to the service and social needs of society such as recreation and group worker, personnel and labor relations worker and therapist. In contrast, the greatest expansion in women's employment during the 1940s occurred in such war-related occupations as chemist, engineer, draftsman and radio operator.

Among the professions in which the number of women more than doubled between 1950 and 1960 were: mathematician, personnel and labor-relations worker, public-relations worker and publicity writer, recreation and group worker, sports instructor and official. The number of women in certain other professional occupations increased from 30 to 60 percent during this period, including accountant and auditor, college president and professor, editor and reporter, librarian, musician and music teacher, nurse, physician and surgeon, teacher, and therapist and healer.

It is apparent that job horizons will continue to widen for the college women in the 1960s. Challenging careers for qualified college women have never existed in such a variety, nor offered so many rewards. News items appeared in the *Wall Street Journal* this spring which indicated a marked increase in the number of business corporations recruiting at women's colleges. The number of company recruiters visiting Mount St. Mary's in Los Angeles, for example, was up 50 percent. However, only 13 percent of their senior class went into business. Most in demand by business are graduates in science, mathematics and economics, but there is a growing need for librarians for corporate libraries.

The number of professional women in federal government service made significant gains during the last two decades. Women comprised 18 percent of all government professional personnel in 1959, contrasted to eight percent twenty years earlier.

The summary of job opportunities for 1965 college graduates prepared by the Department of Labor indicates that the demand is highest for graduates in scientific and technical fields. Men and women with degrees in electrical, chemical and mechanical engineering, in chemistry, physics and mathematics, are most sought after.

FACTORY WORK

While the number of women in factory and other operative occupations was higher in 1962 than ten or 20 years earlier, the increase has not kept pace with the overall expansion in women's employment. In 1962, there were 3.3 million women operatives. About 15 percent of all women workers and about ten percent of all single women workers were in this category. However, in 1950 the smaller number of women operatives, 3.2 million, represented almost 19 percent of the total of all women workers. Much of the demand for women in operative jobs arose during World War II and continued into the high-level economy of the postwar period. However, with recent technical innovations, and the increased use of automatic machinery in mass production, the demand for production workers has not been increasing as fast as that for technician, research and clerical worker, and skilled craftsman.

Women continue to be an important part of the textile industry. Their traditional niche is the world of manufacture, where they constituted 45 percent of all textile workers in 1960 as compared with 40 percent in 1900. Nevertheless, in spite of an ever-increasing number and variety of alternative occupations opening up for women in the past ten years, only nine in every 100 women at work in manufacturing were in textiles in 1960 compared with 15 percent at mid-century.

Almost four out of five apparel workers are women, their number having increased seven percent since 1950. This compares with the overall decrease of 28 percent shown above for the textile industry. Women dominate the sewing occupations. The number of sewers and stitchers rank eighth in the total employment of women in all occupations. There are more sewers and stitchers than there are typists employed in all industries and twice as many as the number of women assemblers.

The decline in employment of women in textile, tobacco, and food manufacturing since 1950 represents the general decline of employment in these industries brought about by technological changes. It is interesting to note that the total employment of women in the nondurable or soft-goods industries, where they have conventionally been employed in the past, has not changed since 1950, while the employment of women in the durable or "heavy" goods industries increased by 80 percent. The overall gain of almost half a million women workers in the durable goods industries in 12 years stems largely from two main factors: marked industrial expansion in response to economic and military needs, and, secondly, developments in industrial technology which have introduced new processes tending to lighten the physical demands on the worker and thus open more industrial jobs to women. As a result, durable goods industries employed two-fifths of the women factory workers in 1962, in contrast to one-third in 1950. The largest employer of women in this industry division is the electrical equipment and supplies industry, which includes firms manufacturing radio and television sets, telephones, electric lamps, electric measuring instruments and household appliances. Almost 700,000 women are employed in the manufacture of nonelectrical machinery for offices, stores, metalworking and general industrial machinery, and service household machines, fabricated metal products, including cutlery, hand tools, hardware, and the manufacture of various instruments, including watches and clocks.

Elizabeth Baker has concluded that as automation advances, increased employment of women may result from relief from dangerous, dirty, heavy and backbreaking jobs, and the reduction of some skilled operations to tasks that require only a few days or weeks of training. Also, the probable decentralization of plants into rural areas whose local workers union organizers largely fail to reach, is likely to result in further employment for women. Automation will also reduce the number of repetitive monotonous and highly specialized tasks on the assembly line and increase the need for better education in order to carry greater responsibility (Baker, 1964).

SALES WORKERS

There are 1,499,000 saleswomen engaged in retail trade, as indicated by the April 1962 employment report. This occupation is second only to secretary in the number of women employed. The increase of 25 percent in saleswomen from 1950 to 1960 was exceeded only by increases in the number of service and clerical workers.

In retail trade, women constitute about one-third the number of managers and officials in apparel and accessories stores and well over one-fifth in general merchandise and five-and-dime stores. It is estimated that between one-fourth and one-third of the executives in department stores are women. Moreover, store buyers should definitely be classified as executives, and their inclusion with other managers and officials would raise still further the percentage of women among department store executives.

The use of automatic vending machines and "self-service" has changed and will continue to change the nature of the selling job. The Women's Bureau concludes, however, that leaders in the retailing field believe that as long as fashion remains a vital factor in sales appeal, the employment of women in the industry is assured. Fashion has become, decade by decade, more important in the 20th century in the marketing of common goods. Today, the latest style, in line, color, design, and ornamentation, has become crucial in the sale of many items.

Over the long run, the number of salespeople employed in retail stores is expected to rise moderately. Rising income levels will probably increase the demand for more expensive merchandise which usually requires the service of an experienced sales person. Little of the expected increase in sales employment is likely to be in routine sales jobs. Much of the demand will be for workers who are skilled in salesmanship and well informed about the merchandise they sell.

Most of the sales jobs that become available outside the retail field, such as in wholesale trade, manufacturer's representative, insurance agent, and real estate salesman, will probably continue to be filled by men. However, women are finding increasing opportunities in some of these occupations. This is particularly true in the real estate field where women find that their familiarity with home features of special interest to housewives, who share decisions on home purchases, is a marked advantage. Employment in this field is expected to accelerate during the early 1970s when the many young people born shortly after World War II will be establishing their own homes.

SERVICE WORKERS

The individual occupation among service jobs, other than private household work, employing the most women, is that of waitress. Over 700,000 waitresses were employed in 1960. Of all the largest detailed occupations of women, waitress was sixth in importance. About 87 percent of all those working as waiter or waitress were women. The second largest occupation among service workers, and the eleventh in numerical importance in the list of occupations of women, is that of cook. Over 350,000 women are cooks and they constitute 64 percent of total employment in the occupation. The number of waitresses and cooks employed is expected to increase fairly rapidly over the long run.

Other important service occupations for women are hospital attendant, hairdresser, charwoman, and practical nurse. The demand for hairdressers, practical nurses and hospital attendants is expected to continue to expand rapidly.

Employment of service workers, exclusive of household workers, increased by 48 percent from 1950 to 1960. This was the largest expansion of any occupational group.

There are over two million private household workers. The number of women so employed is exceeded only by the number of female secretaries and retail saleswomen.

Private-household jobs increased by 24 percent between 1950 and 1960. Although this traditional occupation of women remains numerically important, it should be recognized that only one woman in ten is so employed today, compared to two out of every five in 1900. In contrast to earlier days, a large proportion of these women live outside the households in which they work, and almost two-thirds work only part-time. Less than a fifth are employed a full 50 to 52 weeks a year.

FARM WORKERS

Farmwork is the only large occupational group in which women's employment has been declining both proportionately and numerically. The number of women classified as farm laborers dropped almost 50 percent between 1950 and 1960. In April 1961, 120,000 women were classified as farmers and 539,000 as farm laborers. However, the number of women employed as farm laborers more than doubles during peak seasons.

ECONOMIC TRENDS

Recent industrial trends conclusively point to an increased employment of women. The shift has been from primary growth in the production industries (manufacturing, agriculture, construction, and mining) where comparatively few women are employed, to the service industries (trade, government, finance, insurance and real estate) where a higher proportion of women are used. The related shift from blue-collar occupations (operative and laborer) to white-collar occupations (clerical, sales, professional and managerial) has also resulted in increased employment opportunities for women.

The impact of automation upon future jobs for women cannot be forecast with any certainty. We have noted increased employment of women even in the telephone industry where great technological advancement has been made in recent years. Technological change will continue to displace workers in specific occupations while other types of emloyment will continue to grow. For example, while there was a decrease in the number of women telephone operators between 1945 and 1960, there was at the same time a much greater increase in the number of women employed in the telephone industry as clerical, business office, sales, professional and semiprofessional employees and as managers.

The technological innovations of the future are expected to require the development of new skills, to reduce the need for workers engaged in routine tasks, and to result in the temporary displacement of some workers. Yet, a contraction in total employment opportunities is not expected to occur as long as the economy continues to grow. Moreover, automation is not likely to have a drastic effect in the near future upon women's employment in service, sales and secretarial jobs, or in professional occupations such as teaching, nursing and social work.

Despite these industrial and occupational trends, which have resulted, and should continue to result, in the expansion of employment opportunities for women, we find some disturbing elements which must be considered. The most serious of these is the high rate of unemployment which has existed for a number of years. The rate for women has been above six percent for four years and has not been below four percent since 1953. The situation is even more serious when broken down by age and color. The unemployment rate for nonwhite girls, age 16 and 17, was 40 percent in 1963 and 36.5 percent in 1964, compared to 18 and 17 percent respectively for white girls of this age group.

There are two major trends which account for this serious unemployment problem. Our economy is not expanding rapidly enough to compensate for productivity increases and to absorb, in addition, increases in the size of our labor force, which will average 1.4 million per year for the rest of the decade (Buckley, 1965). The number of women age 14 to 24 in the labor force increased by only 6.5 percent from 1950 to 1960 while it will increase by 55 percent between 1960 and 1970.

The second element which aggravates the unemployment problem is the changing nature of the white collar jobs which are expanding. These are jobs in trade, finance, government, and central offices which require education, pleasing appearance and bearing, and reasonable language skills. The routine clerical, factory, or service jobs which formerly existed are now largely being performed by machines. On the other hand, domestic service jobs are increasing at a slower rate than clerical and sales jobs. As a result, we find a large number of young unemployed girls, 16 to 21 years of age, with little formal schooling. Relatively more of the nonwhite unemployed girls (22 percent) than white girls (15 percent) have no more than eight years of formal schooling. It is estimated also that about two-thirds of the unemployed girls are not married.

The existence of a labor surplus has enabled employers to raise their hiring standards. A number of employers have made a high school diploma a prerequisite for employment irrespective of the actual job requirements. This is done simply as a screening device to cut down the number of people to be interviewed, or to ensure "a better class of workers." A study of females age 16 to 21 years of age in the labor market in 1963 indicated that white high school graduates had an unemployment rate of 13 percent and those with less than four years of high school had a rate of 26 percent. The unemployment rate for female nonwhite women in this age group was 36 percent for those with four years of high school and 27 percent for those with less than four years of high school.

As a result of these divergent trends, we have the paradox of unemployment among young women traditionally employed in the service industries and great shortages of qualified applicants in such occupations as secretary, stenographer, flight hostess, typist, practical nurse, general office clerk, dental hygienist, registered nurse, social worker, counselor, librarian and teacher.

One of the more encouraging aspects of the existence of shortage occupations is the increased cost of indulging in race and sex discrimination. Recently I spoke before a group of accountants and noticed the absence of Negro or female members in the group. I predicted then that the color and sex composition of this group would change as the result of the shortages of qualified white males. Because of the great need for trained personnel, an increasing number of employers are finding it advantageous to break with tradition in the employment of women. They are more likely today, and in the years to come, to consider women applicants for positions in such expanding shortage occupations as accountant, engineer, mathematician, chemist and physicist.

Another development which may further open doors to job opportunities for women as well as Negroes, is the Civil Rights Act of 1964. This act makes discrimination in employment unlawful if it is as a result of an individual's sex, race, color, religion, or national origin. It must be recognized, however, that this section of the Act applies at this time only to employers of 100 persons, although eventually it will apply to employers of 25 or more employees.

The major trend in the shift of employment patterns for Negro women workers is away from the traditional home-service types of work. This reflects recent gains in employment and educational status. There has also been a drop in the percentage of Negro women workers in farming and factory occupations and an increase in the percentage of those in clerical, professional and sales occupations, and in service work other than household.

A recent study made by the Women's Bureau indicated that while the number of employed Negro women reached 2.5 million in 1960, an increase of 31 percent since 1950, the percentage of private-household workers among Negro women workers dropped from 60 percent in 1940 to 41 percent in 1950 and to 36 percent in 1960. On the other hand, the percentage of Negro women clerical workers rose from one to five percent between 1940 and 1950 and to nine percent in 1960. The increase of Negro women service workers outside households progressed from ten percent in 1940 to 19 percent in 1950 and 21 percent in 1960. A significantly greater number of Negro women also have been employed in banking, retail trade, medical and other health services, public administration, and in some branches of manufacturing that are expanding.

TRAINING OPPORTUNITIES FOR WOMEN

One answer to the problem of "structural" unemployment is to provide women with the education they need to qualify for the jobs which are going begging at the present time. The Women's Bureau emphasizes that women's goal must be to develop their individual talents to the fullest extent possible. I agree with the conclusion reached by Elizabeth Baker in her recent study of technology and women's work that "surely in this age of revolutionizing technology more and more education is the most promising route" (Baker, 1964, p. 442).

Fortunately, action is being taken to expand and improve training opportunities in which women and girls may participate. Training programs under the Manpower Development and Training Act of 1962 (MDTA) are expanding in occupational areas where current shortages of trained women workers exist. Women account for 41 percent of all unemployed workers. Correspondingly, two out of five MDTA trainees in 1964 were women. Over one-third of the women trainees in 1964 were under 22 years of age, about the same proportions that they constituted of all unemployed women. Over one-third of the women enrolled in institutional MDTA training programs in 1964 were nonwhite, a substantially higher proportion than their 23 percent representation among all unemployed women workers.

Training under the MDTA is geared to upcoming needs as the occupational requirements change. Relatively fewer women are being trained for work as factory operators and more for the expanding service sector of the economy. An additional 100 training occupations opened up for women in 1964 under the MDTA beyond the 150 in which training was offered in 1963. For example, women are being offered refresher courses in teaching and in technical illustrating. Among the new clerical and sales occupations were console operator and grocery checker, and, in the service category, special diet worker, geriatric-nursing assistant, and attendant at children's institutions. More women continue to be trained as stenographers than in any other occupation.

There are other important recent Federal legislative enactments which are assisting in better preparing young people for the changing world of work. These include the Vocational Education Act of 1963, and the Economic Opportunity Act of 1964, which have provisions for adult basic education and work training.

CONCLUSION

Education and training may well be the key to our future. For individual women seeking paid employment, good occupational preparation can lead to jobs which allow for full expression of personal talents and interests. It can enable the worker to achieve the literacy and the skills needed to find a place in this automated world of work. As Pope John XXIII emphasized, the economic system must "allow and facilitate for every individual the opportunity to engage in productive labor" (John XXIII, 1961, No. 55, p. 426). Until this objective is achieved, we cannot maintain that the recognition of human dignity is a practical reality in all parts of American life.

REFERENCES

Baker, Elizabeth. *Technology and woman's work.* New York: Columbia University Press, 1964.

Buckley, L. F. Automation: master or servant. *Cath. Mind,* 1965, *63*, 36-41.

John XXIII. Mater et magistra. Encyclical letter of May 15, 1961. *Acta Apostolicae Sedis,* 1961, *53*, 401-464. English translation: Christianity and social progress. *Cath. Mind,* 1961, *59*, 411-479.

National Manpower Council. *Womanpower.* New York: Columbia University Press, 1957.

Smuts, R. W. *Women and work in America.* New York: Columbia University Press, 1959.

United States Department of Labor, Bureau of Labor Statistics. *Occupational outlook handbook.* Bulletin No. 1375. Washington: U.S. Government Printing Office, 1963.

United States Department of Labor, Women's Bureau. *1962 handbook on women workers.* Bulletin No. 285. Washington: U.S. Government Printing Office, 1962.

United States Department of Labor, Women's Bureau. *Negro women workers in 1960.* Bulletin No. 287. Washington: U.S. Government Printing Office, 1962.

Sexuality and the Single Woman

GEORGE HAGMAIER, C.S.P.

Father George Hagmaier, C.S.P., is Associate Director of the Paulist Institute for Religious Research, and professor of religious education at the Catholic University of America. He holds an A.B. degree from Santa Clara University, California, an M.A. from St. Paul's College, Washington, D.C., and an Ed.D. from Teachers College, Columbia University. He is the first priest to have been awarded the doctoral degree by the department of marriage and family life at Teachers College, Columbia. Father Hagmaier is co-author of the well known Counselling the Catholic *(1959), and is a frequent contributor to magazine and journal articles, particularly in the areas of marriage counseling and religion and mental health. Father Hagmaier is a director of the Religious Education Association, an advisor to the American Foundation of Religion and Psychiatry, and a member of the Academy of Religion and Mental Health, and the American Catholic Psychological Association.*

Sexuality, if it is to be validly considered, must be seen as touching in some way every major area of human life. Because of its pervasive presence, therefore, a paper such as this cannot possibly limit itself to mere genital or stimulatory considerations, so characteristic of much writing today on "sex and the single girl." Regrettably, however, the very scope of the subject requires that we speak only in the most general terms about the category "single woman," lest we stereotype a group made up of individual women as varied and unique as any found among the married.

Very little has been written about the sexual conflicts of the single woman attempting to live the Christian life. What has been written is, by and large, pretty bad. Preachers, confessors, and religious guides seemed so often to be saying that to remain single one must become sexless. Hence, there was little left to be done, other than to avoid scrupulously any "person, place, or situation" which could lead to stimulation or involvement. In practice, this often implied that a prayerful, "deeply spiritual" personal life plus a heady involvement in "good works" were to substitute for warm, close, and affectionate relationships with others.

Often enough, too, the Catholic writer presumes that there are only two respectable categories into which our single women fall. These would be a wholehearted and dedicated service to others "in the world," or the obvious alternative, entry into religious life. Rarely considered are those who are called to neither. Through no fault of their own they are unable to find a husband, and remain for a lifetime keenly conscious of their unfulfilled and lonely state. The encyclical of Pius XII (1954) on Holy Virginity is an example of the pious literature that offers little consolation and may even create additional conflict for those virgins who are *not* content with their lot. Contemporary psychology suggests that some widows resent the exhortation not to remarry, and that the description of marriage as a spiritually "inferior" state of life does not effectively reassure those who yearn fruitlessly for a husband.

It may be helpful, then, to remind ourselves of the variety of types found under the heading "the single woman." I suggest that we consider two general groupings: those who have chosen celibacy through a process of careful and reasoned deliberation, and therefore freely, and then a second group who are celibate chiefly because of some unconscious block to marriage, indicating a less-free and poorly reasoned choice. Let us look more closely at these two groups.

FREELY CHOSEN CELIBACY

Among those in the first category (celibacy-freely-chosen) is the *lay* apostle. This is the individual who dedicates her life to the service of others, particularly as she dispenses the corporal works of mercy to those in need. She foregoes the opportunities for marital happiness fully aware of the sacrifice she is making in terms of the ascetic, contemplative, and apostolic goals she pursues. Secondly, there are the *religious* women and members of secular institutes who further particularize the goals mentioned above by pursuing that mode of personal perfection made possible by formal commitment to the evangelical counsels of poverty, chastity and obedience, and by life together in community.

Finally, there is a third group characterized by a certain basic immaturity or neuroticism *consciously* acknowledged by them as the chief reason for their remaining unmarried. They feel—and in many instances quite rightly so—that marriage would only complicate their lives beyond the tolerable, bringing unhappiness to their spouses, and casting real doubt on their potential abilities for parenthood. Precisely because they do have such prudent and commendable insights into their own limitations, these women are able to live far happier and productive lives than if they had assumed what for them would be a precarious adventure with matrimony.

We might indicate, in passing, that it is possible for these free commitments to celibacy to be *temporary* as well as permanent. There are certain women (the average teenager is one of them!) who are freely celibate for a time. As circumstances, insight, and readiness of various kinds develop, they then opt for marriage. This happens, on occasion, even with the immature or neurotic adult who, through therapy or other developments, re-examines her potential for marriage. In rare instances, though more and more frequently today, members of religious communities have second thoughts about celibacy some years after their profession, particularly if they were not given the opportunity during their formative years to consider other alternatives to the vowed life they were choosing. The whole question of temporary vocation must be dealt with in a theological context, of course. From the psychological point of view, there seems to be no reason why certain souls who have lived the religious life with dedication cannot at some future time feel themselves called to the pursuit of perfection within the marriage state. We await with eagerness the further conclusions of those theologians and behavioral scientists who together are deliberating these matters.

This is the place, perhaps, to mention a somewhat elusive type of single woman who does not fall easily into any of the rather clearly defined groups above. I refer to the classic career woman—the executive administrator, the artist, the scholar, and others—who is so absorbed in her profession that she puts her work above all else, including marriage. She is an extremely capable and often very personable individual, but there is nothing very altruistic about her motives. Her keen mind, her great powers of concentration revel in the pursuit of her professional objectives, and all else is secondary. Currently a debate centers on the question: Is such a woman completely mature and capable of clear motivation? Or does the fact that she foregoes without regret the consolations provided by husband, children, and family suggest that she is at least slightly neurotic, immature, or emotionally unfulfilled? We shall certainly not attempt an answer!

ENFORCED CELIBACY

Let us turn to the second general category, namely those whose choice of celibacy has not been a particularly free one.

Obviously, there are first of all the *very young* who yearn for marriage and yet are for the moment prevented by some important detail of our highly complex twentieth-century culture from making a marital commitment. High school or college must be completed first, a better job must be secured, finances are precarious, parents object—these are only a few of the external factors which mercilessly impinge upon the yearnings of the young. They need our generous solicitude which might help them to use the time of waiting as a time for growth rather than of alienation and of bitterness.

Next, we must consider those who make up perhaps the largest group living in "enforced celibacy." I speak, of course, of the hundreds of thousands of women of all ages who through no fault of their own have been unable to find a husband. They are victims of the *numerical imbalance* of the sexes. In our culture there are a great many more women than there are men. What percentage of these unmarried females falls into some of the earlier-mentioned categories is hard to assess. But it seems certain that a great number are free from many of the motivations characteristic of others who remain deliberately unmarried. They ache for the love of a man and they are admirably prepared to return that love. They yearn for the joys of motherhood, and they are acutely conscious of the loneliness which an empty womb and an empty house portend. They feel helpless, cheated, at times even bitter and enraged, especially if they are not particularly pretty, have not been given the opportunity to develop the social graces so essential in certain circles, or have remained home to assume responsibilities for sick or aged parents. Because of these or other reasons they have been passed by.

There is, for this group, a subtle and sometimes dreadful psychological change. They share in their teens the *expectations* of all their companions who look with eagerness to the day when "they will get married." As the years roll on, the "when" becomes "if." In their late twenties and early thirties, expectations give way to *hope,* and hope sometimes to *desperation.* The final phase becomes one of *resignation*, but the quality of this capitulation to the inevitable varies from person to person. The wellspring of hope is never more eternal than in the bosom of many a maiden. The door is still open "if the right man comes along. . . ."

It is this group—those who are ready for marriage but who have had singleness forced upon them—which needs further attention from the Church and from the counselor. Our one gesture has, on occasion, been a "young adults club," operated by a large parish or some religious organization. It usually attempts a program of intellectual, spiritual, and social activities. In several instances, this has been done quite proficiently, and lonely young people, particularly in crowded urban centers, are able to pursue new theological and liturgical trends as well as deal with their loneliness in a kind of pseudo-community. Some fine marriages result in many instances; however, the male participants of such a program are not only in the clear minority, but they are particularly inadequate and immature bachelors who have long avoided marriage and are now dealing, sometimes in desperation, with their own problems. The girls, by contrast, are often more adjusted, and their frustration can become even more acute as they view the meager prospects around them.

Another group of unwilling celibates are the widows, grass and otherwise. They have known the consolations of marital companionship and sexual exchange, and the loss is keenly felt. Many find great difficulty in adjusting to a life without sexual stimulation after years of such gratification. Many widows would like to remarry, but again the supply of eligible males is slight. (There are, incidentally, very few widowers—at least not for long.)

Then there are the very *seriously repressed* or gravely neurotic women who flee from marriage although they do not understand why. Many of them will protest with vehemence that they would like nothing better than to find a man, but these laments are unconscious rationalizations which do not match their basic fears and defenses. Many sociologists and psychologists feel that the majority of single women fall into this category. This seems an unrealistic conclusion, if only in the face of the shortage of males. However, there are a good many who do seem to have basic inhibitions which prevent them from really taking the proper steps. They have many different personalities. Some seem quite lighthearted and companionable, yet when a man becomes serious they will pull away. Others will go along right up to the engagement—or even wedding time—and then balk at some inevitable flaw they discover in their fiancé. This "hard to please" mentality is typical of the anxious and immature woman. Since she will marry only a perfect man, she inevitably protects herself from this eventuality.

COUNSELING THE SINGLE WOMAN

What can we say in regard to the counseling needs of the single woman? To begin with, we must emphasize that the single woman, like human beings everywhere, is very individual. Her own background, conflicts, and opportunities for solutions need consideration. We have no right to lump her into a general grouping, any more than we should a married woman. Certain general observations, however, may be helpful.

If the single state has been freely and maturely chosen, then overt sexual conflicts are likely to be infrequent. For the lay woman, occasional masturbation or a budding affair may be surprising intruders into an otherwise placid and fulfilled life. We must meet these difficulties in the confessional and elsewhere with the same quiet understanding and encouragement which we bring to other counseling situations. In a good many instances, difficulties arise when an absorbing job or an exciting apostolate become routine and uncreative. When such opportunities for sublimation dwindle or vanish, then sexual pressures might emerge with a heretofore unexperienced intensity. (This is also a problem for the reluctantly single girl.) Both groups resent the cheery and naïve suggestions of some confessors or religious guides: "Plunge into your work; get yourself a good job." It is precisely the frustrations of a poor or unsatisfying workload which lead certain professional women to seek compensations through sexual experimentation.

The Kinsey studies (1953), which on this score we have no reason to question, indicate that when the single woman engages in overt sexual activity, masturbation is by far the most frequent practice. It is important that confessors and spiritual guides meet this problem with the same patience and understanding we bring to the counseling of the adolescent and the married.

The observations we have made in other publications (Hagmaier & Gleason, 1959) concerning the unconscious dynamics underlying the habit of masturbation are particularly applicable. So often priest and penitent alike will dwell too much on the external circumstances assess-

ing guilt: e.g., number of times, degree of resistance, exposure to harm-
ful reading, recreation, companions, etc., when in reality the difficulty
is rooted in other matters—often not sexual in essence.

The vulnerability of the single woman to loneliness, boredom, frustration, and hostility can often be a far more telling reason why tensions
build, and compulsive, though shameful and unsatisfying, release is
sought in this fashion. If ways are found to involve these individuals in
a more real, warm and satisfying life with other people—in other words,
a more human and less 'humanoid' existence—then many of the pressures may abate or vanish, and the symptoms will lend themselves to
more adequate control.

Let us consider now the lay woman who is an unwilling celibate. Of
all groups in the church, hers is perhaps the most neglected. To begin
with, she resents very much being spoken of as no different from the
bobby-soxer, the widow, the neurotic spinster, or the nun. Encouragement, consolation, and direction, which might be appropriate for one
or the other of these groups, have little or no meaning for her.

If she continues to dream of marriage, her search for sexual identity
is surely different from that of the confirmed celibate or the nun. She
has not yet (if ever) made a lifetime commitment to the single state
and therefore her openness to potentially fulfilling sexual relationships
presents different problems. The quality of her "temptations," the frequency of falls-due-to-weakness may be more troublesome, and she must
live with an ambivalence about the future over which she has no control.

Some of the typical advice she has been getting, often enough from
spokesmen in the Church, particularly irritates her. It would include some
of the following: Single women should live a "protected life" at home
until married. Single women are needed by their parents. Single women
should sublimate sexuality through work. (Most of them do not enjoy
the drudgery of an unimaginative job any more than the married!)
Single women should fill their free time with charitable enterprises. (One
confessor was quoted as saying to a single office worker: "I know you
are a statistician, but what are you doing to save your soul?") Each of
these observations has its place, but none of them is by any means
universally applicable.

Particularly unrealistic are many pieces of advice regarding the single
woman's social life. She is urged to seek her friends among other single
people, preferably other women. She is specially cautioned to "watch
out for the married man." On the other hand, unduly anxious religious
guides who have met an occasional lesbian problem may also warn
against the dangers of a too intimate relationship with other women.

In practice, then, the single Catholic woman sometimes finds herself hemmed in by almost contradictory attitudes, expectations, and advice. A good many of her contemporaries, including some priests, hint that "there is something wrong with you if you're not married." So often single women are not welcome in mixed company, but if invited to a party they are expected to bring "a friend" on their own. (The "Noah's Ark" concept, one described it!) Married women often resent friendships between their husbands and a single woman. Because of these, and many other oversights, the unmarried are often very lonely and unhappy people, particularly when they are prevented from establishing a deep, ongoing involvement with the married community.

It is my impression—purely a guess—that some priests find it particularly difficult to counsel objectively with the single woman. I would wonder, in terms of the psychological factors involved, if certain priests are not unwittingly threatened by the "free" status of the single woman. Since she has no prior commitment to a spouse, the discussion of sexual matters in particular may be unsettling to the clergyman who has not yet faced all of his own unconscious sexual conflicts.

THE SINGLE NON-CELIBATE WOMAN

Before concluding this paper, it seems appropriate to mention, at least in passing, a category not included in the groups mentioned above. These are women who are single but not celibate. Most of them are complex psychiatric types, and for this reason we are not attempting an analysis of either their dynamics or the counsel process by which they may be helped. They would include the *prostitute* and the lesbian, both of whom basically fear and resent men; their personalities were usually affected in the very early developmental years. The *unwed mother* produces a child "by accident." She is so often a little child herself, searching for a loving father figure whom in many instances she has never known.

Two other types are special problems of our age. One is the "enlightened" or "emancipated" unmarried female *who needs a man but not children*. Simone de Beauvoir (at various times the companion of Jean-Paul Sartre and Norman Mailer) is an example. Then there are a considerable number of women *who seem to need children but not a man*. These mothers, often with many offspring, are found particularly among the underprivileged groups in the United States and Latin America.

Obviously all of the above require special educational and psychiatric services before the priest can be of help. The priest's knowledge of the proper professional resources, should he be called upon, will probably be his most effective ministry for them. As confessors, priests should, of course, be particularly reluctant to play a strong judgmental role in these cases. To insist, for example, that a common law marriage be *immediately* rectified, or that two lesbians who have set up a "housekeeping" arrangement must immediately break up if absolution is to be granted, is often totally unrealistic. We must not be misled into thinking that the sexual relationship is always the key one, when in reality occasional sexual experience is frequently a by-product or side effect of other companionable needs which these deeply lonely people are seeking to assuage. In so many instances they will eventually split up by themselves, but only after they have come to see the value of separation. As long as they are willing to search for further answers, and particularly when they involve themselves in psychotherapy, the priest should be in no hurry to tamper with the present *status quo,* even though sexual acting out may on occasion be a part of the picture.

Finally, let us say just a word or two about a vast group of temporarily single women who are re-examining, along with their male counterparts, the very substance of Christian sexuality. These are the adolescents and the young adults who are no longer content with the atrophied moral casuistry of past generations. Most of them (many more girls than boys) have genuine inclinations to preserve their virginity until marriage. However, they are demanding that the Church give them better reasons for remaining celibate. Paradoxically, the personalist revolution which has touched theology, liturgy, and the whole scope of pastoral concern has opened the windows in this area as in so many others.

Young people are being urged to resolve their own consciences in knowledge and prudence in moral matters. They do not respond reflexively to the traditional list of *do*s and *don't*s so typical of our earlier catechesis. Our young people want clear answers to their direct questions. They want to know why it is that "suddenly with marriage what was formerly bad becomes good." They want, further, to be told why, for truly devoted and mature young persons, the marriage *contract* makes all the difference.

We must not belittle or dismiss this earnest questioning. For one thing, our young men and women have come a good distance from some of the less mature and hypocritical standards of the past. Thoughtful young people today deplore the adolescent double standard and the playboy ethic which encourages enjoyable sexual activities without deep personal involvement or responsibility. Youngsters and young adults are seeing sexual love as an intense interpersonal communication, a way of expressing affection, a way of finding self in and with and through the other. The theologians and the behavioral scientists must put their heads together and present meaningful rationales for remaining aloof from these kinds of involvement. I feel certain that valid arguments are there, not perhaps as universally and rigidly as we have presented them in the past, but with more of the flavor of the acceptable absolute than is presently noticeable in these deliberations.

SUMMARY

In summation, then, we have suggested that the single woman cannot be easily categorized. Each woman must be approached as a unique individual. Those who remain celibate because of conscious or unconscious anxieties should be helped through education, guidance, and therapy to become more liberated and fully human. Those who remain single through conscious and mature choice, or because of the tragic lack of opportunity, must be helped to survive as *complete* women and bring their individual feminine qualities to bear on the world, including the married world, around them. And hopefully all of this will be done with greater and greater effectiveness as the deliberations of churchmen and the insight of social scientists fuse to produce the more and more refined meanings that sexuality must have in the life of the Christian celibate.

REFERENCES

Hagmaier, G. (C.S.P.) & Gleason, R. W. (S.J.) *Counselling the Catholic.* New York: Sheed & Ward, 1959.

Kinsey, A. C., Pomeroy, W. B., Martin, C. E., & Gebhard, P. H. *Sexual behavior in the human female.* Philadelphia: Saunders, 1953.

Pius XII. Sacra virginitas. Encyclical letter of March 25, 1954. *Acta Apostolicae Sedis,* 1954, *46*, 161-191. English translation: On holy virginity. *Cath. Mind*, 1954, *52*, 491-509.

The Spiritual Life of the Single Woman

JOSEPH G. KEEGAN, S.J.

Father Joseph G. Keegan, S.J., who is an associate professor of psychology at Fordham University, received his A.B. degree from Woodstock College in 1939 and his M.A. (1943) and Ph.D. (1949) degrees from Yale University. He was Chairman of the Psychology Department at Fordham University from 1949 to 1958, and Director of the Counseling Center from 1961 to 1966. He is a member of many professional organizations, including the British Psychology Society, the American Psychological Association, and the American Catholic Psychological Association, of which he was president from 1961 to 1962. Father Keegan has been intimately associated with the entire series of Pastoral Psychology Institutes, having been a member of the Organizing Committee for each Institute.

If there is any person for whom a personal life must be fashioned and developed along lines that are satisfying and rewarding it is the single woman. Too often both in her own view and in attitudes created in others about her she presents the image of someone neglected and forlorn. Almost by definition she is expected to present not just one problem but a plethora of insoluble problems. And too often her very existence in the single state is assumed to be the resultant of problems that went unsolved. Consequently the person who would counsel or advise her, especially if the counseling is reinforced with spiritual ideals, is likely to be cast in the role of someone trying to recondition a reject and perhaps even of trying to use slightly unfair methods in the bargain!

THE VOCATION OF THE SINGLE WOMAN

It will be recalled from statistics cited in a previous paper [1] that, permitted to project their adult roles, 95 percent of the nation's young girls declare their role expectations will be fulfilled in marriage. If things actually turned out that way we might have more marital problems, but the single woman who is a Catholic would probably be in a religious order. But the situation is otherwise and her existence in such large numbers presents to the Catholic single woman a tremendous challenge— if she is to realize her potential for spiritual growth in her own person and be a resource for the service of God. Yet for such a realization to be accomplished she must be assisted in such tasks as the following: dealing with the stereotype or prejudice that she is ungenerous and self-centered; surmounting the implication that society and the Church expect her to submit passively as a kind of victim of circumstances; cultivating constructively her human and feminine capacities, and striving to spiritualize her motives for meaningful achievement. Here is an ambitious program and in this paper we can refer only indirectly to the other issues as we address ourselves to the challenge of her personal sanctification.

Concerning avenues of sanctification perhaps the Catholic girl has been overindoctrinated in respect to two of the options available in life: to be sanctified through a husband and family, or to be sanctified through religious vows constituting her espousal to Christ. If this dichotomy recurs to her later on in her adult singleness, what would prevent her status from appearing to be a form of commitment to ambiguity?

Precisely because her situation may appear ambiguous, the priest or religious counselor who would be concerned in helping the single woman formulate a spiritual orientation in her philosophy of life and shape her goals realistically must be thoroughly convinced that hers can be a vocation and not merely a fortuitous and unfortunate happenstance. To conceive our task in discussing the situation of the single woman and her need for spiritual development within it as a mere quest for morale-building techniques would be to foster rather than rectify prevalent confusions.

[1] Woman and marriage expectations, p. 97.

What is needed is a forward-directed and objectively based spirituality which accepts her being and existence as having meaning for herself as well as for society. It must be based on a frank recognition of value in her way of life with its proper ideals and the multifarious avenues open to her for achieving ideals objectively accepted as primary, not as mere substitutions. To the single woman the useful counselor will be one who in theory as well as in practice accepts the objective reality that the single state is an option or choice that a sane and healthy woman can make. It appears obvious that his usefulness in counseling many if not all will be hampered through his acceptance of the position indicated by the statement that "the single life lacks its own ideal, its own *mystique*, its own end" (Dohen, 1960, pp. 160-161). Granting that singleness can be the state of those who have not as yet chosen a definite vocation, or the condition of those more mature persons who have been impeded in their choice, one can also envision other possibilities. But having once conceded that the single state is necessarily a state of privation, one is hard pressed to devise any more suitable spiritual means than pietistic palliatives! Incidentally, in this area as in certain others, I believe we must move away from the more supine mood of "adjustive psychology" in the sense that it would present singleness as a condition to be endured. To be sure, one will encounter instances where there are or have been handicaps to marriage, some indeed psychologically and others situationally determined. There will be instances wherein it will be the strategy of the counselor to substitute new ideals for vanished hopes. But to say that singleness in and of itself must be without a goal or aimless would be a vast generalization.

Given the possibility that the single state can be a feasible option for a woman, what are the available principles and the steps to be taken in preparation for living it well? And, if such can be found, they should also be available for restructuring and redirecting the life that is single through factors other than conscious choice. In the foreword to a very stimulating book edited by Marion T. Sheehan, Anne O'Hare McCormick observed:

> Before woman can play her proper part in the struggle of our time, she has to take a fresh look at herself and decide in what fields her contribution to society can make the strongest and most lasting impact upon the community. Her first responsibility is to know herself and have a philosophy of life to guide her inner thoughts and her outer actions [McCormick, 1955, p. xiv].

In unison with eminent women from many fields of endeavor who contributed chapters to this book, Mrs. McCormick would summon the women of our time to a greater understanding of the spiritual heritage that is theirs to share in the work of creating and molding a better future. As alert as anyone else to the enormously expanded opportunities for women in our era, she was yet alive to the heightened worth of every human person achieved through the Christian ideal of human nature. And she saw woman as trustee of those spiritual treasures which have made it possible for her sex to achieve the place now held in Western society.

INNER SPIRITUAL LIFE

In thinking about the spiritual formation of the single woman one must seek to bring into focus her emotional, psychological, and spiritual potential as a woman, and the ideals toward which it is realistic to direct her aspirations as a person. No one could possibly claim that this is to be conceptualized in a straightforward manner or worked out in highly structural formulations. Accepting all that sociologists and social psychologists tell us about the essential communality of the human nature possessed by men and women respectively, we still suspect that she will best develop her potentialities as a woman. The task is further complicated by the very realistic consideration that for some single women their singleness may not be permanent. Nevertheless, while they are single and maritally unengaged their current status will carry those obligations and responsibilities which characterize the single life as such.

It would seem that one basic consideration for the efficacy of any personal spiritual development would be the realistic acceptance by the single woman and the person who would direct her of meaningfulness in the life she is leading. Her dignity as a human person, her deep motivation to realize her potential as a woman in the setting of what her talents and environment permit to her, as well as the societal and eternal value of her temporal efforts, must be respected and preserved.

Whether it be God or man (the opposite sex!) who made her so, the woman does well in our society to cultivate her sense of trusteeship and to enhance those qualities of modesty and reserve, refinement, and compassion in her spiritual outlook which will enable her to complement the roles of her colleagues. Whether the predominant aspects of her own role be designated as instrumental or expressive she must remain a woman. Be she physician or nurse, executive or administrative assistant, principal or teacher, her role expectation will, in our culture at any rate, be conditioned by the simple and obvious fact that she is also a woman.

When we attempt to generalize we must be cautious, but there are certain emotional, psychological, and characterological qualities which seem to appear more naturally—or should I say congenially—in women than in men. She has more perception of the needs of others and usually is more readily available in helping others. She has greater enlightenment in respect to social needs, though she is not necessarily as resourceful and aggressive as man in devising plans of ameliorating social conditions. More patient and resigned, she is also more durable and enduring in sacrifice. She is more prone to sympathy and compassion. Finally she is more capable of sustaining a mood and therefore also more faithful in sustaining a cause once she has committed herself. Of course, it is a psychological truism that these and other traits, to be laudable, must also be suited to circumstances. Therefore it is appropriate that in the Common of Virgins of the Divine Office she is declared worthy of an anointing with the oil of gladness because she has loved what is right (justice) and hated what is wrong (wickedness).

Generalizations are deceptive and no doubt every individual single woman will develop a spiritual orientation that is personalized, appropriate to her. But looking at single women as a class there must be some spiritual functions which they will discharge after the manner of women rather than after that of men. If the manner of her approach to reality is via spontaneous understanding, if her perception penetrates to the human element in every situation, if she combines intuition with reason, then let her decision-making be based on these. By no means is she to be persuaded that her femininity exempts her from spiritual realization if the related capacities assist her in the discharge of the many roles woman is fulfilling in our culture. Whatever may be said of femininity and passivity in antiquated biology, it was never true to set the goal of woman's spiritual fulfillment in passive acceptance.

Furthermore the image of woman is poorly presented when too much emphasis is placed upon "feminine" virtues. The implication too often is that they too are the passive, delicate, or even frail virtues.

For men the world is, in the main, an object for cultivation and reformation, for woman it provides an occasion for loving care and attention. Accordingly woman lives more in a compact world which immediately surrounds her and man in a world which is open and without horizons. The woman's world is not the noise of public life, but the home, the world of things near to the heart, the domestic hearth. And she makes the professional world when she is educator, doctor, welfare worker and nurse into a compact world containing all that is entrusted to her and gives it warmth and a new atmosphere. This world need not be narrow. Compactness does not mean narrowness, but a concentration on what is near at hand [Arnold, 1963, p. 53].

Similar statements are apropos in relation to other aspects of her femininity. If the warmth and protecting features of her personality are a reflection of her adaptation for motherhood, is that a good reason for denying her an outlet for the "maternal" gifts of understanding, sympathy, encouragement, and inspiration to others? Or is alterocentrism such an odious venture in our modern competitive society that a woman must be forced to temper her drive and desist from feminine intervention lest she undermine graft and chicanery? Perhaps we can "not just make the best of it" but be grateful that in increasing numbers women will be contributing their feminine assets to our professional, commercial, and technological enterprises. As one woman has stated:

A godless philosophy ignores the spiritual factors in woman's nature. It does not recognize that woman has the ability to emphasize love above sensuality; the living person above material achievement; the spiritual objectives of life above earthly factors [Sheehan, 1955, p. 158].

With more specific reference to the spiritual role possible to the single woman the same author writes:

And when the single woman consciously uses her spiritual gifts of motherhood, the meager definition of single life becomes obsolete. Everyone has to love and when the power of love in the single state is given a spiritual direction, it does not turn inward to self. In the single woman self can become the idol of love if spiritual elevation is not present [Sheehan, 1955, p. 159].

Obviously the great danger of objectless love is that there will ensue a type of regression to adolescent frivolous or childish simpering modes of loving self. But *a* self that is properly identified to *the* self and seen as acceptable and not rejected will be for the single woman the source of her strength and motivation "to be grasped by an ultimate concern" to love the "ground of all being" and to realize personally that she too has meaning at that decisive point at which the relation between God and man becomes fully actualized, namely, in the Incarnation.

Let the single woman therefore be encouraged and helped to pursue and achieve the spiritual goals that are realistic for her as an individual person. Pursuit is not enough; there must be the reward of some realization. Consequently goals must be set that are attainable. A contributor to a symposium on the potential of woman aptly notes:

Extravagant glorification is not the remedy for traditional degradation. Exploration of the potential of women is part of the world-wide exploration of the potential of humanity generally. Ideals too easily realized do not sufficiently spur us on to optimum growth. But we must distinguish between ideals which stimulate constructive action and the fictional products of dreams and unfulfilled needs. Impossible ideals do not bring out the best in us [Albert, 1963, p. 114].

To bring out "the best in her" the single woman must be inspired to all that is possible to her.

With more opportunity for prayer and more freedom to attend daily Mass and Retreats than married people, she is, in one sense at least, a spiritually privileged Christian. Her prayer, which rises to God from the depths of her needs, which starts from the basis that she "is alone and poor," can gradually develop into a hymn of praise and thanksgiving for all His goodness to her and to all mankind [Dohen, 1960, p. 192].

Though the author of this quotation makes her observation in the context of noting also the single woman's lack of a "channel for her love" I believe that as counselors we shall act more realistically and constructively through encouraging the single woman to accept and value her "spiritually privileged" position.

HER APOSTOLIC ROLE

It should be frankly recognized that personal salvation involves a mysterious cooperation with a munificent and merciful God who through Jesus Christ offers to each and every human person an option to be accepted in freedom and aided through grace. The Church's office of mediation and her role in preaching the word and dispensing the sacraments are not really calculated to eliminate or diminish the dynamic relationship of communion between God and man. The Church's hierarchical constitution must be presented in terms of what it really is, not an obstacle but an aid to, and bulwark for, Christian freedom and love. It is not intended to be masterful and compelling but to provide service and ministry. And to the extent that the Church is seen in its character of service and community she will the more readily be appreciated by woman. While it is perfectly true that historical factors such as revolt and misunderstanding forced the Church to strengthen her position of authority, it is equally Christian to consider that modern women share the blessings of living in an era of expanded charity and ecumenism.

Of their very nature hierarchy and priesthood are member and organ, a function and a "service" in regard to their brethren. The Holders of office in the hierarchy are told: "He who will be the first among you, will be the servant of you all." And there could be no more deplorable bankruptcy of religion than an outwardly vital but inwardly paralyzed priesthood which tried to set up its own human dominion over consciences and had lost sight of the words: "we are not masters of your belief but servants of your joy" [Arnold, 1963, p. 73].

It is a truism to remark that in the strictly organizational or administrative structure of the Church at present there is no room for women. Perhaps one can say that, because of her special personal orientation and preference for contemplation, much can be made in the spiritual guidance of women of the more recent recognition of the "I-Thou" approach to God. Again the greater realization of the meaning to be assigned to the membership of all baptized in the Body of Christ and the union of all in His priesthood can be profitably proposed so as to emphasize woman's participation as well as man's in the apostolate of the laity. We should be bold enough to recognize the application to woman also of what Pope Pius XI proposed in the early years of his reign and later reiterated—the participation of the layman in the hierarchical apostolate of the Church. In a letter to Cardinal Bertram, Pius XI began by asserting that what he calls "Catholic Action" is not a new thing but has its roots in St. Paul's Epistle to the Philippians in which he is mindful of his fellow laborers: "I entreat Evodia and I exhort Syntyche to be of one mind in the Lord. And I beseech thee also, my loyal comrade, help them for they have toiled with me in the gospel, as have Clement and the rest of my fellow-workers whose names are in the book of life" (Phil 4:3). And in his letter to Cardinal Bertram Pius XI goes on to state:

In view of the public good, which is principally moral and religious, Catholic Action will not exclude the participation of its adherents in public life in all its phases. On the contrary, it will render them better fitted for public office by a serious preparation for holiness of life and the fulfillment of their Christian duties [Pius XI, 1929, p. 83].

The Church as mediator serves the process of salvation and sanctification. It is in this setting that in her vocation the laywoman shares with the layman the priesthood of the New Covenant. In this sense it is no more temerarious to speak of the priesthood of woman than of that of the layman in the community of believers. For the character imparted through baptism and reinforced through confirmation is as truly hers as it is the layman's. Therefore whatever degree of participation in the hierarchical apostolate and whatever position of authority and dignity of mission accrues to man would seem to be woman's also. What remains to be clarified is the implication of this degree of membership and mission for active participation in the work of the Church. Such activity, as here understood, must be seen as a more personal and vital participation in the Church's hierarchical apostolate on the part of some—those generous and courageous persons, male and female, who will accept the challenge. But the basic point is that participation in the priesthood of Christ provides the theological foundation for the call.

It will help at this point to be specific and cite some of the elements in what Pius XI called Catholic Action that would be particularly appropriate for the woman's apostolate. In the first place her participation must not only recognize but must also strengthen the unity between hierarchy and the people of God. Perhaps she better than man (better than the cleric as well) can be more perceptive of undesirable advances of so-called clericalism in the total work of the Church. Because she is, at least by cultural definition, a "helpmate," it would be my guess that sooner than man she would recognize the futility of that devisive approach which seeks to separate a social and a so-called secular function, assigning the former to the cleric and the latter to the layman. Where this view gains prevalence the very notion of participation would be changed and the laity would be deprived of the truly kerygmatic and religious involvement which Pius XI stressed in his call for Catholic Action.

Another important aspect of woman's participation in Catholic Action is that it so much needs religious and moral renewal. Its effectiveness can never be vested exclusively in what may be called its organizational features. Organization and administration must be there; but its reform of the temporal order will be achieved not so much by political measures as through spiritual renewal, a surge of faith, and an urge for service through faith and love.

Finally the impetus to Catholic Action is an inner conviction of vocation, a consciousness of social responsibility beyond the call of duty. The value for woman of this particular motivational force must not be lost or overlooked. She can safely be assured both of her position in the priesthood of all believers and of her equality with man in a more meaningful collaboration with the hierarchy. Again safely, she can be assured of her close and intimate association with the aims of the Church. For her too there is meaning and relevance in the program proposed: "Faith then depends on hearing, and hearing on the word of Christ" (Rom 10:17). She too can witness and proclaim the word of salvation, just as she can know "that for those that love God all things work together unto good, for those who, according to His purpose, are saints through His call" (Rom 8:28). For a single woman it might seem that such direct kerygmatic activity is not as notably available as it is for the woman who is wife and mother. However, precisely because she lacks such immediate familial claims upon her spiritual resources, the single woman should be in a better position to exert a more forceful apostolic role in the classroom, in the office, and in the parish.

In the invitation to exert her role and throughout her performance therein, it is important that the single woman be encouraged to regard it as a vocation. Because of the many age-old prejudices associated with her sex, there still exists the danger that even her role of witness will be robbed of its proper Christian dynamism, and for her the connotation will be diminished responsibility and assignment to uncreative chores. Hence it is interesting to note that a modern woman author singles out the concept of vocation as one which has received emphatic renewal in the modern Church. Far from being limited to the religious life its application has been extended considerably.

> Every Christian's vocation extends beyond his specific state and category. An attempt to penetrate to the mystery of the Church in this world has begun, and many of the old juridical and tidy categories are transcended. The Church today returns to Scripture and sees the early Church working as a community with a minimum of hierarchical divisions. Their unity in love and realization of themselves as the people of God was more important than lines of command, states of life and specialization. "Each had his gift" or talents, but these were to be used in concert with others to build up the whole community. The glory and mystery of the body of Christ is that each member developed to his fullest can still be knit into a functioning unity of a whole. With God the giver of every good gift, every good gift can be developed to the full and given back to Him [Callahan, 1965, p. 171].

Of singular significance in this context of being a witness in proclaiming the faith is the pivotal position women have taken as lay catechists. It must be that many more could be inspired to become concerned about this sphere of endeavor and to offer themselves for training as assistants in such important instructional programs as the reclaiming of youth and the preparation of mothers who would in turn impart a higher level of religious instruction to their own children.

> As far as the sphere of the work of the lay apostolate and Catholic Action and the aims of its activity are concerned, both aim and extent are exactly those of the Church itself. It is work for the kingdom of God,

the attempt to realize the kingdom of God in mankind [Arnold, 1963, p. 78].

Furthermore, greater stress must be placed on woman's potential for participation in the liturgical and eucharistic life of the Church. Praise of God, His glorification, and rendering thanks to Him are surely not reserved to men. Adoration in spirit and truth is the work of the entire *sancta ecclesia,* of the whole priestly people of God. The eucharist must be seen as the adoring and thankful prayer of all the faithful gathered around the celebrant. The celebrant, of course, is unique as Christ's minister and without his priestly functions there would be enacted no *mysterium fidei* with the faithful participating. But insistence upon the public character of this eucharistic sacrifice involves besides Christ Himself, the Holy Spirit, the Body of Christ, and the communion of saints.

Given the basic *raison d'être* of her participation through faith and of her responsible share in proclaiming the word of God through her liturgical and sacramental life of adoration and thanksgiving, woman's role in the works of charity will be much enhanced. To be convinced that such works are essentially works of *agape* and the outcome of the Christian parish's union of hearts and sense of community, stresses the awareness in the laity that they thereby exercise a pastoral role. It is a discharge of the pastoral function that the priest alone cannot fulfill, but the realization is needed that to discharge it is to fulfill in actuality precisely that kind of service which faith and sacramental union demand. The office of shepherd and the fertility of *agape* would be diminished without such flowering as is evidenced in the works of charity. For charity too is a function of the entire *sancta ecclesia.*

Who can fail to see in the field of charitable activity, the works of love, a special domain for feminine devotion? The giving of one's own, of oneself in active love and untiring action corresponds most highly with womanly concern for generous and unsparing unselfishness. Married or single, she has stores of unspent resources precisely because of her peculiar capacity of being maternal and concerned for all those whose needs would go unfulfilled unless she, acting for *sancta mater ecclesia,* fulfilled herself in responding to need.

With specific reference to the single woman we must remember that in every woman there exist interwoven, as it were, the propensities for the three valid forms of her existence: as unmarried virgin, as wife, and as mother. Doubtless each form contains elements of the others, and it would be unwise and wasteful not to appeal to, and rely upon, the potential contributions of each. We would lose too much of woman's total being if we were to claim that it is only the mother who fulfills the essential feminine role. The childless marriage, for instance, is not lacking in validity, for therein woman as wife fulfills her role of companionship. So also virginity of the unmarried state is not to be regarded independently as something to be dealt with as a problem. It definitely has relevance for the single woman's self-image as the potential spouse of Christ and his kingdom. Incidentally this is the point of contact for her sanctification and for the communication to her of the dynamic flow of grace. In the Church she is wedded to Christ, and thereby are all of her human, womanly, and personal forces made vital and significant.

It is essential to keep in focus the fact that any one of the three forms of existence (wife, mother, or single state) can provide expression for the fulfillment of woman's life. To think otherwise would be to subject in a certain way woman's totality as a person to a contingent mode of existence, and thus, to a degree at least, subordinate her dignity as a person to her use value to society. It is of particular importance that this principle be stressed in talking to and about the single woman. She may or may not have hope of fulfillment in a marriage wherein her role will be the mutuality of care and protection to be exercised conjointly with a man, but this is not inevitably the meaning of her life. To hold any other view is automatically to reduce her status, her self-esteem, and her spiritual value as a unique person. And we see this "reduction" all too often in the aura of resignation or rejection associated with the life of the "bachelor girl" or "maiden lady." These adverse associations are negative in that they highlight the absence of optional roles. Our attitude toward her should rather be positive in stressing her choice or acceptance of virginity.

What seems needed here is a certain revisionary attitude toward the distinction between the unmarried state as such and virginity. Too often the acceptance or the interpretation of St. Paul's words: "Therefore both he who gives his virgin in marriage does well, and he who does not give her does better" (I Cor 7:38) is purely negative and representative of immature Christianity. It seems to sanction the empty notion that bodily integrity or ascetic abstinence are end values in and of themselves. It omits the view that Christian virginity has its meaning in the positive setting of the heroic striving for a fulfillment in undivided service. Why is it that this, or at least a comparable nobility, cannot be proposed to the single woman with significant purposefulness toward her service in God's kingdom? Is it perhaps because too many of us have feared that such positive proposals would somehow divert vocations from the religious life? If so, we had better revise the theological

basis for asceticism in general rather than accept *in obliquo* the unthe-
ological notion that asceticism is an end in itself.

Should we not rather frankly and straightforwardly transfer to the
single life the value resident in virginity, namely, that it is altruistic self-
sacrifice generously offered for the sake of the kingdom of God? For the
unmarried woman too Christian virginity need not be lived to avoid
obligation or simply to attain heaven more easily. Rather its value
should be to provide exemplary devotion and selfless service in the
kingdom of God and for the good of the members of Christ's mystical
body. For who are more capable of undivided service, who more eligible for the kind of untiring devotion required in these days for apostolic activity and the spread of God's kingdom on many fronts?

It should be clear, I hope, that in no part of what I have said, do I
imply that virginity rather than marriage is for man or for woman the
more natural fulfillment or the norm whereby the person is to reveal
in existence the mystery of creation and sanctification. But the fact
faces us and looms large that in the modern world there are many single
girls and women whose being and existence would be left sterile and
meaningless if we so emphasize the norm as to leave no operation in
the extension of God's kingdom open to them.

REFERENCES

Albert, Ethel M. The roles of women: a question of values. In S. M. Farber
& R. H. L. Wilson (Eds.) *The potential of woman.* New York: McGraw-
Hill, 1963. Pp. 105-115.

Arnold, F. X. *Woman and man: their nature and mission.* New York:
Herder & Herder, 1963.

Callahan, Sidney C. *The illusion of Eve: modern woman's quest for identity.*
New York: Sheed & Ward, 1965.

Dohen, Dorothy. *Women in wonderland.* New York: Sheed & Ward, 1960.

McCormick, Anne O'Hare. Foreword. In Marion T. Sheehan (Ed.) *The
spiritual woman: trustee of the future.* New York: Harper, 1955. Pp.
xiii-xvi.

Pius XI. Letter to Cardinal Bertram. *Cath. Mind,* 1929, *27,* 81-84.

Sheehan, Marion T. Woman's spiritual role in society. In Marion T. Sheehan
(Ed.) *The spiritual woman: trustee of the future.* New York: Harper,
1955. Pp. 153-167.

V

TOWARD WOMANLY PERFECTION

Psychological Fulfillment for the Woman

VIRGINIA STAUDT SEXTON

Virginia Staudt Sexton received her A.B. degree from Hunter College in 1936 and her master's (1941) and doctoral (1946) degrees in psychology from Fordham University. Since 1958 she has been teaching in the psychology department of Hunter College of the City University of New York, where she is now professor of psychology. Dr. Sexton is co-author of two books, Catholics in Psychology *(1954) and* History of Psychology *(1966), and has contributed upwards of 25 articles to professional journals. She is a fellow of the American Psychological Association, the American Association for the Advancement of Science, and the New York Academy of Science, in addition to being a member of a large number of professional organizations. She was president of the American Catholic Psychological Association from 1964 to 1965.*

Psychological fulfillment, that is, self-actualization or the development and realization of one's potentialities, is a vital need and an essential goal of both men and women. However, "fulfillment" is a highly subjective, hence very imprecise, term. It denotes a sense of inner and outer balance or adjustment for a person. Yet it is not mere self-centered indulgence. Perhaps we might best define "fulfillment" as a feeling or awareness that you are in the world, that you are actively participating in life, and that you are accomplishing something worthwhile.

Self-discovery and the achievement of identity are prerequisites to such fulfillment. In addition, true fulfillment requires recognition of the self as process, as a dynamic cluster of potentialities, rather than as a static, fixed, finished product. To know oneself, to be oneself, and to become oneself, these are the essentials to psychological fulfillment, and thus to the ultimate happiness of each person. To choose "to be another than himself" can only result in deep despair with one's human lot, as Kierkegaard cautioned more than a century ago.

In discussing "what it means to become a person," Carl Rogers (1956) emphasizes that it is an individual's principal responsibility to be the self which one truly is. His implication for our discussion is that a woman who wants to become herself must discard masks or roles with which she has disguised herself in confronting life. A person's life, or much of it, in Rogers' view, may be motivated by what she thinks she *ought* to be rather than by what she actually *is*. When a woman recognizes that she exists, that she is motivated, only in response to the demands of others, she knows that she has forsaken her identity. When she sees that she is moved to think, feel, and act only in the way that others say she should think, feel and act—or worse, in the way she imagines that others think she should think, feel, and act—then she has abandoned her duty to herself. Perception of self and perception of her role are crucial to woman's becoming a person and to attaining psychological fulfillment.

DIVERGENT VIEWS ON PSYCHOLOGICAL FULFILLMENT IN WOMEN

Women's roles have undergone more changes, and more radical changes, than have men's roles in recent years. As a result, women's psychological fulfillment has posed more persistent and perplexing problems in contemporary life. During the last two decades in America, the topic of "psychological fulfillment for women" has received unprecedented attention in both professional and popular literature. Psychologists, psychiatrists, sociologists, educators, editors, and writers have expressed themselves at length and in detail, especially in women's magazines. These spokesmen have announced to American women what their roles should be, and their viewpoints, on analysis, are in clear opposition.

On one side, we find Phyllis McGinley (1964), author of *Sixpence in her shoe*, and her fellow protagonists. Theirs is the three-dimensional approach to feminine fulfillment—marriage, motherhood, and home-making. Confronting them are Betty Friedan (1963), author of *The feminine mystique,* and her cohorts. They advocate for women's fulfill-ment the pursuit of a fourth dimension: her own identity as a person in society. The McGinley group espouses the cause of domesticity and the praise of its glories. The Friedan group opprobriates Freudian psy-chology, Margaret Mead and the functional sociologists, motivation re-searchers, advertising agencies, and journalists. They draw a blanket indictment against these persuaders for victimizing women by a "sexual sell" and by using the old shibboleth, "woman's place is in the home," to discourage women from achieving their identity as persons, and their fulfillment as persons. Is it any wonder that American women, under a barrage of two such disparate views, find themselves confused and distraught? What, indeed, is the real role for woman, a role by which she can attain fulfillment?

BACKGROUND OF THE PROBLEM

Perhaps a brief recapitulation of the events leading to the current concern and confusion about the psychological fulfillment of women is in order. It will be recalled that under the impact of the Industrial Rev-olution the home ceased to be the center of industry and education. Homebodies became, literally, displaced persons forced into the com-munity for schooling and employment. Women left at home were bereft of their traditional chores and were socially isolated. Their mounting discontent ultimately erupted in the violent feminist campaigns for equal rights and for women's emancipation. In the late nineteenth and early twentieth centuries, women organized a revolt which effected drastic changes in women's roles. According to Havighurst (1956), the nine-teenth century roles—the princess, the beast of burden, the fragile flower, the mother, the no-sex, the all-sex, the spinster, and the bluestock-ing—yielded to the twentieth century roles—the house manager, the career woman, the factory worker, the bachelor girl, the mother, the club woman, and the citizen. Shortly after American women achieved great feminist gains, such as suffrage, the victory was lost through the twin impact of a great economic depression and a second world war.

The late 1940s and the 1950s saw a marked change. This post-war milieu was characterized by great indecision on the part of women. Many were troubled by the difficult choice between marriage and a career. Yet a new era of domesticity emerged. In part, this was occa-sioned by the long estrangement of American men and women during the war years. Perhaps domesticity was further intensified by the admiration expressed for the femininity and charms of foreign women by our returning servicemen, who in some cases brought home foreign brides, both Occidental and Oriental. In any event, for whatever reason or complex of reasons, the post-war period was characterized by a renewal of kudos for the domestic role, by a substantial increase in the birth rate, and by a general exodus of families to suburbia.

By the early 1960s, the national mood again shifted. This shift was undoubtedly precipitated by our competition with Russia in the "race to space," and by related developments in atomic energy, and electronics. It had been known in the nineteenth century that women were a significant reservoir of thinking capacity in nations with high cultural indices. But emphasis on woman's domestic role in the post-war period had obscured this important fact. Now American women were urged by educators, employers, and government officials to continue their education, and to enter the professional and occupational life of the nation. They were reminded pointedly that their Russian sisters, in great numbers, were doctors, engineers, and scientists. So pressing did the question of women's role become that the late President Kennedy appointed a commission to study the status of women in the United States. Its report, published in 1963 (President's Commission on the Status of Women, 1963), affirmed in no uncertain terms that the nation's future good demanded the enlistment of womanpower in increasingly larger measure.

Contemporary America, with its increased educational facilities, its rapid technological advances and industrial expansion, has offered women both new and traditional opportunities for achievement in the professions, arts, sciences, business, and industry. A summary consideration might suggest that these recent developments have facilitated the possibility of women's fulfillment. Today's women surely have a broader choice than the traditional roles of marriage, motherhood, and homemaking. Vast employment opportunities are offered them, on both a part-time and full-time basis. Older women—those in their middle years—are now welcomed as a more stable type of employee than their younger sisters for certain types of employment. Universities and colleges are adjusting programs for older women who want to return to classes. A combination of roles has thus become increasingly available. Today the young married sophomore and the older married woman who has raised her family can sit side by side in college and university classes. Employment statistics show ever-increasing numbers of married and single women of all ages in business and industry.

Yet the broader opportunities for education and employment have not yet enabled American women, collectively, to attain psychological fulfillment. In fact, there are some who would argue that American women today are more dissatisfied and unhappy than ever before in our nation's history. On the surface, such dissatisfaction and unhappiness hardly seem warranted. American women have a high standard of living, and excellent housing with a minimum of drudgery. They are well educated. They are well dressed. They have a general freedom enjoyed by few women around the world. They have notoriously indulgent and generous husbands. Their possibilities for competition with men in our economy were never brighter. Still, the evidences of woman's unhappiness in our society are blatantly apparent: high separation and divorce rates; increased incidence of alcoholism, suicide, and mental disorder; excessive use of tranquilizing nostrums and other drugs. Lundberg and Farnham (1947, p. 221) have also observed that "the sense of self-realization constantly missed is shown, for example, by the overstress on youth in advertising and literature." They point out that to many women youth, in retrospect, seems "to have been a time of potential fulfillment beyond all other times." Many older women feel that if they could recapture youth they might be able to fulfill themselves. The cosmetic syndrome is evidence enough of the scope of this urge in older women to maintain or recapture youth, to obliterate the traditionally respected middle years, by externals of decoration and behavior.

It is quickly apparent when one studies the material circumstances of the 1960s, and the expanded opportunities for women to fulfill themselves psychologically, that the sources of any lack of fulfillment must be sought in woman herself, in the society in which these women live and in which they participate, or in a combination of both. Perhaps it would be worthwhile to have a look at the women themselves and at what society can do to improve women's chances for psychological fulfillment.

WOMAN'S ACCEPTANCE OF WOMANHOOD

Obviously, the first step that American woman must take for fulfillment is to determine her own identity. This means that she must define a conception of herself and a role for herself in our particular society which will enable her to be satisfied and happy. Most fundamentally, it would seem she must begin by accepting the uniqueness of her own womanhood, and by resisting any impulse to mimic men. *She must be a real woman*: "A real woman," says Robert Graves (1964, p. 151), who at 70 has surely attained the age of wisdom, ". . . neither despises nor worships men, but is proud not to have been born a man, does everything to avoid thinking or acting like one, knows the full extent of her powers, and feels free to reject all arbitrary man-made obligations." In a negative translation of Mr. Graves, the road to feminine fulfillment is certainly not in emulation of men, or in pursuing the route of male achievement competitively. As Graves asserts: "When women organize themselves intellectually on masculine lines, they merely stimulate the feminization of men, who, for terror of husband-hunting viragoes, are apt to seek refuge in the cul-de-sac of homosexuality" (1964, p. 154). Neutralization of the sexes—whether in thinking or in social behavior of action or dress—is a deterrent to the psychological fulfillment of women, and, it might be added, to that of men as well. And yet, even though women must concede that they are still an "out group" in a society whose standards are principally determined by men, they would do well to avoid the practice of most out groups, that is, imitation of the dominant "in group," the men. Perhaps Kierkegaard's warning is again in order: to try "to be another than himself" can only lead to despair.

In her search for fulfillment, woman does well, not only to accept, but to acknowledge, her womanhood. For most women, and undoubtedly, such acceptance and acknowledgment will probably always involve marriage, motherhood, and homemaking. Admittedly, in the future as in the past, a domestic career will remain the fulfillment of the majority of women. Yet, it would be the greatest indiscretion for the married woman to delude herself into thinking that she has achieved herself in the act of marriage. On the contrary, she might well remind herself even in marriage, that her self-recognition of women's role— hence of her possible fulfillment as woman—is a continuing process. Thus she is in the state of becoming even when she has assumed the role of wife and mother. She is never, that is, a fixed entity. She must continue her efforts toward self-development—a development which she must never abandon, lest she relegate herself to the ranks of those appallingly ignorant American women who dote on trivialities. Above all, in responding to the demands of husband and children, she must hold fast to her own identity as a human person. If she preserves herself and cultivates her mind, she need not make apologies ever for being "just a housewife." In that status she can remain a fulfilled person playing one of many roles available to women, happily and satisfactorily. Contentment with her role will best be judged by her own inner peace as wife, mother, and homemaker. Yet it will also be shown by her acceptance of the role, and by her lack of envy of the role of women who seek their fulfillment outside the home.

NO ONE ROLE FOR ALL WOMEN

Although people, especially men, are wont to speak of women categorically, it is a psychological fact, as well as a fact of social experience, especially among men of religion, teachers, and police magistrates, that there are marked differences among women. Margaret Mead, of whom we have spoken, has described the basically different conceptions of women's roles from culture to culture (Mead, 1949). But even in a monocultural setting there are striking individual differences among women. Consequently, a pattern of life and an individually fulfilling role that may be totally absorbing for one woman, may lead another to the very brink of despair.

Individual women must therefore be alert to, and resistant to, the propaganda, so generously disseminated from all sources in our society, which seeks to convince them of any single, appropriate role or roles for women. It should be pointed out here that young women should not feel constrained to make forced choices, as Catholic girls so often in the past were encouraged to do: to get married or to enter the convent. More recently Catholics have given evidence of acknowledging the single state—what with Bethany conferences [1] and such. We should never forget that many single women have experienced and are experiencing fulfillment in caring for aged parents and/or in making it easier for their sisters and brothers to fulfill themselves in the married or religious life. Such single women deserve our respect—not pity, contempt, or denigration.

Clearly, *there is no one role for all women*. Each woman must search for what is meaningful to her as a person, and what is in accord with her values. When she acts in conformity with her own self-perception and self-commitment and with her personal, social, and spiritual values, only then can she find psychological fulfillment as an individual woman. This

[1]The Bethany Conference is designed especially for the mature (25-30 years of age and up) single woman in business and professional life. The name *Bethany* suggests the friendship depicted in the Gospels of Mary and Martha of Bethany with Christ. It seeks to help women think through and discuss the essential role of woman, and to see how this may be fulfilled in the life of a woman who is neither married nor in the religious state. For further information write: The Bethany Conference, 305 East 40th St. (10-A), New York, New York 10016.

self-directed and self-realizing action must be her objective, whether she remains in the single state, or whether she marries or enters the religious life, or whether she is widowed, separated, or divorced. Stated simply, her supreme obligation for fulfillment is knowing herself, and living by the standards to which her individual, unique self commits her in personality and conscience.

One principle must be the enduring keystone of a woman's psychological structure: There is *not only no one role* for all women, but there is rarely, and certainly *not* necessarily, *one single role* for any given individual woman. Woman's life, more than man's, tends to be characterized by discontinuity; therefore, woman's life demands flexibility. Ordinarily, assumption of the role of wife and mother entails the end of the role of employee, even if ever so temporarily for some women. A real problem emerges when a woman tries to combine, satisfactorily, her personal desire or need for a vocation outside her home with the roles of wife and mother. Although some married women have always continued their vocation—either from necessity or choice—yet, as Bowman (1964, p. 3) validly observes ". . . the role of wife as earner is a new phenomenon with which we have not yet learned how to live." The modern married woman who takes employment outside the home is still obliged to weigh many factors beyond her immediate personal satisfaction; for example, the possible threat to her husband's self-image and role, and adequate care of their children in her absence. In the situation of the working wife, the important consideration is not so much the employment itself; it is rather the kind and quality of relationship the employed wife and mother establishes and maintains with her husband and children.

While, fundamentally, the search for her psychological fulfillment is the deepest responsibility of each individual woman—whether single or married—she must also be able to function in a society that will enable her to grow and to realize herself. It is strange that in our country, which has always prided itself in its concern with the development of each individual's potential, and which in the last decade has been especially sensitized to the handicaps of race and class, that there should persist social and economic handicaps occasioned by sex—too obvious and too well known for us to detail here. Let us consider what features of society might help women chart a more realistic and satisfying course to fulfillment. Assuming that the state will provide the necessary legal supports and protections for women, we shall briefly consider three other aspects of her life in the community—educational, economic, and social.

EDUCATION AND WOMANLY FULFILLMENT

Education for a woman is of two kinds: domestic and formal. Domestic education is that which she receives in the home—principally from her mother. Formal education is the training which she receives in school. A mother's role in the life of her daughter is an extremely significant one—as is well known both from experience and from the vast literature on the subject. From her mother, the daughter learns directly —by word and domestic behavior—how complex, and how fulfilling or disappointing, the role of wife, mother, and homemaker can be. Every girl reared at home is assured some first-hand education in the roles of wife and mother, and homemaker. Perhaps it is well from time to time that mothers remind themselves of the influence and training they provide by the images they project to their daughters. Daughters perhaps should similarly be reminded of the educational aspects of domestic life—it is surprising to observe how frequently young married women are challenged or overpowered by the routine realities of marriage—realities of wifehood and motherhood which have been before their very eyes in their own homes during their pre-marriage years. There is no more direct, however incomplete, education for marriage than life in one's own home. Furthermore, the home and family in many, many ways influence the thinking of young women in respect of their own choice of marriage or the single life, just as they are influenced by their own personalities and career-objectives.

In formal education, especially in high school and college, young women should receive expert guidance counseling. Too often girls are short-changed in this respect. Because it is assumed they will marry anyway—by themselves, if not by their counselors—too little attention is given to careful direction of their career objectives. Although the probability of marriage for young girls is great, still the possibility of their need or desire for professional and business career skills is similarly great—even though they marry. Despite their youthful fantasies, girls must be prepared for the eventuality of not finding—or being found by—a spouse. They may require a means of supporting themselves. So, too, will many of those married women, who through the various turns of fate may become breadwinners. In other words, the young woman must be alerted to the possibilities of her life in maturity, if she is to face it adequately and fulfill herself. Guidance counselors and course program directors have a particularly weighty responsibility in their vocational work with young women in the immediate future. Theirs is the job to encourage girls to make the most of their education, and to fortify them with appropriate knowledge and skills—not a mere watered-down version of a male-oriented curriculum or a course in home economics for the potential bride. Educators and counselors would do well to heed the words of the following authors:

> While a young woman should not be deflected from thoroughly enjoying her motherhood and homemaking, she should be helped to see that we make our choices in one period of our lives and that the regrets, if any, come later. She needs to be helped to understand both what choices there are and what these choices imply for her long life ahead [Gruenberg & Krech, 1952, p. 109].

In the economic area, society will have to increase its concern with women. Not only will this require more careful vocational preparation in the schools, but the business world will be forced in the next decade to be more "woman-oriented." As has already been stated, the 1963 President's Report on the Status of Women indicated that womanpower must be enlisted in increasingly larger measure in the national interest. More specifically, the U.S. Bureau of Labor Statistics predicts that 13.5 million more workers will be needed in 1970—almost half of them women. In this figure the increase in women workers will be 25 percent against a 15 percent increase in men. The Bureau also predicts that nine of ten young women will join the labor force. Under these circumstances, through every possible means, the female youth must be alerted to their own opportunities and responsibilities in the economic sphere for their own psychological—as well as economic—self-knowledge and future fulfillment.

Business itself will have to promote its own interest in respect of woman's place in the economic future of America. This means that a more informed and better-planned allowance must be made for the often discontinuous life patterns or work patterns of women in business. This discontinuity has already been alluded to in our previous mention of flexibility as an essential of women's development. Businesses which employ women—certainly women under 40—must be more than ever willing to allow for their movement in and out of jobs because of marriage, childbearing, and the rearing of young children. At times the married woman may return to business by choice. More often she returns to the labor force through necessity—unemployment, illness, death of her husband, or desertion, separation, or divorce. Rising costs of educating children are an additional serious motivation for woman's return to the labor market. Such necessities are a far cry from the stereotype of the married woman who works simply to avoid the frustrations of housekeeping and tight budgets. This stereotype now has less validity than most men are willing to admit.

Woman, then, will bear a greater share of the future operations of business. Inasmuch as her economic and her psychological fulfillments are interrelated in her work, business must be responsibly concerned with both. This means two kinds of improvement for the position of women in business. They must be given better job opportunities, opportunities in keeping with their talents and training. Perhaps, even more importantly, they must be compensated on the principle of equal pay for equal talents and training.

INFLUENCE OF SOCIAL ATTITUDES ON WOMANLY FULFILLMENT

Finally, some social attitudes relating to the psychological fulfillment of women are worth a brief consideration. Let us consider first the current attitudes toward roles which women assume in their quest for human fulfillment. The ultimate source of such attitudes is society itself. A role is usually assumed by a woman if it is culturally acceptable, and rejected when it is culturally unacceptable. Some of us will remember the psychological bruises given women who were needed for industrial jobs during the Second World War. Comedians of sorts—professional and amateur—made women industrial workers a prime source of their humor. Those women who were the comic targets took their abuse, took their good wages, and took psychological wounds in the bargain. They adopted emergency roles temporarily available, but retreated from them as soon as possible because these roles are normally unacceptable in our society. It is a social and psychological truism that a role can be accepted and embraced by an individual only when other people recognize, accept, and reciprocally respond to the role. It is equally true that most women do not want to be trail-blazers; they do not want to be the targets of criticism from family, friends, and neighbors. When their potential roles bring unsatisfactory responses from their own society, they suffer a burden of guilt. When family and neighbors actively thwart or reject their attempts to venture off on something new, most women become discouraged from exploring new roles.

Men have characteristically rejected woman's attempts at career fulfillment—thus psychological fulfillment—outside the home. Without the encouragement of men, in the enrichment of her economic role in society as well as her romantic, domestic, and maternal role, woman can not attain her psychological fulfillment as a person. Until meaningful work is accepted as a worthy objective for women as well as for men in our society, women will continue to regard the most meaningful work for which they are competent as a mere stopgap before marriage. At the same time, young women will continue to regard higher education, professions, and careers as handicaps to their sole remaining objective, marriage. On this point, specifically regarding the dearth of women scientists in the United States, Alice Rossi writes of the need to change the attitudes of young women on career objectives, both for their own good and for the good of society. She urges one possible persuasive technique, and suggests that

> the views of young and able women concerning marriage and careers could be changed far more effectively by the men who have found marriage to professional women a satisfying experience than by exhortations of professional women, or manpower specialists, and family-living instructors whose own wives are homemakers [Rossi, 1965, p. 1201].

Virginia Woolf pinpointed a basic obstacle to women's achieving a more expansive and productive role in society—an obstacle somewhat of woman's own making—some thirty years ago. Said Miss Woolf, in cold irony,

> Women have served all the centuries as looking glasses possessing the magic . . . power of reflecting the figure of man at twice its natural size [Woolf, 1929, p. 60].

In the matter of choosing her own role for her own fulfillment woman must not only reduce the power of the mirror in which she views the figure of man, but she must turn the mirror to include the "separate but equal" image of herself. If it is true that she needs man's approval to realize her own potential in "The New Society"—and clearly it is true—then man's approval must include a willingness to encourage the application of women's talents in business and the professions. Great advantage to our society would accrue from a transfer of the energy of women from proliferating community activities of questionable merit to more productive areas in our economy. Some of these community activities are designed to exhaust the animal energies of the kiddies, while their mothers are enabled to exchange miseries with their fellow-matrons. An unfortunate side effect of the social malaise of the mother in community service is her demand that the business and professional woman, who is also a mother, engage in similar frustration-cures. Usually the business and professional woman has avoided the frustration itself by her own satisfying work.

As much as society is responsible for a narrow conception of woman's role—hence of woman's fulfillment—it must be woman's own responsibility to modify the conditions which maintain that narrow conception. The success of the feminist movement proves that woman can improve her own access to broader opportunity in the society in which she lives. She must, as a social being, respect her own dignity and needs and give like respect to the dignity and needs of other women. She must give greater energy to developing her personal talents in directions that will enrich her contributions to the whole of society. She must work to alert society at large to an awareness of women's potential in the great present movement to build and improve that society. But she needs the help of society in planning her own social development. In the nature of her potential or actual role of wife and mother, woman must live a more complex existence than man. Yet the complexity of this existence does not prevent—it simply makes more involved—the design of a method by which women can realize themselves to the full in the variety of roles for which they are fitted in a society that needs women's participation in those roles. To realize themselves, as Marguerite Zapoleon (1947, p. 165) has stated, "Women should have full opportunity for development. . . . They need aid that will expand rather than contract the areas of their usefulness."

SUMMARY

In this brief overview of "Psychological Fulfillment for the Woman," we have certainly but scratched the surface of our complete subject. However, there are certain large and vital areas which this paper means to point up for serious consideration. The psychological fulfillment of women depends not on a person alone, not on a state alone, but on the possibilities of fulfillment when that particular person assumes that particular state. To be fulfilled psychologically, a woman must willingly commit a self-perceived identity to a role or roles with which she has familiarized and informed herself. She must know herself, know what she wants, and prepare herself psychologically to assume that role. Only when she foresees the dynamic potential of her own personality, of her own individuality, in the role she adopts, will she achieve fulfillment in that adopted role. Despite the pressures of society, domestic or economic or educational or pastoral, her psychological fulfillment can come only from the success and happiness with which she performs a freely chosen role—a role which meets the objectives and standards set by the person, unique as well as female, that she knows herself honestly to be. Knowing herself and what she can be and wants to be, and willingness to fulfill herself in attaining her objective, is what makes her a psychologically fulfilled woman.

REFERENCES

Bowman, H. A. *The family: its role and function.* Austin, Texas: Hogg Foundation for Mental Health, 1964.

Friedan, Betty. *The feminine mystique.* New York: Norton, 1963.

Graves, R. Real women. *Ladies Home Journal,* 1964, *81,* 151-154.

Gruenberg, Sidonie M. & Krech, Hilda S. *The many lives of modern woman.* Garden City, N.Y.: Doubleday, 1952.

Havighurst, R. J. Changing roles of women in the middle years. In Irma H. Gross (Ed.) *Potentialities of women in the middle years.* East Lansing, Mich.: Michigan State University Press, 1956. Pp. 3-18.

Lundberg, F. & Farnham, Marynia F. *Modern woman: the lost sex.* New York: Harper, 1947.

McGinley, Phyllis. *Sixpence in her shoe.* New York: Macmillan, 1964.

Mead, Margaret. *Male and female: a study of the sexes in a changing world.* New York: Morrow, 1949.

President's Commission on the Status of Women. *American women.* Washington: U.S. Government Printing Office, 1963.

Rogers, C. *Becoming a person.* Austin, Texas: Hogg Foundation for Mental Health, 1956.

Rossi, Alice S. Women in science: why so few? *Science,* 1965, *148,* 1196-1202.

Sherman, Helen & Coe, Marjorie. *The challenge of being a woman.* New York: Harper, 1955.

Woolf, Virginia. *A room of one's own.* New York: Harcourt, Brace, 1929.

Zapoleon, Marguerite W. Education and employment opportunities for women. In Louise M. Young (Ed.) Women's opportunities and responsibilities. *Ann. Amer. Acad. Pol. Soc. Sci.,* 1947, *251,* 165-173.

Opportunities for Service
to the Church and the World

JOSEPH E. HALEY, C.S.C.

Father Joseph E. Haley, C.S.C., received his A.B. degree from the University of Notre Dame in 1937 and an M.A. degree from the Catholic University of America in 1950. The major portion of the interval between the completion of his graduate work at Catholic University and the present has been spent by Father Haley at the University of Notre Dame, where, among other things, he organized and edited the proceedings of the annual Sisters' Institutes of Spirituality from 1953 through 1960. Currently, he is an assistant professor of theology at the University of Portland. In addition to editing the series mentioned above, Father Haley is also the editor of several other volumes, among them Apostolic Sanctity in the World *(1957), a treasure-house of information on secular institutes, and* The Sister in America Today *(1965), containing selected papers from the Sisters' Conferences on Spirituality, University of Portland, 1960-63.*

The search for self-identity and for one's role in life is, for Catholics, inseparable from the inquiry into the nature and destiny of the Church in the world. Further, it is an aspect of the understanding of the very nature and action of God immanent and incarnate in human history in Christ. We never rise to the challenge of our dignity and responsibility until we realize that truly we are Christ redemptively present in our age to renew and perfect all things for the salvation of all men and the glory of God our Father.

Pope Paul VI in his encyclical, *Ecclesiam suam* (Paul VI, 1964), calls us in the Body of Christ to the threefold task of reflective awareness of the true nature of the Church and of its actual imperfect human existence, of reform and renewal, and of effective dialogue and action in the contemporary world. The remarkably frank discussion and cooperation, initiated in the Vatican Council and progressively manifest among all Christian, Jewish, other non-Christian religious and even nonbelieving persons of good will, make us aware that the Word of God lives among us and speaks even through the persons and events of our revolutionary times. The documents of Vatican II, especially the Constitutions on the Church (Abbott, 1966, pp. 14-101), on the Sacred Liturgy (Abbott, 1966, pp. 137-178), and on the Church in the Modern World (Abbott, 1966, pp. 199-308), give us the basic principles of man's communion with God, with all mankind, and with the universe through Christ.

Pope John XXIII in his encyclicals, *Mater et magistra* (John XXIII, 1961) and *Pacem in terris* (John XXIII, 1963), would have us see the secular world as the dynamic creation of God which man is to fashion in justice and charity so that all men can find self-realization in the ordered community of the human family. In particular, we must accept the world of temporal institutions as being secular, democratic and lay in its controlling agents, specialized in its functioning, and progressively unified in its institutions. These features are natural and good. But unfortunately the contemporary world is largely materialistic and secularized by ideologies which discount or reject the relevance of religion, is divided in its understanding of man and his destiny, and is depersonalized by positivist theory and the complexity of our technical, urban, and mobile civilization. Man seeks self-realization through the Christian community which must incarnate itself in all features of secular life and transform them by the sacramental action of Christ, "until we all attain to the unity of the faith . . . to perfect manhood, to the fullness of Christ" (Eph 4:13-14).

THE ROLE OF THE LAITY AND OF WOMAN

The Church calls upon the laity to see the transformation of the secular world as its specific vocation and responsibility, as explicitly stated in the Constitution on the Church:

The term laity is here understood to mean all the faithful except those in holy orders and those in a religious state sanctioned by the Church. These faithful are by baptism made one body with Christ and are established among the People of God. They are in their own way made sharers in the priestly, prophetic, and kingly functions of Christ. They carry out their own part in the mission of the whole Christian people with respect to the Church and the world.

A secular quality is proper and special to laymen . . . but the laity, by their very vocation, seek the kingdom of God by engaging in temporal affairs and by ordering them according to the plan of God. They live in the world, that is, in each and in all of the secular professions and occupations. They live in the ordinary circumstances of family and social life, from which the very web of their existence is woven.

They are called there by God so that by exercising their proper function and being led by the spirit of the gospel they can work for the sanctification of the world from within, in the manner of leaven. In this way they can make Christ known to others, especially by the testimony of a life resplendent in faith, hope, and charity. . . . It is therefore his special task to illumine and organize these affairs in such a way that they may always start out, develop, and persist according to Christ's mind, to the praise of the Creator and the Redeemer [Abbott, 1966, article 31, pp. 57-58].

Priests and laity will find in the entire Chapter IV on "The Laity" of the Constitution on the Church from which the above quotation is taken, as well as the following chapter on "The Call of the Whole Church to Holiness," the basis of inspiration and formation of a dedicated apostolic laity. In particular I would single out for emphasis in terms of the role of women in the Church and the world these points:

1. All Christians are members of Christ and share in the life and threefold mission of our divine Head. The differences of sex, race, Church office and social status illustrate the marvelous diversity and yet basic equality and unity of our life and ministry in Christ.

2. The laity are called to an active share in the growth and sanctification of the Church through Baptism, Confirmation, the Holy Eucharist, and charity. The layman is ". . . a witness and a living instrument of the Church herself . . ." (Abbott, 1966, article 33, p. 60).

3. In addition to this general apostolate of all Christians, the laity can be called ". . . to a more direct form of cooperation in the apostolate of the hierarchy" (Abbott, 1966, article 33, p. 60).

4. In exercising the priestly mission of worship of God and the salvation of men, the laity can render their prayer, work and even relaxation ". . . spiritual sacrifices acceptable to God through Jesus Christ (cf. 1 Pet 2:5)" (Abbott, 1966, article 34, p. 60), particularly with the offering of the Lord's body in the celebration of the Eucharist.

5. The laity exercise their sharing in the prophetic and kingly role of Christ as effective witnesses of the Word of God in their daily life of marriage and the family, in their secular occupation continuing God's creation, in their dedication to the reform and perfection of the whole social order according to the justice and charity of the Gospel.

6. The laity are called to holiness for the glorification of Christ and the edification of all men. This holiness is essentially the same for all: growth in union with God through Christ by the divine life of grace and charity in response to the Holy Spirit. While essentially the same, this holiness is lived according to the various gifts and duties of state in life —the clergy, the married, widows, the single, workers, the poor and suffering.

7. Specific to the single woman, the Constitution, while not explicitly referring to them, sums up the doctrine of the Church found particularly in the important statements of Pope Pius XII on Woman's Duties in Social and Political Life (Pius XII, 1945), on *Sacra virginitas* (Pius XII, 1945), and on Christian Widowhood (Pius XII, 1957a). The Constitution on the Church of Vatican II speaks as follows:

> Married couples and Christian parents . . . offer all men an example of unwearying and generous love, build up the brotherhood of charity, and stand as witnesses to and cooperators in the fruitfulness of holy Mother Church. By such lives, they signify and share in that very love with which Christ loved His Bride and because of which He delivered Himself up on her behalf. A like example, but one given in a different way, is that offered by widows and single people, who are able to make great contributions toward holiness and apostolic endeavor in the Church [Abbott, 1966, article 41, p. 69].

> The holiness of the Church is also fostered in a special way by the observance of the manifold counsels proposed in the gospel by our Lord to His disciples. Outstanding among them is that precious gift of divine grace which the Father gives to some men (cf. Mt 19:11; 1 Cor 7:7) so that by virginity, or celibacy, they can more easily devote their entire selves to God alone with undivided heart (cf. 1 Cor 7:32-34). This total continence embraced on behalf of the kingdom of heaven has always been held in particular honor by the Church as being a sign of charity and stimulus towards it, as well as a unique fountain of spiritual fertility in the world.

> Since the disciples must always imitate and give witness to this charity and humility of Christ, Mother Church rejoices at finding within her bosom men and women who more closely follow and more clearly demonstrate the Savior's selfgiving by embracing poverty with the free choice of God's sons and by renouncing their own wills. They subject the latter to another person on God's behalf, in pursuit of an excellence surpassing what is commanded. Thus they liken themselves more thoroughly to Christ in His obedience [Abbott, 1966, article 42, pp. 71-72] .

8. Chapter VI of the Constitution on the Church contains a full development of that particular form of Christian life dedicated to Christian holiness and the apostolate which is distinguished by the profession of the evangelical counsels in societies approved by the Church and which are called "religious." A remarkable omission without adequate explanation is the absence of any reference to the new form of total dedication by the counsels in secular institutes. These societies were hailed by the documents of approval of Pope Pius XII as providential links between the life of evangelical perfection of the Gospel and the secular world through dedicated persons living and working "in" and "of" the world. We find no reference to the "states of perfection" so loved by canonists: an omission probably due to the laudable desire that all Christians realize they are called to perfection as witnesses to the holiness of Christ and the Church.

WOMAN AND THE APOSTOLATE

The apostolate is an essential part of woman's vocation and spirituality. Her natural orientation toward personal love, service and "motherhood," perfected and supernaturalized by divine charity and the sacramental sharing in the mission of Christ by Baptism, Confirmation, Matrimony and the Eucharist, make her one of the Chosen People sent to witness to and beget Christ in the world of persons and social institutions. The apostolate of the married woman as wife and mother is primarily in the home and is supplemented by auxiliary service to the Church and to the community. The single woman, whether the religious or the secular person, virgin, widow or divorcée, is to dedicate herself to the various works of the Church and secular life such as by teaching, social work, medical and nursing care, and the social and political betterment of society. The Christian woman belongs to God in Christ through the Church in the context of the secular world of her day. Her charity and dedicated service will be the very source of her personal fulfillment and sanctification, and the efficacious means of humanizing and Christianizing the environment.

The suggestion of a separate or special spirituality for women elicits a strong response, mostly negative, from women. Many Christian women in the more significant apostolic circles insist that there is only Christian spirituality, and allow only secondary modifications by reason of sex. Spirituality or holiness is that state of the Christian who has responded to the vocation of the Father to be his child by adoption through the grace of Jesus his Son, and who strives to love Him and all his creatures—self, all mankind, and the universe—as God loves them in Christ. There is but one spirituality, the Christian, which allows of the infinite variations of the human personality, both male and female, reflecting the perfections of God and continuing His work in this world.

The opportunities for service offered in the religious sisterhoods are well known in this country by reason of the number of sisters and their contributions so remarkable as to be the envy of the whole Church and one of the principal factors in the progress of the Church in the United States. While there is room for improvement, most observers agree that the various communities of sisters in our land have done more to carry out the renewal and adaptation to modern conditions than priests, religious men and the laity. Particular credit is due to the energetic leadership in the Sister-Formation Conference, the Conference of Major Superiors of Women's Institutes, the progressive Sister Formation colleges, the Sisters' Institutes of Spirituality, and the developing in-service training programs. Most American women still find their greatest opportunity for lifetime dedication in these communities. Priests can assist in developing vocations, in directing these dedicated women to perfection, and in cooperating with them in their various apostolic works so formative especially of the young.

Less known and appreciated is the single woman in secular life. Since the majority of Christians are called to the vocation of marriage and there is an unfortunate overemphasis on family life as the only means of personal fulfillment, and since most Christians inadequately understand their calling to a vocation in secular life, we must be clear in our concepts and emotional attitudes. Let us admit that for too long the Catholic position has been identified with an other-worldly angelism and eschatology sceptical of the goodness of nature created by God and redeemed by the risen Christ, with an authoritarian traditional conservatism committed to doctrinal formulation and ritual practice irrelevant to the contemporary mind, and with a Jansenistic legalism foreign to true charity and chastity. Women and the young influenced by them have suffered from this negative orientation away from the very providential situation in which they are to find personal fulfillment and effective apostolate. However, remarkable progress has been made since World War II; John XXIII (1962, 1963) and Vatican II (Abbott, 1966) call upon us to make even further advances.

The single woman considered here is (1) a woman who desires marriage but is open to God's will and positively dedicates herself to her present life as a vocation; (2) the woman who has chosen to remain single in the secular world as a lifetime vocation; (3) the widow or the divorced woman who accepts her deprivation of a husband as being a vocation in itself. Undoubtedly, the highest vocation is perpetual virginity chosen and consecrated to God, but celibacy also is held to be superior to marriage. Further Pope Pius XII in his encyclical, *Sacra virginitas* (with St. Thomas Aquinas, St. Bonaventure and the masters of sacred theology) teaches that ". . . virginity does not possess the stability of virtue unless there is a vow to keep it forever intact. Certainly those who obligate themselves by perpetual vow to keep their virginity put into practice in the most perfect way possible what Christ said about perpetual abstinence from marriage . . ." (Pius XII, 1954 p. 494). Insufficiently researched and encouraged is the value of a temporary vow of chastity before marriage and of continence for the unmarried, widows, and divorced. The same pope in his address, The State of Perfection, further suggested private vows of all three counsels even for those not members of societies requiring them (Pius XII, 1957b).

OPPORTUNITIES FOR SERVICE IN THE CHURCH

First place in the life of the Church is for the prophetic role of witness to the faith and grace of Christ incarnate and risen. Called the apostolate of "presence," it is the irrefutable and attractive joy and peace radiating from the spirit of Jesus living in His members. It is the holiness of Christ and His Church and so the vocation of the Christian. This opportunity and apostolate of *being* Christian in every aspect of life is particularly meaningful for women and especially necessary in our age which seeks personal significance in a selfish pragmatism of economic usefulness or physical pleasure. The recent comparison of the life philosophy of Phyllis McGinley (1964) in her poetry and home life with that of Betty Friedan (1963) in her best-seller, *The feminine mystique*, is significant (*Time*, 1965, p. 75). Clare Boothe Luce spoke of the compelling apologetic of the sincere believer radiating the attractiveness of Christ. The spirituality of Charles de Foucauld makes this concept of "presence" its only apostolate.

Opportunities for women to serve within the institutional structure of the Church are as numerous as positions not restricted by Holy Orders or the lack of maturity or competence of the women in question. The most important need is education in all its aspects from the elementary to the university level. This need is greater than ever because of the proportionate lag of priestly and religious vocations and the effectiveness of laity in witnessing to the relevance of religion to secular life. Within the last ten years there has been a notable breakthrough in the opportunity for laywomen to obtain degrees and teaching positions in philosophy and theology. Allied opportunity in the education of the world to the true, the good, and the beautiful lies in the whole field of mass-media communication—journalism, radio, television, movies, and publishing.

In the social-welfare field, hospitals, nursing, child care of the orphan, the mentally retarded and the delinquent, and social work particularly among the poor and minority groups present areas of service for women to express their personal and maternal sympathy and professional competence.

The entire program of religious instruction in the Confraternity of Christian Doctrine in the parish or mission, whether of weekly instruction, summer session, or the new "religion school" associated with the public school in a "shared-time" program to accomodate all the Catholics not in the Catholic school and to test the greater effectiveness of this integration of private-religious and public-secular subject teaching, offer great challenges to women on a part-time or full-time basis.

LAY MISSIONS

Within the last five years in this country, but beginning in 1922 in Europe with the first medical team going from Germany to Africa, the lay mission movement has been a thrilling proof of the generosity of our Catholic lay people completing the centuries of heroic service by priests and religious. The first efforts in this country were largely unorganized until several dioceses such as Oklahoma City and several missionary religious communities invited college students to volunteer their services for the summer or for a year. Since then the summer opportunities have multiplied with both training and service including home visitation, catechetics, nursing, and tutoring. The home mission effort has developed into the National Extension Lay Volunteers which in August, 1965, trained and sent 410 Volunteers into 160 home mission parishes and institutions with $100,000 support by the Extension Society. These carefully screened, trained and highly motivated volunteers give at least one year to the Church and often re-enlist.

The Papal Volunteers for Latin America began in 1960 and is the lay mission aspect of the total assistance being rendered by the Church in the United States to the Church in Latin America. The Latin American Bureau of the Bishops' Committee for Latin America cooperates with the Continental Episcopal Conference of Latin America (CELAM). Some 350 lay volunteers are currently working in 13 Latin American countries. A three-year minimum service including the training period is required, and re-enlistment is encouraged for the benefit of the greater experiences. Training centers are maintained at the Catholic University of Puerto Rico, Cuernavaca in Mexico, the Catholic University of America in Washington, Petropolis in Brazil, and at other places. Normally Papal Volunteers are sponsored by their dioceses or by parishes or colleges.

Other lay mission societies and agencies are worthy of attention as avenues of apostolic service. The International Catholic Auxiliaries was begun in Belgium under the inspiration of the great missionary of adaptation to native culture, Abbè Vincent Lebbe. Over 260 different countries serve on all the major continents to develop the native lay apostolate and to promote the total welfare of peoples in areas of greatest need (Evanston, Illinois). The Grail movement began in Holland and, in its apostolate of forming Christian women and of incarnating Christian values in all the situations in which modern woman finds herself, has centers in most countries (Loveland, Ohio). The Association for International Development interestingly sprang from the separate realization of several laymen and several missionary priests who formed this association of married couples and single men for service in the key institutions of developing nations (Paterson, New Jersey). Women Volunteers Association prepares and sends laywomen to Africa to serve there for at least two years as teachers, nurses and medical-team members (Washington, D.C.). The Catholic Lay Mission Corps, composed of the married and single men and women, devotes itself to teaching, catechetics and community development of the Spanish-speaking peoples of this country and ultimately Latin America (Austin, Texas).

Catholics for Latin America is a recent development for training and sending lay missioners, both married and single, for the apostolate of presence and service (Yonkers, N.Y.). The Lay Mission Helpers founded by the late Monsignor A. J. Brouwers has sent many lay missioners to Africa and Latin America (Los Angeles). The Catholic Medical Mission Board has become an effective liaison service for interesting and placing doctors and providing medical supplies to Catholic medical facilities throughout the world (New York, N.Y.). The Council of International Lay Associations is a coordinating agency of several of the lay mission societies and the Mission Secretariate of the National Catholic Welfare Conference. The annual Conference of the Catholic Inter-American Cooperation Program is a serious effort to bring together the important leaders of the Church in the United States

and Latin America for evaluation and planning. This incomplete listing
must give credit also to the Catholic Student Mission Crusade which has
worked for many years to develop interest in and support for the
missions in Catholic schools (Cincinnati).

SECULAR INSTITUTES

One of the intriguing developments of the Christian life in the Church
is the evolution and approval in 1947 of secular institutes as the climax
of the difficult integration of secularity and the life of Christian perfection, lived by members of societies approved by the Church and
dedicated by the evangelical counsels. The idea is implicit in the nature
of the Church, but awaited the troubled times and persecution of
traditional religious institutes for the founding of two societies, the one
for diocesan priests and the other for laywomen by Abbè Pierre de
Clorivière, S.J. (1735-1820) (cf. Vath, 1957), and the more recent
secularism of the 19th and 20th centuries. The historical, theological,
and canonical development of this state in the Church is fascinating as
a further application of the redemptive incarnation of Christ in the
temporal or secular order through His members who as "the leaven . . .
which always and everywhere at work, mingled with all grades of
society, from the highest to the lowest, strives by word, example and
in every way to reach and permeate them each and all until the whole
mass is transformed and wholly leavened in Christ" (Pius XII, 1948,
p. 139).

Secular institutes are defined as "clerical or lay Associations whose
members, in order to attain to Christian perfection and the full exercise of the apostolate, make profession of practicing the evangelical
counsels in the world" (Pius XII, 1947, p. 133). The secular character
of the life and the total dedication to the apostolate are emphasized in
the Motu proprio, *Primo feliciter*:

> . . . it must be kept in mind that the proper and special character of
> these Institutes, that is, their *secular* character, which constitutes their
> whole reason for existence, must always stand out clearly in everything.
> Therefore, nothing must be withdrawn from the complete profession of
> Christian perfection, solidly founded on the evangelical counsels and
> authentically religious in its substance, but this perfection must be pur-
> sued and professed in the *world*; it must therefore be adapted to secular
> life in all that is lawful and in accordance with the obligations and works
> of this same perfection.
>
> In its entirety the life of the members of Secular Institutes ought to
> be directed towards the apostolate. The exercise of this apostolate in con-

stancy and holiness must derive from such purity of intention, close union with God, generous forgetfulness of self and mortification, from so great a love of souls, that it should reveal the interior spirit which informs it and must continually nourish and renew it. This apostolate, which embraces the whole of their life, is usually so deeply and sincerely regarded in these Institutes, that, with the help and under the inspiration of divine Providence, the burning thirst for souls seems not to be confined to the provision of a suitable opportunity for a dedicated life, but to a great extent to have stamped it with its own form and nature and, even more wonderfully, to have required and brought into being its specific and even its generic purpose.

This apostolate of the Secular Institutes is to be faithfully exercised not only *in the world* but, in some sort, as originating in the world, and as a consequence its profession, activities, forms, places and other circumstances are to correspond to this secular condition [Pius XII, 1948, pp. 140-141].

Most of these societies began as apostolic groups of the laity who progressively saw the value of a lifetime and total dedication to personal holiness and the apostolate through the evangelical counsels while retaining their secular character. A similar development has taken place among secular priests who retain their status in the diocese under their bishops. There has been a rich, even exuberant, growth of such groups in number and variety. Their approval by the Church follows the same general lines as with religious institutes (Sacred Congregation of Religious, 1948).

Among the Institutes having pontifical approval and active in the United States are: the Company of St. Paul for priests, laymen and laywomen, dedicated to the apostolate of the transformation of modern life through dedicated Christians (Washington); the Society of the Heart of Jesus originally founded by Abbè de Clorivière and later revived as a secular institute for secular priests (Putnam, Conn.); Opus Dei (Sacerdotal Society of the Holy Cross and Opus Dei), the largest institute having two branches, one for priests and laymen and the other for laywomen, seeking to diffuse in every class of civil society, especially the intellectual class, the life of Christian perfection in the world (Chicago); Caritas Christi which provides for laywomen a life dedicated to Christian perfection and the apostolate in secular life (Chicago); the Missionaries of the Kingship of Christ which follows the Franciscan spirituality and is made up of three divisions for priests, laymen, and laywomen (Washington); the Society of Our Lady of the Way for laywomen dedicated to personal perfection and the Christianization of occupational fields under the special patronage of the Blessed Virgin Mary (Los Angeles); the Teresian Institute for laywomen dedicated to the goals of Catholic education in both private and state schools (Boston). Other approved Institutes of significance are the rapidly growing Oblate Missionaries of Mary Immaculate for laywomen (Hartford, Conn.); the Cordimarian Filiation for laywomen (Chicago); the three Institutes founded by the Very Reverend James Alberione under the patronage of St. Paul (Boston); the Schoenstätt Sisters of Mary of the Catholic Apostolate (Madison, Wis.); and the Jesus-Caritas Fraternity of women dedicating their whole lives as an apostolate particularly to the poor in the spirit of Charles de Foucauld.

Several indigenous American developments of special interest are: the Secular Institute of St. Pius X for laymen and associated married grew out of a Y.C.W. group (Wincester, Mass.); the Madonna House Apostolate for priests, laymen and laywomen founded and directed by the indomitable Catherine de Hueck Doherty and dedicated to the restoration of the world to Christ through "preaching the Gospel with our lives in the market place" (Combermere, Ont.); Caritas for laywomen devoted to the sanctification of the members and the world culture through the parish structure (New Orleans); Pax Christi for laywomen seeking personal perfection and the Christianization of institutions and the betterment of the needy, especially in the interracial apostolate (Greenwood, Miss.); the Rural Parish Workers of Christ the King (Cadet, Mo.), and the Daughters of Our Lady of Fatima (Lansdowne, Pa.).

Comparing lay mission groups and secular institutes reveals several similar tendencies:

1. The integration of priests, the married and single persons into distinct teams for the purpose of a more effective apostolate of witness and a new breadth to the complementation of men and women, priests and laity.

2. The concept of "movement" with extending circles of incarnation or penetration of the environment beginning with a nucleus of fully dedicated persons through vows or their equivalent.

3. The practice of group living and apostolate depending on the purpose of the society but giving greater emphasis to the concept of spiritual community of common purpose and means.

4. The more rapid increase of societies of laywomen than of laymen especially in Europe and the Latin countries, possibly due to the relative traditionalism of religious sisterhoods there.

5. The common quality of "universal apostolate" both horizontally in the whole world and vertically in all levels of society and so the invalidity of contrasting lay mission societies and secular institutes from the scope of their apostolate.

SERVICE IN SECULAR LIFE

The specific role of the laity is in the secular order with opportunities and responsibilities for service to persons and to the entire range of social institutions—domestic, economic and professional, cultural and political. Women are finding the doors progressively opened to them in various cultures which until recently restricted them to the home. Each woman must determine her own participation in this secular world. Women are particularly endowed and consequently called to an apostolate of service and influence in protecting and enhancing the personal values of women, children and the family (Pius XII, 1945).

As developed previously, the professional areas of education, law, journalism and communications, nursing, medical service, and social work offer splendid opportunity for service to the community, especially to the underprivileged. Economic life in its range of agriculture, manufacturing, marketing, advertising, banking, labor unions and cooperatives and credit unions offers not only financial security but also a challenge to maintain truly human and Christian values in the business world. Government service and political office from the local to the international levels need women to inspire political life with respect for the human person and the spiritual factor of the common good. The Peace Corps and the Vista Volunteers parallel the foreign and domestic lay mission volunteers and are highly effective forms of the lay apostolate in the secular institutional area.

Christian women can do much to impart motivation and direction to the efforts which otherwise may discount religion in the legitimate concern for the material welfare of peoples. The Job Corps program, the Red Cross, United Good Neighbors, Great Decision Councils, etc., enable women to contribute on either a part-time or full-time basis. Many public-spirited women further culture in music, art, drama and the dance and so offset the jaded tastes so prevalent, especially among the young. Public figures such as the late Eleanor Roosevelt, Mrs. John Kennedy, Mrs. Lyndon Johnson, Edith Green, and Clare Boothe Luce illustrate the effectiveness of women in public life.

INTEGRATION OF SERVICE IN THE CHURCH AND IN THE WORLD

The description of the various forms of life and apostolate for women in the Church and the secular world shows the variety of opportunity of the feminine vocation. Women should be active in both spheres, or either one or the other will lose the value which the masculine-feminine complementation is divinely ordained to preserve. This applies particularly in the secular order if it is not to become impersonal, materialistic, pragmatic, technical and homocentric. Let women preserve a sensitivity to the truly human, the holy, the cultural, the eternal and the divine.

Two critical suggestions are relevant. Careful coordination of effort will lessen the duplication of activity and institutional effort in Church-private and secular-public agencies. Secondly, the Decree on Ecumenism of Vatican II (Abbott, 1966, pp. 341-366) calls for cooperation of Catholics with non-Catholic Christians and non-Christians in prayer, dialogue, and social action for the welfare of all peoples, and is a welcome departure from the exclusivist self-sufficiency marking our past attitude toward other religious bodies and secular agencies and governments. Talent, money, and the pressing needs of the temporal order dictate this integration. An amazing example of such cooperation is the coordination of local diocesan and civic, Peace Corps and Papal Volunteer personnel in the Instituto Campesino development in Northern Ecuador among 10,000 families in 45 communities of Indian people, 65 percent illiterate, 50 percent eating only one meal a day, and 70 percent living in one-room huts. The success of the project stems from the latent tradition of cooperation in the Indians and the new integration of the religious and secular volunteers.

CONCLUSION: FORMATION OF WOMEN FOR SERVICE

The vocation of woman is fruitful love expressed in personal union with God and service of Christ in redeemed mankind. She needs to develop the emotional and spiritual qualities of maturity rather than the egoism of self-pity or pampered adulation as she passes through the various climacterics, especially of adolescence and menopause. This maturing is best ensured by a full sharing in the Christian community oriented toward God in liturgical prayer and toward fellow men in fraternal charity and apostolic involvement. The family lays the principal foundation and is aided by the parents' participation in such efforts as the Christian Family Movement. The school in its entire curricular and co-curricular program can and must challenge the woman to develop her whole personality through formal learning and commitment to service in and beyond the campus. Specialized apostolic movements are available for the woman after graduation. The directive in *Mater et magistra* that the laity are to be formed in the mind of Christ for social action largely through the small group-inquiry method pioneered by the Specialized Movements is a responsibility of both the clergy and the laity (John XXIII, 1961, Part IV). New approaches to the formation of single women, such as the Bethany Conference for the unmarried and the Naim Conference for widows and widowers, and Divorcées Anonymous, parallel the successful Cana Conference. Much progress has been made; new approaches and greater efforts need to be used. We live in a changing world and Christian women must conserve the best of the past and be the soul imparting the love and grace of Christ to the future.

REFERENCES

Abbott, W. M. (S.J.) (Ed.) *The documents of Vatican II.* New York: Herder & Herder, 1966.

Considine, J. J. (M.M.) (Ed.) *The Church in the new Latin America.* Notre Dame, Ind.: Fides, 1964.

Friedan, Betty. *The feminine mystique.* New York: Norton, 1963.

Haley, J. E. (C.S.C.) (Ed.) *Apostolic sanctity in the world: A symposium on total dedication in the world and secular institutes.* Notre Dame, Ind.: Univer. Notre Dame Press, 1957.

John XXIII. *Mater et magistra.* Encyclical letter of May 15, 1961. *Acta Apostolicae Sedis,* 1961, *53,* 401-464. English translation: Christianity and social progress. *Cath. Mind,* 1961, *59,* 411-479.

John XXIII. *Pacem in terris.* Encyclical letter of April 11, 1963. *Acta Apostolicae Sedis,* 1963, *55,* 257-304. English translation: Peace on earth. *Cath. Mind,* 1963, *61,* No. 1175, September, 1963, 47-62, and No. 1176, October, 1963, 45-63.

McCarthy, T. P. (C.S.V.) (Ed.) *Total dedication for the laity: a guidebook to secular institutes.* Boston: St. Paul Editions, 1964.

McGinley, Phyllis. *Sixpence in her shoe.* New York: Macmillan, 1964.

Paul VI. *Ecclesiam suam.* Encyclical letter of August 6, 1964. *Acta Apostolicae Sedis,* 1964, *56,* 609-659. English translation: The paths of the Church. *The Pope speaks,* 1965, *10,* 253-292.

Perinelle, J. (O.P.) *God's highways: the religious life and secular institutes* (trans. by D. Attwater). Westminster, Md.: Newman, 1958.

Perrin, J. M. (O.P.) *Secular institutes* (trans. by L. C. Sheppard). New York: Kenedy, 1961.

Pius XII. Woman's duties in social and political life. Allocution to the women delegates of the Christian Societies of Italy, October 21, 1945. *Acta Apostolicae Sedis* 1945, *37,* 284-295. English translation in: Monks of Solesmes (Eds.) *Papal teachings: the woman in the modern world.* Boston: St. Paul Editions, 1959. Pp. 127-142.

Pius XII. *Provida mater ecclesia.* Apostolic Constitution concerning canonical states and secular institutes for the attainment of Christian perfection, February 2, 1947. *Acta Apostolicae Sedis,* 1947, *39,* 114-124. English translation in: J. E. Haley (C.S.C.) (Ed.) *Apostolic sanctity in the world.* Notre Dame, Ind.: Univer. Notre Dame Press, 1957. Pp. 127-137.

Pius XII. *Primo feliciter. Motu proprio* in praise and approbation of secular
    institutes, March 12, 1948. *Acta Apostolicae Sedis,* 1948, *40,* 283-286.
    English translation in: J. E. Haley (C.S.C.) (Ed.) *Apostolic sanctity in
    the world.* Notre Dame, Ind.: Univer. Notre Dame Press, 1957. Pp. 139-
    142.
Pius XII. *Sacra virginitas.* Encyclical letter of March 25, 1954. *Acta
    Apostolicae Sedis.* 1954, *46,* 161-191. English translation: On holy vir-
    ginity. *Cath. Mind,* 1954, *52,* 491-509.
Pius XII. The glory of widowhood. Address to the Congress of the Inter-
    national Union of Family Organizations, September 16, 1957. *Acta
    Apostolicae Sedis,* 1957, *49,* 898-904. English translation: *Cath. Mind.*
    1958, *56,* 374-380.(a)
Pius XII. The state of perfection. Address to the Second World Congress
    of the States of Perfection, December 11, 1957. *The Pope speaks,* 1957,
    4, 264-272.(b)
Reidy, G. (O.F.M.) *Secular Institutes.* New York: Hawthorn, 1962.
Sacred Congregation of Religious. *Cum sanctissimus,* March 19, 1948. *Acta
    Apostolicae Sedis,* 1948, *40,* 293-297. English translation: Instruction on
    secular institutes, in: J. E. Haley, (C.S.C.) (Ed.) *Apostolic Sanctity in the
    world.* Notre Dame, Ind.: Univer. Notre Dame Press, 1957. Pp. 143-148.
Time 1965, *85,* No. 25 (June 18, 1965), 74-78.
Vath, J. G. Historical development of secular institutes. In J. E. Haley
    (C.S.C.) (Ed.) *Apostolic sanctity in the world.* Notre Dame, Ind.: Univer.
    Notre Dame Press, 1957 Pp. 83-92.